FAMILY QUESTIONS

FAMILY QUESTIONS

REFLECTIONS ON THE AMERICAN SOCIAL CRISIS

Allan C. Carlson

Transaction Books
New Brunswick (U.S.A.) and Oxford (U.K.)

Library of Congress Catalog Number: 87-31007
ISBN: 0-88738-206-1
Printed in the United States of America

Library of Congress Cataloging in Publication Data

Carlson, Allan C.
    Family questions: reflections on the American social crisis /
Allan C. Carlson.
        p.   cm.
    Includes index.
    ISBN 0-88738-206-1
    1. Family—United States.   2. United States—Social
conditions—1945-   3. Family policy—United States.   I. Title.
HQ536.C37   1988
306.8'5'0973—dc19   87-31007

to Elizabeth Cecelia

Contents

Foreword

This book may set something of a record for the number of persuasive debunkings per chapter. Debunkings are, of course, a dime a dozen, but persuasive debunkings are quite another matter. Allan Carlson does more than maintain a critical distance from established opinions. With a bemused skepticism and with awesome patience, he takes them apart piece by piece. One is impressed by the doggedness with which he has read through so much patent nonsense, and by the care with which he presents his findings. It is as though he would assure us that he is not making this up. People in positions of great influence, he wants us to know, really are saying these crazy things about the family, sexuality, cultural oppression, and much else. Not only that, but what they are saying is reflected in social policies that are having the most doleful effect upon the gullible affluent and the vulnerable poor.

This is an iconoclastic work in the service of tradition. Carlson writes less in alarm than in droll puzzlement at the ways in which the over-educated of our cultural elites have succeeded in obscuring the self-evident. If populist can still have a positive meaning, Allan Carlson is something of a populist. These pages evidence a refreshing respect for ordinary people and the ways in which they try to live their lives in the worlds of which they are part. Carlson encourages us to muster the intellectual courage to challenge the intellectual dandyism that makes anti-intellectualism seem the course of common sense. The answer to regnant wrong thinking, he insists, is better thinking that holds itself accountable to the facts. *Family Questions* bristles with facts—many of them unhappy facts about the consequences of ideas that have been liberated from their moorings in human behavior.

Where social policy inserts itself into the interstices of intimate human relationships, the law of unintended consequences takes a fearful vengeance. Nowhere is this more evident than in the history of family policy. Carlson's firm grasp of the history of family policy, both in America and elsewhere, helps him illuminate the ways in which we keep repeating the mistakes of the past. As often as not, today's proposed remedy is a retread of the remedy that produced the pathology it is intended to cure. Carlson's concern, however, is not just with unintended consequences and historical amnesia. He also has important things to say about intended consequences that sensible people should know better than to intend. Not to be missed, for example, is his critique of the proponents of depopulation, and of the advocates of an androgynous social order. A great strength of the present work is the author's diligent documentation of what architects of culture and policy have said and now say about the kind of world they would design for others to live in.

This is an unabashedly biased book. The bias is unabashed, but not unexamined or unexplained. Carlson's attachment to the "traditional family" comprehends the fact that it is not traditional in the sense of being forced upon us by nature or irresistably imposed by the past. The family that he would defend is an historical and cultural achievement. It can only be sustained by understanding the forces that brought it into being—and the forces by which it is now besieged. No doubt some readers will think it quaint, while others will find it refreshing, that Carlson affirms "bourgeois values" and asserts that some patterns of behavior are "wholesome and decent," while others are not. In a world that has undergone the famous "transvaluation of values" who but the hopelessly naive can speak of wholesomeness and decency? It will be objected that Carlson speaks of policies and attitudes that have "stripped the old of their dignity and the young of their innocence" as though words such as dignity and innocence had a clear meaning today.

Allan Carlson, however, is keenly aware of how much has been thrown into questions by the ravages and achievements of modernity. If he at times strikes a note of seeming naïveté, it is what philosopher Paul Ricoeur has called the "second naivete" of those who have understood the disillusionments of our time. Yet another philosopher, Alfred North Whitehead, wisely wrote that the only simplicity to be trusted is the simplicity that is on the far side of complexity. *Family Questions* is, in largest part, an argument on the far side of complexity. It is also an exposé of false complexities that have served to obscure the "family answers" that have been there all along.

Allan Carlson is a colleague and friend. Many of the issues engaged by this volume we have discussed and debated at great length. Because of my intense involvement over the years with what is called the black underclass, I wish the book had more on the price exacted from the poor by the chic ideas and misguided policies that Carlson so devastatingly dissects. But any book can only do so much, and it is no criticism to express a wish for more of what this book does so well. On another question Carlson and I will likely have to agree to continue to disagree, until he sees the light. I sympathize with much that he says about suburbia as a refuge from the failure of our cities. But I believe he fails to appreciate sufficiently the role that the city has played and should play in human civilization. For instance, he professes not to understand how New York City is the historical preview of the New Jerusalem of biblical promise. Friendship notwithstanding, I take that to be just short of a moral failing.

Family Questions is aptly titled. It contains, both implicitly and explicitly, answers aplenty. But the chief contribution of this iconoclastically traditional book is in challenging the ways in which intellectuals and policy-makers have framed the questions. Without a bold reframing of the questions, we can be sure that none of our answers will turn out right.

—Richard John Neuhaus
New York City

Acknowledgements

The ideas and interpretations found in this essay are, in significant measure, the product of conversations with my colleagues at The Rockford Institute: John Howard, Richard John Neuhaus, Thomas Fleming, Bryce Christensen, Richard Vaughan, Michael Warder, and Momcilo Selic. The Institute's publication *Persuasion at Work* provided me an outlet in which I could begin to think through the components of the contemporary American family issue.

Other individuals, in conversations and their writings, have helped to shape my approach to the subject: Carl Gustavson of Ohio University, who taught me how to use history as an analytical tool; the late Gunnar Myrdal, the subject of my doctoral work and this century's foremost expositor of the components of Western Civilization's family crisis; George Gilder, the writer with the clearest understanding of what is at stake in the gender question; Robert Nisbet, the ablest interpreter of the tension between modernity and community; and Friedrich Hayek, whose devotion to human liberty is balanced by personal compassion.

I have also drawn insight or inspiration from William Gribbin, Brigitta Berger, Carl Anderson, Juanita Duggin, Stellan Andersson, Joseph Piccione, and Ann-Katrin Hatje.

For believing in this manuscript, I am most grateful to Transaction's Irving Louis Horowitz, whose intellectual powers are matched by his courage. For the typing, I need thank Heidi Bradford and Anita Fedora.

From my own family, I have gained more than a taste of the sweet joys to be found in this world. To my children Anders, Sarah-Eva, Anna, and Miriam, I extend the hope that this book helps shape, in some small way, a better future for their families-to-come. To my wife, Elizabeth, I offer my boundless gratitude for her example and her affection and support.

Introduction

For a decade, "family" has been a political word. Among politicians and pundits, the family issue has usually been equated with the welfare problem or, more recently, the so-called "underclass." Of course, these labels are usually polite euphemisms for "Blacks," and are symbolic of the rapid disintegration of urban black family life in America, a phenomenon first analyzed by Daniel P. Moynihan in 1965.

However, this popular reduction of the family issue to a welfare or ethnic matter is grievously misleading. The family in America—black, white, Hispanic, and Asian—is actually in the throes of basic upheaval. A crisis point, in the sense of an unstable condition portending abrupt change, may have already been passed.

The statistical evidence, while fairly well known, bears repeating. The number of divorces in America climbed from 393,000 in 1960 to 1,213,000 in 1981, with the divorce rate rising 140 percent. The number of children annually involved in divorce rose from 463,000 to nearly 1.2 million over the same period. The rate of first marriage (new brides per 1,000 single women) fell 30 percent; among women ages 20–24, the decline was an astonishing 59 percent. The birth rate (births per 1,000 women ages 15–44) tumbled from 118 in 1960 to 65.6 in 1978, a figure which has since remained fairly constant. The total fertility rate, which measures the ability of a society to reproduce itself, slipped into the negative column in 1973. Even these low numbers are sustained only through an increase in the number of illegitimate births from 224,000 in 1960 to 715,000 in 1982. Among Blacks, 21.6 percent of all births were out-of-wedlock in the former year; by 1982, 48.8 percent were. Among Whites, the increase was from 2.3 percent to 21.1. Meanwhile, the number of legal abortions in America climbed from 745,000 in 1973 to 1,577,000 in 1981.

Such massive swings in the statistical measures of family life for a nation are unprecedented. Even among countries crushed by war and occupation, such as post-World War II Japan and Germany, we find greater resilience. How could the United States of America, once considered the most family centered of nations, give witness to such developments?

Offering tentative answers to that question is the goal of this volume. As a prelude to that investigation, several background assumptions and basic themes should be identified.

To begin with, the author believes that a central purpose of human existence—perhaps *the* central purpose—is the reproduction of the species. This belief derives from readings of the natural law and the disciplines of sociology, psychology, anthropology, genetics, and biology. The family serves as the source, protector, and incubator of these human children. All other institutions, be they economic, educational, social, or political, exist to support, preserve, or defend that primary social form.

Second, the family is a universal institution, and not distinctly American. The phrase once commonly used in discussions such as this—"the American family"—is misleading, carrying precisely the wrong connotation. The family formed by a man, a woman, and their children is an institution that is prior to any existing nation or state, including this one. Accordingly, the appropriate phrase is "the family in America." Before the tribunal of history, the United States, like all other lands, will be judged on how the universal family fared in this time and place.

Third, governments or the state have an infinite capacity to harm or disrupt the family and very limited ability to help it. This means that government attempts to save the family through aggressive schemes or intervention will have unintended and usually negative consequences. More disturbingly, since governments almost always grow in order to compensate for society-wide family decline, state bureaucrats have a perverse stake in promoting decay in family life. For these reasons, programs of family policy must be viewed with suspicion.

Fourth, the American system of liberal capitalism holds an unusual relationship with the family institution. A capitalist economic system is critically dependent on the successful functioning of the family. The nuclear family of father, mother, and their children provides the critical matrix for human reproduction while also serving as a highly mobile unit, able to follow the market signals that would raise their incomes while also increasing market efficiency. Moreover, the family contains within its bounds the necessary positive incentives which make human beings behave in economically useful ways. As industrial capitalism cut persons off from the economic protections provided by kin and village, the family system made each male aware of his responsibilities to protect and provide for his mate as she performed her maternal task. This arrangement generated economically and socially constructive anxiety, ambition, and imagination, while keeping the baser human instincts and the individual ego under control.

Yet it is important to note that this relationship runs primarily one way. Capitalism needs the family as a regulator, or control, over the economic system's baser instincts. In contrast, the family does not need industrial capitalism to the same degree. All other things being equal, capitalism's benefits—the generation of extraordinary wealth, extended lifespan, the creation of new opportunities, the restructuring of wealth and rewards according to democratically determined merit—aid the universal family. It is also true, though, that the precapitalist, predominantly agrarian economy provided a more natural setting for the family unit, where issues of gender roles and the value of children were not questions at all. Moreover, an industrial economy, resting on market determined wages, makes no natural accommodation to the needs and structure of the universal family. In short, the decay of family life necessarily threatens capitalism; yet the disappearance of capitalism does not necessarily threaten the family.

Fifth, a free society resting on the precepts of liberty easily accommodates family life only so long as the family is seen as the repository of unique rights and obligations. As wives and children gain new rights independent of their husbands and fathers, and as the state takes on responsibility for the protection of those rights, family autonomy necessarily suffers and the state grows.

Finally, it is apparent that the negative turn of family statistics in the 1960s, cited above, was to some degree illusory, and merely a return to much older and more pervasive trends. The 1945–60 period in American history was exceptional in many ways. Particularly noteworthy was the apparent resurgence in family values. The U.S. fertility rate, for example, which had been declining since before 1850, nearly doubled between 1940 and 1957. The divorce rate, which hit a war-induced peak in 1946, gently declined through the 1950s. These positive family developments were concentrated primarily among the American middle class. Social observers were astonished at the time, and in retrospect we can appreciate their surprise.

Even granting the exceptional nature of the post-World War II era, though, the family traumas evident in the 1960s and 1970s were something more than historical artifacts. This was an extremely ideologized era, and more than a handful of newly competing political persuasions were implicitly or explicitly hostile to family life. Partisans of the new left, Maoists, radical feminists, Neo-Malthusians, sexual liberators, inhabitants of the counterculture, and others all found a common enemy in the natural community and biological vitality of the universal family. Moreover, the cultural and economic arrangements, carefully constructed over a hundred years, which had protected the family from the full impact of radical individualism, unraveled during this period. In some combination, these developments created the family crisis which now marks this nation.

This volume explores the situation of the family in America by dividing the matter into a series of questions. "The gender question" asks how the relationship between man and woman fares in modern America, with a focus on the influence of ideology on both the sciences and government. "The population question" assesses the effects of the family crisis on family size and birth of children. "The economic question" highlights the state of family well-being, looking primarily at the family's recent loss of economic protection. New attempts to control sexuality in the midst of moral revolution are addressed by "the sexual question." "The community question" looks at the altered relationship of the family in America to other forms of human attachment and control, specifically focusing on the decline of agrarian community and the rise of suburban America as the incubator of family life. "The age question" explores the vast recent alteration in the place of the old within the family circle. "Questions of state" assesses past attempts by governments to aid or replace the family unit. The volume concludes with an attempt to define the proper role of a government of free people, relative to the family. Its primary focus is on the creative disengagement of the state from family life.

Part I
THE GENDER QUESTION

1

The Triumph of Social Parenting

Since 1962, motherhood has faced subtle attack under the terms of the so-called "child care debate." Pressure is now growing for a new wave of "reform." Numerous conference results, reports, and research findings have been released in recent years demanding substantially higher federal subsidies for the nonparental care of children. Moreover, despite a common rhetorical affirmation of the family, the 1984 platforms of both major political parties pledged to support schemes transferring more income from families that care for their own children to families that do not. The Democrats called, in addition, for corporations to assume the responsibilities of child care. Accordingly, it's an appropriate time to review how we arrived at this point, and to ask whether this is the way Americans want to order their common life.

For the first 185 years of its existence, the United States of America was characterized by a cultural system that considered child rearing the responsibility of each family. Children, it was assumed, were properly raised in the home. Governmental intervention was justified only in cases of family malfunction. Nonmaternal child care, in particular, was considered to be a mark of abnormality. As the 1909 White House Conference on Children succinctly put it: "Home life is the highest and finest product of civilization." Theodore Roosevelt warned that "sins against pure and healthy family life are those which of all others are sure in the end to be visited most heavily upon the nation."

During the 1920s, though, a new ideology of "social parenting" began to take shape in America. It drew on the arguments of the "Chicago school" of sociology, spearheaded by Joseph Folsom, Ernest Burgess, and William Ogburn. Under modern industrial conditions, these men argued, the family was losing its functions. Experts needed to fill the vacuum. This ideology also absorbed the arguments of social psychologist George Herbert Mead, who posited that "social roles" such as "father," "mother," and "competitive businessmen" were learned through play. Gender-free, non-

3

competitive playthings properly presented in a daycare center, he suggested, could produce a new generation of children, trained to be independent in their moral judgments yet cooperative in their social activities.

Seen this way, the view of nursery or daycare was transformed in some professional circles from a limited service for families in trouble into a desirable stage in every child's life. The 1930 White House Conference on Children hinted at this new spirit: "If the grouping of little children for a few hours each day for educational activities and for habit-training through nursery schools is found to be desirable in itself, then this service should be extended on behalf of children generally, regardless of the economic status of their family." So the experts laid their claim that "social parenting" was superior to the "inexpert" nurturing of very young children by their parents.

Experimental daycare centers sprang up throughout the United States during the same decade, many of them attached to universities. Crucial funding for these new "child development centers" came from the Laura Spelman Rockefeller Memorial Fund. Although there were fewer than fifty of these institutions, it is hard to overestimate their importance. By applying a new doctrine to real children and training the first generation of child development specialists, these experimental centers laid the foundation for future expansion. An unknown number of charity and proprietary daycare centers also began operation in this period. While the former served children from low-income and immigrant families, the latter rose in response to the needs of middle-class working mothers. The turn of these business and professional women toward social parenting proved to be an omen for the future.

Emergencies on a national scale stimulated the first federal intervention into the care of small children, and a consequent—although unintended— weakening of the maternal care norm. The Works Progress Act of 1933 resulted in the creation of over 1,500 government-run nursery schools. Rather than experiments in alternative child care, these WPA centers were designed solely to provide work for unemployed teachers, nutritionists, and other personnel. Their target populations were children from families on relief and similar low-income families. Most units operated on a full-day basis, five days per week, year round. By 1937, 40,000 children were enrolled in WPA nursery schools.

War brought a similar result. As the United States entered World War II, large numbers of women moved into the defense factories and reports of "latchkey" children grew common. At first, federal child welfare authorities in the Children's Bureau and Office of Education sought to establish a national policy discouraging the employment of mothers with small children. However, the War Manpower Commission overruled them and instead set a policy leaving the decision to work or not to work up to each mother. The consequences of this decision were soon clear. In July 1942, the WPA received $6 million to restructure its nursery school system to meet the needs of working mothers. The Community Facilities Act of 1941 (Lanham Act), concerned primarily with housing and public works projects for the defense industry, was reinterpreted so as to permit expenditures in support of daycare programs. By July 1944, 129,000 preschoolers were enrolled in 3,102 Lanham centers. In addition, the Farm Security Administration spent large sums developing daycare facilities in rural areas. The U.S. Maritime Commission also funded child-care centers at two Kaiser Corporation shipyards. They operated seven days a week, 24 hours a day, had large staffs of specialists, and offered mothers a food service allowing them to pick up both children and a take-home dinner at the end of a work shift.

All of these programs were terminated shortly after the war's end. Yet they had set a significant precedent, suggesting that if the national interest was served, public funds should help working mothers pay the cost of the daycare. The concept of social parenting had taken a key step forward.[1]

Surprisingly, peace brought a strong resurgence of the maternal-care norm within the United States. The advocates of daycare found themselves in retreat over the next 15 years. Shifts in the dominant flow of ideas played a role in generating this change. Instrumental was the 1950 publication of John Bowlby's *Maternal Care and Mental Health* under the auspices of the World Health Organization. After reviewing studies of the effects of institutionalized care on children, Bowlby concluded that the "warm, intimate and continuous" care of the mother or permanent mother substitute—the "provision of constant attention day and night, seven days a week, and 365 in the year"—underlay "the development of character and of mental health." He labeled the state of affairs where the child did not enjoy this relationship as "maternal deprivation." While focusing largely on the traumas inflicted by orphanages and similar institutions, Bowlby hinted that the "full-time employment of mother" was among those causes resulting in "neglect" or "maladjustment of the child."[2]

At the same time, Harvard sociologist Talcott Parsons was leading American sociology away from the grim analysis of the "Chicago school" and toward a renewed celebration of the American family. For the first time in the nation's history, he wrote, "there has emerged a remarkably uniform, basic type of family," the nuclear family. Crucial to this family form, he argued, was a complex elaboration of sex roles, with women taking on the emotive, nurturing, and managerial functions of the household.[3] The majority of social workers in the federal Children's Bureau, never happy with the WPA–Lanham programs, also joined in this reaffirmation of maternal care, believing that federal involvement in daycare would eventually prove destructive of the family and contrary to basic American values.[4]

As it touched on the family, public policy during the 1950s reflected this maternal preference. Aid to Dependent Children (later renamed Aid to Families with Dependent Children, or AFDC), for example, remained in the tradition of the earlier widows' pensions, subsidizing mothers to stay home and rear their children. Day-care centers entered a period of traumatic decrease. Publicly funded institutions almost disappeared. The number of philanthropic programs for children of the poor declined from 1,500 in 1951 to 1,109 in 1960. Modest growth came only in the private or proprietary sector serving an upper-middle-class clientele. By 1960, this sector accounted for 64 percent of all licensed daycare centers.

In that same year, the Child Welfare League of America defined daycare narrowly as a service "to protect children . . . when their families are unable to meet their needs without some assistance from the community." The 1960 White House Conference on Children recommended "alternative methods" of child care only when "the understanding, loving care best provided by mother" was not available.[5] Maternal care again seemed secure.

Yet behind this reaffirmation of motherhood, two social developments were working to undermine the cultural foundations of the historic family system in America. The first of these was the steady increase in the number of married women in the labor market, including those with preschool children. Between 1948 and 1966, the labor force participation rate of married women with husbands present and with children under the age of six increased from 10.8 percent to 24.2 percent, a number that would double again in the next twenty years. The second change was the dramatic increase in the number of fatherless households with children present. Caused primarily by rising levels of illegitimacy and divorce (and statistically amplified by a decline in marital fertility), the phenomenon was first noticed during the early 1950s among black urban populations. For example, the "non-white" illegitimacy ratio (the number of illegitimate births per thousand live births) rose from 164.7 in 1948 to 229.9 in 1962. By the late 1950s this development had spread to the white population, with a 50 percent jump in its illegitimacy ratio between 1957 and 1963 alone (from 19.6 to 30.7). In consequence, the number of children on AFDC with fathers absent through illegitimacy, divorce, desertion, or separation rose from 334,000 in 1946 (41.8 percent of all recipients) to 1,016,000 in 1956 (59.5 percent) to 1,889,000 in 1963 (64 percent). The "feminization of poverty" had occurred, a program of widows' pensions was quietly transformed into a welfare scheme, and the "child care" question took on an acute urgency.

The first sign of renewed interest in daycare came from an unexpected place. Symbolic of the unrecognized role played by the military in social experimentation after World War II, the U.S. Army established in the mid 1950s a series of daycare centers on posts here and abroad. Their purpose was "to enhance the morale of servicemen and their families," a broad statement hitherto foreign to federal policy. The Army provided the buildings and land for these centers, while operating funds came from Post Exchange profits and daycare fees. By 1966, an estimated 20,000 American children were enrolled in Army daycare.

1962 was the year in which ideas about motherhood once again began to shift. An opening round came from psychologist R.G. Andry, who argued that Bowlby's emphasis on "maternal deprivation" as the major pathogenic factor in personality development overlooked a host of other causal factors, particularly the role of the father. Mothers, he said, were simply not that important. The same year, anthropologist Margaret Mead implicitly criticized the "provincialism" of Bowlby's work and his tendency to "over-attribute" developments to single causes "such as breast-feeding or its absence, [or] separation from a mother-figure." Things were more complex. Indeed, Mead went on to suggest that full-time mothering actually was somewhat abnormal, being possible only "under highly artificial urban conditions" and involving the "isolation" of the child and "the artificial perpetuation, intensification or creation . . . of exclusive mother-child dependence." In fact, she continued, cultural anthropology showed that there was "security in a larger number of nurturing figures." In this era, when "[p]reparation for change—radical, rapid change—is the greatest single educational requirement," there was ample evidence "to warrant the advocacy of such public measures as . . . provision of daycare . . . for the children of working mothers" and other new ways of childrearing "which would establish a new level of human existence."[6]

These back-door assaults on the importance of motherhood were not exactly honest. They relied, in fact, on serious logical distortions used elsewhere during the era to deny any linkage between broken homes and juvenile delinquency or between female-headed families and negative school performance by children.[7] Nonetheless, the message that mothers were not terribly important to children quickly took hold. Social workers, for example, began looking for a new definition of daycare that would rid it of existing pathological connotations. They soon "discovered" that daycare often assured children "better care than they would receive if they remained at home" and could, paradoxically, even "be the means of keeping families together."[8] Writing in *Child Welfare*, one social worker concluded that "daycare can offer something valuable to children *because* they are separated from their parents."[9] In short, the celebration of motherhood among child welfare professionals was over.

Policy consequences soon followed. A key breakthrough came in 1964, when staff members of the U.S. Senate Subcommittee on Education came up with a gimmick for overcoming hitherto solid congressional opposition to funding preschool, elementary, and secondary education: the targeting of categorical funds to "areas of substantial unemployment with unemployed parents." Education dollars would follow welfare dollars. During early 1965, Lyndon Johnson administration officials wove "Child Development Centers"—subsequently labeled "Head Start" programs—into the planned "war on poverty." Early, apparently positive results from the Perry Preschool Project in Ypsilanti, Michigan added to the sense of optimism. The federal government was soon aggressively back in the preschool/daycare business.

Congress amended Title IV of the Social Security Act in 1967 to provide funds for the daycare of AFDC children. In 1970, $109 million was spent on this program. Four years later, daycare for AFDC children cost $695 million. With soaring expenses and a spiraling number of "welfare mothers" and children, policymakers also began to reconsider the long-existing policy of subsidizing full-time maternal care. The 1967 law actually removed "a large measure of choice about working" from AFDC mothers. In 1972, physically well AFDC mothers with children in school were required for the first time to register for work or work training. The concept of "Workfare" slowly triumphed, and motherhood suffered another blow, this time for fiscal reasons.

The latter part of the decade also witnessed the emergence of radical feminism, and the first American linkage of child care to the demand for total sexual equality. The theme would eventually dominate the debate.

An early, widely publicized salvo came during the 1970 hearings on "Discrimination Against Women" before the House Special Subcommittee on Education. Wilma Scott Heide, then chairman [sic] of the board of directors of the National Organization for Women (NOW), laid out the two imperatives for radical change in America. The first, she said, was U.S. "overpopulation," which threatened "the quality of people and our total environment." "Superimposed" solutions such as "coercive family limitation" did not get to the heart of the problem, she added. "Unless women have, from the moment of birth, socialization for, expectations of, and preparation for a viable significant alternative to motherhood . . . women will continue to want and reproduce too many children." The second imperative, Heide maintained, was "the women's rights liberation movement," which promised "the creation of an androgynous society to replace our androcentic culture, and . . . a viable democracy to replace male supremacy values."[10]

Government-funded, collective, gender-neutral child care was seen as necessary to meeting both imperatives. At NOW's 1970 annual conference, the organization declared that "Child care must become a political priority," and it called for the building of an action coalition "to exert pressure on the power structure in labor, industry and government to immediately make available facilities, funds, etc. and to grant tax deductions for quality child care." The 1970 "Platform on Women's Rights" of the New Democratic Coalition demanded that government "provide child-care centers as a matter of right to all children whose mothers need it," and "generous tax deductions" for child-care expenses.[11]

The report of the 1970 White House Conference on Children also turned against maternal care and toward social parenting. Decrying existing federal legislation resting on a "narrow and static" concept of the family and celebrating "our pluralistic culture of varying family forms and a multiplicity of cultures," the conference found the "traditional model of the biological mother as the sole and constant caretaker" to be "unusual." It cited "new" research demonstrating daycare to be "highly beneficial to the social and intellectual functioning of children." Ignoring Mom and Dad, the report declared that "Society has the ultimate responsibility for the well-being and optimum development of all children." Day care was, the report's authors admitted, "a powerful tool," granting to those who ran it "over 8,000 hours to teach [a child] values, fears, beliefs, and behaviors." Yet, they added, it was a necessary tool, needed not just so that mothers could work, but so that children might also be trained to appreciate "the changes that we as individuals are living, changes in our views of family roles." In short, the panel recommended that the federal government establish a network of "comprehensive developmental child-care centers" to accommodate 5.6 million children by 1980, and to fund and train an additional 500,000 child-care workers.[12]

Congress, rocked by urban riots and antiwar protests and locked in a fever of reform, was only too happy to oblige. In consequence, 1971 witnessed the great "child development" debate, one of this century's most fascinating and ideologically charged domestic political events. At the time, motherhood seemed to win the contest. In fact, it won a battle but lost a war.

Originally sponsored by Congressman John Brademas and Senator Walter Mondale, the child development bill reflected several impulses. The "success" of Head Start, for example, loomed large (although in retrospect, this was primarily because even mediocre performance looked good relative to the overall failure of the War on Poverty), and the concept of "child development" was in vogue. Even President Richard Nixon had called in 1969 for "a national commitment" to give "all American children an opportunity for healthful and stimulating development during the first five years of life." Second, feminist influence was growing, and needed to be appeased. As Representative Bella Abzug warned her colleagues: "The women of this country are no longer willing to be the involuntary source of cheap labor that the absence of adequate daycare facilities has dictated." And third, Congress was prepared to declare the traditional family system dead. Republican Orval Hansen of Idaho put the news bluntly: "The American family today is not any longer—if it ever was—the Norman Rockwell-*Saturday Evening Post* stereotype complete with a mother waiting at the door with hot apple pie for the children after school."[13]

The bill, eventually attached as an amendment to the reauthorization of the Economic Opportunity Act, declared comprehensive child development programs with "a full range of health, education, and social services" to be "essential to the achievement of the full potential of the Nation's children." It authorized spending $2 billion in 1973 for the creation of such programs in localities with populations over 5,000. These centers would be open to all preschool children. Those from families with an income under $4,320 would attend free, while a fee schedule would be set for children of families above this line.

Opposition to the child development proposal was unusually bitter. Senator Carl Curtis of Nebraska accused social planners of tearing children from their families and mothers. Senator James B. Allen of Mississippi saw the measure as evidence that America was "rapidly shaping up as a socialist, collectivist society under an authoritarian central government." In a brilliant oration, Senator James Buckley of New York charged that the bill would make the federal government the "arbiter of child-rearing practices in the United States ... producing a race of docile automatons." In the lower chamber, Congressman Schmitz of California noted that Congress toyed here with "elemental fire" and declared: "A Nation of orphanages cannot endure, and should not. It is an offense to God and men."[14]

Interestingly, though, even this vociferous opposition laid the groundwork for later expansion of federally funded social parenting. The concept of child development centers was so radical that it drew virtually all of the hostility. Most opposing congressmen, it turned out, bent overboard to endorse "ordinary daycare for the children of working mothers."[15]

The measure eventually passed by a wide margin in the Senate; and by a lesser one in the House. Yet Nixon vetoed the bill. "For the federal government to plunge headlong ... into supporting child development," his veto message said, "would commit the vast moral authority of the federal government to the side of communal approaches to child rearing as against the family-centered approach." The Senate subsequently sustained the veto.

Many have assumed that that put an end, temporarily at least, to the push for social parenting. In fact, it merely diverted the campaign into less divisive, but no less revolutionary, channels. These changes were such that, within only a few years, historian Bernard Greenblatt could write: "For the first time in the nation's history, social parentage competes effectively with families on a mass basis for influence over the preschool-age child."[16]

In the very year of Nixon's veto, for example, Congress quietly approved the other half of NOW's child-care agenda by liberalizing income tax deductions for child-care costs, labeling them "business expenses." For annual family incomes under $18,000, working families could now declare up to a $400 deduction each month for such costs. With higher family earnings, the deduction was prorated downward, reaching zero at $27,600. Governmental leverage against maternal care now extended for the first time to nonwelfare mothers of the middle class.

Three years later, Congress approved the largest single federal program in direct support of child care, Title XX of the Social Security Act. Designed to provide or purchase social services that would enable low- and moderate-income families to "achieve or maintain economic self support," Title XX supported 800,000 children in daycare by 1977, at a cost of $800 million.

In 1976, Congress replaced the child-care deduction with a 20 percent tax credit for work-related child-care expenses. Granted for annual costs of up to $2,000 for one and $4,000 for two or more dependents, the measure allowed taxpayers to credit against taxes up to $800. The bill also eliminated the income limit and extended the credit to married couples where one spouse worked part-time or was a student.

This measure was sold publicly as a means of simplifying tax returns. In truth, it represented a major extension of federal support for social parenting to middle- and upper-income families. As Senator Edward Kennedy acknowledged during floor debate on the measure, "We have a child care program in the tax laws." The credit, he added, was "an extremely important work incentive" for women. When Senator Allen of Mississippi charged that the proposal inappropriately mixed social programs and taxation, Senator Mike Mansfield replied: "I do not see how we can differentiate between taxes and social programs." Senator Hathaway bluntly admitted that "what we are actually doing is giving an $800 subsidy" to parents who placed their children in someone else's care.[17] No consideration was given to the financial pressures and child-care problems facing one-income or schedule-juggling two-income families. In fact, Congress implicitly decided that parents who cared for their own children would henceforward be taxed at a higher net rate than those who hired someone else to provide the care.

At times, it is true, backsliding by federal officials to older attitudes occurred. In 1977, for example, Assistant Secretary of Labor Arnold Packer advocated the one-per-family allocation of public service jobs, in order to sustain "the traditional American family structure with two parents and children in which the family head goes out to work and makes enough of a living to keep the family together." He was pilloried in the feminist press.

Indeed, the late 1970s and early 1980s brought enhanced attention to the "civil rights" aspects of subsidized child care. In an important 1981 report, *Child Care and Equal Opportunity for Women*, the U.S. Commission on Civil Rights declared "that women's traditional family role—and in particular their responsibility for child care—constitutes a significant barrier to equal opportunity." While the commission said that it did not intend to suggest that women "should make extrafamilial child care arrangements," it quickly went on to use the fact that many women did choose to be full-time mothers to be prima facie evidence that women were discriminated against. The report noted, for example, that "mothers are the group of women least likely to be in the labor force," which it interpreted as proof of discrimination. Among its conclusions, the report also stated that the subsidy provided by the child-care tax credit was so low "that some women may still choose to remain at home rather than to seek employment." The very existence of nonworking mothers had, in this view, become an affront to basic civil rights.[18]

Once again, Congress was eager to oblige the partisans of change. In 1984, it raised the child-care credit for those families making $28,000 or less. For adjusted gross incomes of $10,000 or less, Congress increased the maximum credit to $720 for one child and $1,440 for two. At $20,000, the figures were $600 and $1,200 respectively. For incomes above $28,000, it stood at $480 and $960. Families that sacrificed a potential second income or that, through the pains of juggling job schedules, chose to care for their own children again received nothing.

Even more aid for nonparental care has been promised. The 1984 Republican platform took pride in the increase of the child-care credit and pledged to raise it further. The Democratic platform called for expanded daycare facilities, paid for by the federal government or business corporations. Presidential candidates, looking to 1988, see an expanded daycare subsidy as the core of a modern family policy.

Social parenting, in short, now stands virtually unopposed as official United States policy. By way of contrast, caring for and raising one's own children in America has become a privilege for which one must pay.

Is this the situation that a majority of the American people desire? The truth is that the question has never been honestly placed before the nation. In contrast to Sweden, for example, where the turn to social parenting was a conscious, open act motivated by socialist principles, the American policy embrace of social parenting has proceeded surreptitiously under labels such as "welfare reform," "tax equity," and "tax simplification."

Moreover, it remains true that the effects of widespread, universal daycare are still unknown. The American research used to justify the vast expansion of social parenting has been based largely on results found among the most deprived elements of the population, where group care usually is better than a brutal or nonexistent home life. It has been a fundamental error, though, to transpose results achieved among a specific target group to the nation-at-large.

There is also substantial research suggesting that the depersonalization inherent in the group care of children under the age of three commonly causes "anaclitic depression" and other psychobiological disorders. Jay Belsky of Pennsylvania State University, an early child development center enthusiast, now believes that children placed in daycare when under 18 months are far more "insecure in their attachment to their mothers," which often results in "aggression, non-compliance, and withdrawal." Medical researchers have documented higher rates of meningitis and infectious hepatitis among children receiving social parenting. A new study from the University of Alabama reports that even *unborn* siblings are imperiled by daycare, as children carry home from daycare centers the once rare cytomegalovirus infection.[19] Viewed internationally, strong evidence exists suggesting that universal daycare in the Soviet Union—in place for many decades now—has resulted in an epidemic of psychological disorders. In Sweden, where twenty years of pressures and incentives have statistically eliminated the full-time mother, results are also not encouraging. Public daycare there was recently attacked by Swedish writer Margareta Zetterstrom as "a loveless storage place." The failure of daycare to create the promised "new" individual has also led to calls for more coercion aimed at "breaking down the isolation of families as units" and forcing men to act more like mothers.[20]

Why have feminists clamored so intensively for federal subsidy of social parenting? The simple fact is that reasonably good daycare is quite expensive, annually costing from $3,000 to $6,000 per child over the age of three and up to $18,000 for infant care. Studies by Gad Shifron at the University of Wisconsin's Institute for Research on Poverty have shown, moreover, "that most middle- and upper-income families are not willing to cover the full cost of quality group child care."[21] Hence it was only with state subsidization that social parenting became rational economic behavior. And it was only through federal subsidization that social parenting could grow so as to challenge parental, family-based care as the dominant form of child rearing in America. Indeed, it is probably no coincidence that the most dramatic, "normative" jump in the labor force participation rate of married women with children under the age of six (from 30 percent in 1970 to 48 percent in 1981) came only after the federal government began its net transfer of income away from families caring for their own children and toward those that hired others to provide this care.[22]

It is undeniable that about 50 percent of the mothers of preschool-aged children now work (although a large portion of them do so on a part-time or seasonal basis). It is equally undeniable that 50 percent do not. Unless one accepts the charge that the mere existence of a mother-at-home is a social crime (this is the Swedish and Soviet view), there is no compelling reason for the federal government to penalize through the tax code such a choice of child care. Nor is there any justification for forcing business corporations to pay the bill for daycare. In fact, a strong case could be made that federal policy should encourage, rather than penalize, the parental care of small children. In short, the pressing need in America is to expand the debate beyond daycare, into the whole realm of family policy.

Notes

1. On this period, see: Bernard Greenblatt, *Responsibility for Child Care: The Changing Role of Family and State in Child Development* (San Francisco: Jossey-Bass, 1977), pp. 41–69; and Margaret O'Brien Steinfels, *Who's Minding the Children?: The History and Politics of Day Care in America* (New York: Simon & Schuster, 1973).
2. John Bowlby, *Maternal Care and Mental Health* (New York: Schocken Books, 1950), pp. 11, 67, 73–74.
3. Talcott Parsons, "The Normal American Family," in *Man and Civilization: The Family's Search for Survival*, ed. Seymour M. Farber (New York: McGraw Hill, 1965), pp. 31–49.
4. Greenblatt, p. 61.
5. Steinfels, p. 72; and *Recommendations: 1960 White House Conference on Children and Youth* (Washington, DC: Government Printing Office, 1960), p. 62.
6. R.G. Andry, "Parental and Maternal Roles and Delinquency," and Margaret Mead, "A Cultural Anthropologist's Approach to Maternal Deprivation;" reprinted in *Deprivation of Maternal Care: A Reassessment of Its Effects* (New York: Schocken Books, 1972), pp. 223–51.
7. See: Travis Hirschi and Hanan C. Selvin, "False Criteria of Causality in Delinquency Research," *Social Problems* 14 (Winter 1966): 254–68; and Allan Carlson, "Sex According to Social Science," *Policy Review* 20 (Spring 1982); 129–32.
8. John R. Hanson and Kathryn Pemberton, "Day Care Service for Families with Mothers Working at Home," and Viola G. Gilfillan, "Day Care as a

Therapeutic Service," in *Day Care: A Preventive Service* (New York: Child Welfare League of America, 1963), pp. 1, 7.

9. Quoted in Steinfels, p. 78.
10. Catharine R. Stimpson, *Discrimination Against Women: Congressional Hearing on Equal Rights in Education and Employment* (New York: R. R. Bowker, 1973), pp. 21–22.
11. *Ibid.*, p. 542, 549.
12. *Report to the President. White House Conference on Children* (Washington, DC: U.S. Government Printing Office, 1970), pp. 227, 277–79, 283–84, 286.
13. *Congressional Record*, Dec. 7, 1971, pp. H45091–93.
14. *Congressional Record*, Dec. 2, 1971, pp. S44113–58; Dec. 7, 1971, pp. H45069–101.
15. For examples, see: *Congressional Record*, Dec. 7, 1971, p. H45090; Dec. 2, 1971, p. S44141.
16. Greenblatt, p. 270.
17. *Congressional Record*, July 21, 1976, pp. S23144–17.
18. United States Commission on Civil Rights, *Child Care and Equal Opportunity for Women* (Washington, DC: U.S. Government Printing Office, 1981), pp. vii, 3, 10, 26.
19. Jay Belsky and Russell Isabella, "The Effects of Infant Day Care on Social and Emotional Development," ms. accepted for publication in *Developmental and Behavioral Pediatrics*, Vol. 9, ed. M. Wolraich and D. Routh, (JAI Press); and Robert F. Pass, et al., "Young Children as a Probable Source of Maternal and Congenital Cytomegalovirus Infection," *The New England Journal of Medicine* 316 (28 May 1977): 1366–70.
20. See: Dale Meers, "International Day Care: A Selective Review and Psychoanalytic Critique," reprinted in *Congressional Record*, Dec. 2, 1971, pp. S44128–34; Hilda Scott, *Sweden's Right to Be Human: Sex-Role Equality: The Goal and the Reality* (Armonk, NJ: M.E. Sharpe, 1982), pp. 99–116; and "An Eden in Sweden?" *Newsweek* (Sept. 10, 1984): 20.
21. Gad Shifron, *Sources of the Mounting Pressure to Subsidize Preschool Child Care*, Discussion Paper No. 234–74 (Madison, WI: Institute for Research on Poverty, 1974), p. 5.
22. U.S. Department of Commerce, Bureau of the Census, *Population Profile of the United States*, Series P–20/370 (1982), p. 42.

2

The Working Family

The relatively new concept of "comparable worth" is a full-scale assault on a market economy. If triumphant, its end result could only be governmental control of the wage-setting process, administered either by "equal opportunity" bureaucrats or federal judges.

Pushed by feminist groups—indeed frequently labeled *the* feminist issue of the 1980s—comparable worth rests on the premise that deep-seated discrimination confines, or "crowds," women into certain low-paying jobs. As a result, advocates say, market wages are basically sexist, a favorite statistic being that the average working woman receives only 60 percent of the wage paid to the average working man. To overcome such "institutionalized sexism," they add, pay scales need to be readjusted to reflect true "job value" so that positions held primarily by women pay as much as "comparable" jobs held by men. Schoolteachers, for example, might be as highly valued for their instruction of children as corporate managers are for their efforts at facilitating production; nurses ought to be compensated for their physical and emotional treatment of patients to the same degree that doctors are for their technical manipulations.[1]

Champions of the comparable worth doctrine received an enormous boost in late 1983 when U.S. District Court Judge Jack E. Tanner ruled that the state of Washington was guilty of "pervasive wage discrimination" against women. He ordered the state to award back pay and higher wages to over 15,000 of its employees, at a potential cost to taxpayers of $1 billion. Buoyed by this success, the American Federation of State, County, and Municipal Employees, AFL-CIO, is pursuing similar litigation in other states. A half-dozen states already have comparable worth legislation on the books. Another fourteen states have comparability language in their equal pay statutes, adopted during the 1960s, and advocates see great potential in urging the courts to reinterpret those laws in line with the comparable worth doctrine. On the federal level, Senators Edward Kennedy and Alan Cranston have led the push for congressional action.

Reacting to this flood of activity, opponents of the comparable worth doctrine have raised a host of counter arguments, largely economic in nature.[2] They contend that the free market is in fact working well, and that the pay differential between men and women can be readily explained by legitimate market factors, including the lower average education and skill levels of women, the higher turnover rate of female employees as they leave jobs to have babies or follow their husbands to a different location, the recent oversupply of workers in occupations such as elementary teaching, the preference of women for indoor work, and the proven tendency of married men to work harder and longer hours to support their families. Opponents of comparable worth also argue that no real evidence exists to support the doctrine and that comparable worth rests on the precapitalist, almost medieval belief that jobs have an intrinsic value that can be measured independent of supply and demand.

Significantly, though, these opponents have all but ignored the underlying cultural and ideological contexts of the comparable worth campaign.[3] Such an omission is understandable, for this broader view raises uncomfortable questions which the American political process is ill-prepared to handle. Nonetheless, unless the hidden agenda behind the comparable worth doctrine is exposed and confronted, the American social order will fundamentally change—not by decision but by default—and comparable worth will by one means or another almost certainly become the law of the land.

From this broader perspective, the comparable worth debate is merely one battle line in a war of ideas over how to organize family life and sex roles in contemporary society. As Swedish feminist Alva Myrdal noted back in 1966, such controversy "is largely ideological in character," representing a conflict between the "bourgeois" or middle-class family model and the individualistic, or atomistic, model advanced by Marxists, radicals, and social libertarian thinkers alike.

While the middle-class model had its roots in the seventeenth and eighteenth centuries, it emerged as a numerically significant phenomenon only in the nineteenth century, as the wealth-creating miracles of modern capitalism lifted a growing proportion of the population out of crushing poverty. Women were able to leave fields and primitive factories to give greater attention to the upbringing of children. The natural working family, bonded to a rural economy, became the modern child-centered family, focused on the protection, health, and education of the young. Child care practices among the bourgeoisie improved notably, and infant mortality rates declined.

During the early twentieth century, non-Marxist labor leaders in the West also began demanding payment of a "family wage" to workers, calling for an income sufficient for a male laborer to support his wife and children in modest comfort. Western nations responded in different ways. In France, for example, industrialists took the lead in creating a voluntary family allowance system—later nationalized—which paid an increasingly higher wage according to the number of dependent children in the family.

In the United States, another, less precise and nonstatist type of "family wage" emerged through both cultural pressures and political action.[4] Among the cultural forces, it is undeniable that deeply ingrained assumptions concerning sex roles in the family stratified the American labor market. With but modest exceptions, the highest-paying job categories were reserved by convention for men, as "heads of households." Moreover, the real pay differentials that existed between men and women were justified on the rationale that most men "had a wife and children to support." Put another way, the market internalized cultural assumptions about the importance to society of maternal care of children, and directed resources toward families so engaged.

On the policy side, the Social Security system created in the 1930s presumed this middle class family as the norm, and provided widows' pensions and Aid to Dependent Children as specialized family allowances. The 1948 restructuring of the federal income tax system created the joint return, which favored married couples living on one income and set the personal deduction at $600, acts that removed the vast majority of American families from any significant tax liability.

As late as 1965, such attitudes still prevailed in most Western countries. An International Labor Organization report issued that year found many governments reluctant to encourage further female participation in the wage market. West Germany, for example, felt that female employment should be encouraged only "in so far as the family responsibilities may permit." The United States affirmed "the basic legal principle which places on the husband the primary responsibility for support of his wife and family with secondary liability devolving on the wife."[5]

Opposed to this vision is the atomistic model, resting on full equality in sex roles and predicated on a devaluation—even elimination—of the family as an intermediate social structure. The origins of this ideology lay in the radical-liberal and Marxist writings of the late eighteenth and nineteenth centuries. In this vision, men and women have no separate roles. Rather, they can claim but one shared role: being human. Parenting is viewed as a joint responsibility to be shared equally by men and women. Advocates of this model condemn the sex roles of the bourgeois family, even characterizing the full-time "wife-mother" as a "legal prostitute." Such a wife-mother lives "the humiliating existence of a parasite," they argue; she is "a spiritual cripple." The demand for equality between the sexes means that both men and women should be expected to labor outside the home throughout their working lives, while those advantages previously enjoyed by women—legal protection, the right to be supported through marriage, custody of the children in cases of divorce, widows' pensions—should also be eliminated. In sum, in place of the child-centered family resting on differentiated sex roles, advocates of the atomistic vision call for the return of the working family, one surprisingly similar to that found in the preindustrial era.

In our century, this latter ideological vision has won its most complete victory in Sweden. It is not a coincidence that comparable worth advocates also look to that land as the model for American emulation, as the one place where the comparable worth doctrine has been successfully implemented.[6]

The campaign to eliminate sex roles in Sweden first took on public significance in 1935, with creation of a Parliamentary Committee on Women's Work. In a twist of irony, it was actually set up at the insistence of conservative parliamentarians dedicated to the "family wage" concept and concerned about the inequities of what they called the "double wage" earned by families with working wives. Yet dominated by socialists and left-liberals, the committee quickly turned the ideological table. Its 1938 report emphasized the inevitability and necessity of women's labor outside the home, and the "right" of women to be paid laborers despite marriage and motherhood. The committee urged, among other proposals, expansion in the number of daycare centers, the preferential hiring of women to remove the effects of past discrimination, and an unspecified "new" wage system that would insure that women were paid as much as men.

Interestingly, though, such ideas lay mostly dormant in Sweden for another twenty-five years. Official rhetoric notwithstanding, the Swedish nation shared in the resurgence of "bourgeois domesticity" that characterized virtually all Western lands in the 1945–60 period. As late as 1965, only one-quarter of Swedish women with children under age seven were employed, and a majority of those working did so only part-time. Day care centers were few, serving less than 12,000 children. Maternal care remained the norm.

All that changed during the 1960s. Open, public debate on "sex roles" began early in that decade and became a national passion by 1968. According to one analyst of the controversy, the conservative position was weakly represented: first, by a "traditional" ideology "anchored in the Judeo/Christian religion and in talismanic concepts" of man as woman's lord and master; and second, a "romantic" or middle-class ideology, which saw men and women as essentially different, yet equal and complementary, with the latter principally occupied with the virtues of marriage and motherhood.

Significantly, the writer noted that the conservative viewpoint was "seldom championed at the 'expert' level of debate," finding expression only "in the letters to the editors of weekly magazines and in the views expressed by employees, supervisory personnel and employers"—*i.e.*, among the grass roots and in Sweden's private economic sector.

The Swedish "experts," instead, were arrayed on the side of the "moderate" and "liberal-radical" ideologies. The former position aimed at giving every woman the "right" to choose freely between children and career, "to remove as far as possible the conflict between these two roles." The "liberal-radical" position embodied the atomistic vision outright, denying that women could balance their "two roles" without total social reconstruction necessitating the leveling of sex roles.[7]

Predictably, as the debate progressed, the conservative position—undefended by "experts"—virtually disappeared, while the "moderates" gradually gave way to the "liberal-radical" perspective. In truth, the moderate position proved to be built of sand, and it was simply swept aside by both the compelling logic of the "liberal-radical" view and the passion for equality. In consequence, Swedish middle-class culture began to dissolve under persistent ideological attack. In the mid–1960's, school officials adopted "an emphatic policy of not only refusing to perpetuate but actively counteracting the traditional view of sex roles."[8] Sweden's 1968 report to the United Nations on the status of women declared that "A decisive and ultimately durable improvement in the status of women cannot be attained by special measures aimed at women alone; it is equally necessary to abolish the conditions which tend to assign certain privileges, obligations or rights to men." In order to ensure that "every individual" has "the same responsibility for his or her own maintenance," it continued, "a radical change in deep-rooted traditions and attitudes must be brought about among both men and women, and active steps must be taken by the community to encourage a change in the roles played by both."[9]

Early on, Swedish advocates of the atomized social order recognized that their ideological vision necessitated a basic change in the wage system, a move toward comparable worth. In 1956, Alva Myrdal argued that "a new wage system is required, based on the character of the job to be done."[10] A decade later, two other Swedish writers maintained that wage differentials between "male and female occupational areas" had been established "without regard to the relative requirements of skills, responsibility, etc., of the different areas," and that removing this differential required changes in pay policies "to raise the wage levels in traditional female job zones."[11]

As recast over the course of the 1970s, the Swedish goal became creation of "the working family," a social system wherein every adult would work regardless of married or parental status. In an article for the Swedish Information Service, editor Monica Boethius has defined this family type as one where "two grown-ups (or one, in a one-parent family) spend most of their working day outside the home" while "the children have to be cared for by somebody else." It is a social system in which both men and women view their careers as long-term life commitments, "while caring for a growing family is for both sexes primarily an interlude."[12] It is a vision, moreover, that has vast public policy consequences. As Swedish Undersecretary for Labor Britt Rollen recently put it, the Swedish government now aims at eliminating the bourgeois ideal, "where a man goes out and earns the money his family needs." Instead, "We [now] want to make it possible for everybody to find a paid job and to achieve economic independence. . . . Our aim is to apply this attitude to the whole of society, to working life but also [sic] to politics and family life. . . . [We] realize that this will call for changes in the way in which society, workplaces and the home are organized."[13]

Indeed, much of the 1970s was given over to this radical reconstruction task. With the homemaker declared to be "a dying race,"[14] legal changes removed the special protections afforded women in marriage. Changes in Swedish tax law essentially eliminated the joint return for a married couple, and have left all persons paying the same tax, whether alone, married but childless, or married with children. Moreover, marginal Swedish income taxes were increased in the period (such rates soon approached 80 percent at even a modest income level), making extra personal effort to support a family on one income virtually impossible.

Swedish welfare policy was also altered to discourage maternal care of preschool children. A generous "means-tested" housing allowance, for example, is available to families with children. However, under new law, the housing allowance is denied to families where one or the other parent chooses to care for his or her children and refuses to place them in a daycare center. Choosing *not* to use heavily subsidized government daycare, moreover, represents an implicit rejection of benefits such as free children's meals and diapers. Even economic changes over the last two decades have conspired against parent-raised children, making the single-income family impossible. In 1984, for example, the Swedish "poverty line" for a family of four was 131,000 *Kronor*; but the average annual wage for a Swedish worker ranged between 75,000 and 94,000 *Kronor*, truly making two incomes mandatory. In effect, the market compensated for the massive entry of women into the lifetime labor force by eliminating the "family wage" through the attrition of inflation. Finally, a combination of state pressures and labor union demands have effectively implemented the comparable worth principle. In the Swedish manufacturing sector, for example, women now earn over 90 percent of the male wage, proving to American advocates that "it can be done."[15]

Admirers of the Swedish system point to its "parent insurance" program, which guarantees parents six months of paid leave from work following childbirth and another six months paid leave to be used during the pre-school years. They also cite its child allowance program, which pays a modest sum annually to parents for each child.

In truth, these provisions do little to blunt the effects of a coercive social order dedicated to the destruction of the middle class. The reality of cultural war against the capitalistic laggards is clearly admitted in official Swedish publications, which regularly cite "private enterprise" and "private firms and companies" as the major bastions of continuing sex discrimination, albeit ones already slated for radical change. The fact that most men in the private sector did not use their parental insurance, one writer notes, meant that the law had to be changed to "force them to shoulder their responsibilities." The fact that school girls still tend to choose occupations in traditionally "female" fields, another says, means only that school officers must redouble their efforts "to challenge conventional stereotypes."[16]

The results of this unrelenting social, political, and economic pressure are beginning to show. Between 1965 and 1980, the proportion of women with preschool children who work rose from 27 to 64 percent. Four years later, according to one report, the full-time mother could "no longer be found among young women"; indeed, "the highest employment participation rate is to be found among mothers of infant children."[17] Only 60,000 Swedish children were enrolled in all types of government childcare facilities in 1960; by 1980, 413,000 were.

But the negative consequences of this "sex role" revolution are also pouring in. The Swedish marriage rate began falling in 1966, and is now at the lowest level in recorded world history. Similarly, Sweden's birth rate has tumbled to new lows, and today stands well below the level needed to achieve even zero population growth. Having drained marriage and child-bearing of any moral and social significance, Sweden faces an increasingly sterile future. With the uprearing and character-education of children largely socialized, creating a family and bearing babies simply makes little sense in that land today.

Indeed, most Swedes have even forgotten how to ask moral questions. As Monica Boethius cheerfully notes, the growing refusal of young couples to have children has resulted in "no, or at least very little, speculation that the reason is because women work outside their homes to such a large extent. Nor are there any illusions that they lack responsibility or that they are too materialistic. These arguments would have been very common in many quarters a decade ago. The content of opinions expressed now have dealt ... with such questions as why young people feel they want to live without children or perhaps with only one child."[18]

If her reporting is correct, Ms. Boethius has unwittingly authored her requiem for a doomed society.

In the United States, we are far along the same path toward the "working family" social order. Yet in contrast to Sweden, where the debate over "sex roles" was at least open, honest, and conclusive, our moral and legal "revolution" has often been fought in closed rooms and dark corridors, hidden from public view.

Symbolic of this, the "comparable worth" doctrine derives whatever federal legal status it has primarily from Title VII of the Civil Rights Act of 1964, which prohibits discrimination in employment on the basis of sex. Yet this critical provision, which is serving as the crucial wedge for the wholesale, government-enforced transformation of sex roles in America, was adopted by Congress without hearings, after less than half a day of confused debate, and somewhat as a joke. Indeed, it was introduced as an amendment to the Civil Rights bill on the floor of the U.S. House of Representatives by Democrat Howard Smith of Virginia, who hoped to scuttle the whole measure by attaching to it an embarrassing, confusing, and silly provision. When he proposed his amendment, it was actually met by a gale of laughter (dutifully recorded in the *Congressional Record*); Smith had to reassure his colleagues that he was "serious about this thing." Moreover, implementation of Title VII has proceeded primarily through regulatory action, divorced from public debate. Between 1968 and 1971, one writer sympathetic to feminism notes, the Equal Employment Opportunity Commission "converted Title VII into a magna carta for female workers, grafting to it a set of rules and regulations that certainly could not have passed Congress in 1964, and perhaps not a decade later, either."[19]

Even the Equal Pay Act of 1963—the measure assuring "equal pay for equal work" which no significant politician challenges today—was premised on an unresolved contradiction, one fully revealed in the report of President John Kennedy's Commission on the Status of Women released the same year. On the one hand, the report "presupposed that the nuclear family unit was vital to the stability of American society and that women have a unique and immutable role in the family unit." On the other hand, the report urged that "every obstacle" to women's "full participation in society must be removed." As feminists have correctly argued, this deep tension and implicit contradiction between women's "two roles" could be removed only when men and society at large were fundamentally changed and took on vastly augmented responsibility for childrearing and home-making.[20]

Indeed, by fits and starts, America has moved toward such a "working family" order, predicated on the atomistic view of society. As the Swedish experience suggests, public policy can favor either the middle-class family model or the "working family" model; it cannot be "moderate," favorable to both, or neutral. From the early 1960s on, the trend in the United States has clearly been toward the "working family." Between 1960 and 1984, changes in federal tax law and the seldom visible effects of inflation raised the average tax rate of a married couple with four children by over 200 percent; in contrast, working couples without children saw no change in their average rate. As noted earlier, Congress has granted a generous tax credit to working couples who place their children in daycare centers. Parents who have sacrificed extra income to care for their own children enjoy no comparable tax benefit. Some tax theorists even talk of taxing households for the unpaid services of a full-time mother. Legal changes, from "no-fault" divorce laws to "joint custody" of the children of divorce, are removing most of the protections and privileges once enjoyed by women in marriage. Feminist leadership has taken aim (so far unsuc-cessfully) at Social Security benefits premised on the "middle class" family model, encouraged the elimination of the joint income tax return, and renewed the push for more federally funded daycare. Moreover, the rising cost of housing and high mortgage interest rates, both driven by inflation, have meant that two incomes are increasingly necessary for securing home ownership and other facets of the faltering "American Dream."

As in Sweden, then, the direction is not toward "choice," but rather toward a new kind of "coercion"; toward a society where maternal care of small children is legally difficult and financially impossible; toward the postbourgeois, "working family" order.

In blindly accepting the terminology of "sexism," "discrimination," and "equality" as a given, opponents of the comparable worth doctrine have already conceded most of the battlefield. It is possible that they may be able to stem the floodtide of comparable worth initiatives by stressing thor-oughly logical, statistically solid, and economically sound free market ar-guments. Yet it is unlikely. For logic and freedom are but frail reeds against the passion for equality, particularly when the religious and family norms that undergird a free society have been weakened and are ignored. Com-parable worth opponents are facing a social conflagration, but they insist on trying to put out an economic brushfire.

Notes

1. The latter examples from: Clarice Stasz, *The American Nightmare: Why Inequality Persists* (New York: Schocken Books, 1981), p. 188.
2. "Comparable Worth—Part 1: A Theory With No Facts," and "Comparable Worth—Part 2: The High Cost of Bad Policy," *Backgrounders #336 and #337* (Washington, D.C.: The Heritage Foundation, 1984); Deborah Walker, "Value and Opportunity: The Issue of Comparable Pay for Comparable Worth," *Policy Analysis (CATO Institute)*, May 31, 1984; Phyllis S. Schlafly, "Equal Pay for Comparable Worth," *The Phyllis Schlafly Report* (January 1984); Michael Levin, "Comparable Worth: The Feminist Road to Socialism," *Commentary* (September 1984): 13–19; and Rita Ricardo-Campbell, *Women and Comparable Worth*, (Stanford, CA: Hoover Institution, Stanford University, 1985).
3. The only public opponent regularly to touch on these points is Phyllis Schlafly, who has correctly noted that "the target group which the Comparable Worth advocates believe are *over*paid are the blue collar men (who are generally supporting their families.)"
4. It should be noted, though, that private "family allowance" systems were not unknown in the U.S.A. One 1943 study found a large number of public school districts paying a significantly higher wage to married male teachers, as heads of households.
5. *Woman in a Changing World*; quoted in: Annikea Baude and Per Holmberg, "The Positions of Men and Women in the Labour Market," *The Changing Roles of Men and Women*, ed. Edmund Dahlstrom, trans. Gunnilla and Steven Aulerman (Boston: Beacon, 1962), pp. 106–07.
6. As example, see: Tamar Lewin, "A New Push to Raise Women's Pay," *The New York Times*, January 1, 1984, p. 15.
7. Edmund Dahlstrom, "Analysis of the Debate on Sex Roles," in Dahlstrom, pp. 170–81.
8. Baude and Holmberg, p. 124.
9. *The Status of Women in Sweden: Report to the United Nations, 1968*; appendix in Dahlstrom, pp. 213–15.
10. Alva Myrdal and Viola Klein, *Women's Two Roles: Home and Work* (London: Routledge & Kegan Paul, 1956), p. 113.
11. Baude and Holmberg, pp. 121–22.
12. Monica Boethius, "The Working Family," *Social Change in Sweden* 30 (May 1984): 2.
13. Berit Rollen, "The Working Family: Work and Family Patterns," paper presented at the seminar, "The Working Family: Perspectives and Prospects in the U.S. and Sweden," sponsored by the Swedish Information Service and the Swedish Embassy, Washington, D.C., May 1984, pp. 1–2.
14. Rollen, p. 2.
15. A chilling portrayal of life in "The Working Family" state, written by a young mother, is found in: Krister Pettersson, "Sveriges forstatligade barn," *Contra* 10, No. 3 (1984): 16–17.
16. From: Boethius, p. 5; "Equality Between Men and Women in Sweden," *Fact Sheets on Sweden: Published by the Swedish Institute* (December 1983): 1–2; and Rollen, p. 4.
17. Rollen, p. 3.
18. Boethius, "The Working Family," p. 3.

19. On the origins of Title VII, see: Donald Allen Robinson, "Two Movements in Pursuit of Equal Employment Opportunity," *Signs: Journal of Women in Culture and Society* 4, No. 3 (1979): 427.
20. See Judith Hale and Ellen Levine, *Rebirth of Feminism* (New York: Quadrangle Books, 1971), pp. 18–24, 28–30.

3

The Androgyny Hoax

We are all androgynes now. Or so the popular media would have us believe.

In the last decade and a half we have witnessed a wave of attention to androgyny, the blending of masculine and feminine traits into a reputedly new human type. Proponents of androgyny deny that there is any meaningful biological base to male and female sex roles. Rather, it is social conditioning that determines human behavior. Each person reflects his or her unique mix of male and female behavioral traits. Yet androgynes, they quickly add, display the best of masculinity and femininity. They are flexible, open, free, happy, and terribly effective: almost the long-promised Nietzschean "superpeople."

Many journalists quickly embraced the androgyne as social messiah. *The New York Times* reported that spiritual androgyny delivers to men "a kind of freedom" denied to those locked in the old male stereotype. *U.S. News & World Report* argued that the return of the macho during the Reagan era is merely a blip in the long-term trend toward androgyny: Boy George and Michael Jackson better represent our future. *Newsweek* chronicled the hugging, highly "sensitive" activities of the National Organization of Changing Men, who reject "the enslaving macho code of honor." Androgyny represents "the full potential of the sexes . . . a perfect representation of cosmic unity," reported *Cosmopolitan*. There are not two sexes, but rather "a spectrum of individual proclivities more or less male and more or less female." *Vogue* celebrated the bisexual rocker/actor David Bowie—"a golden blaze lissome gesture, seraphic facial expression, satin hair"—as the androgynous ideal. *Saturday Review* reported that the nation's turn to a service-oriented economy necessitates more androgyny. As one psychologist put it: "We're going to need more deviation from the two-sex role scheme if our culture is to survive." *People* magazine concluded that "these days, androgyny seems almost as American as, well, Dad and apple pie." As the manager of a West Hollywood female-impersonator club explained:

29

"When we first opened, only the elite turned out. Now we have the 'give me a beer and skip the glass' crowd as well."[1]

The drums beat most furiously at *Psychology Today*, which has elevated androgyny to orthodox, normative status. Joseph Pleck complained in the magazine's pages that the old male sex-role identity has damaged men, women, and society as a whole. Male attributes such as rigidity, contempt for weakness, and intolerance of deviance cause fascism, he said. Society is at fault for imposing "unrealistic male-role expectations" on American men. In another piece, executive editor Howard Mason argued that macho test pilots are no longer needed for space exploration. The future of space travel, he maintained, lies with androgynes, men and women able both to meet goals and to show emotional warmth. The magazine also concluded that the androgynous soul was the most "well-rounded and flexible lover," probably the highest compliment that its editors could bestow.[2]

Such popular enthusiasm did not emerge in a vacuum. Rather, it reflects changes in the theories of personality dominating the psychology and psychiatry professions. This shift in ideas began during the 1960s and won a kind of dominance during the 1970s. The battles were fought in professional conferences and specialized journals, largely out of public view. Between 1974 and 1985, for example, there was a 500 percent increase in the number of journal articles listed in the standard indexes that dealt with masculinity, femininity, and androgyny. The subject acquired its own publication, *Sex Roles*. Only later did the androgynous vision spread to the general-interest magazines and pop culture.

Curiously, just as its victory seemed secure, the theory of psychological androgyny began to stagger and fall on the intellectual level, the victim of new and honest social, psychological, and medical research. The popular proponents of the androgynous ideal continue to assert that we are entering the Age of Androgyny. Yet if they are correct, the new evidence strongly suggests that Americans are becoming a very disturbed people.

The rise of androgyny theory needs to be set in the context of the remarkable restoration of traditional values during the 1945–60 period. Defenders of the family in this era saw feminism as the enemy. Their primary goal was the reassertion of strong male and female sex roles as a guide to normal behavior and mental health.

One of the firmest popular statements in this regard was the 1947 book *Modern Woman: The Lost Sex* by Ferdinand Lundberg and Marynia Farnham, M.D. The authors acknowledged that the rise of modernity, as symbolized by the industrial and French revolutions, has undermined the home and the place of women within it. Yet the result, Lundberg and Farnham said, was a shell-shocked culture which had unsettled male identity and "converted a large number of women into harpies."

The authors reserved their sharpest words for feminists. Such activists, they said, sought not justice, but masculinity. "And a female who attempts to achieve masculinity is psychically ill in the same way as a male who attempts to achieve femininity." Feminists feared and despised children, Lundberg and Farnham reported, and pursued an ideology that was "the very negation of femaleness." Insofar as feminists achieved their goal, "it spelled only vast individual suffering for men as well as women, and much public disorder."[3]

With less rhetoric, scientists rallied to support the contention that men were men, and women were women. Researchers in the 1950s began to explore the effects of hormones on animal behavior, discovering, for example, that the cyclic regulation of menstruation in female rats was mediated through the brain. Such work provided a model for theorizing about human sex differences in areas such as aggressivity, intelligence, and sexuality. In the field of sociology, Talcott Parsons led his colleagues and students back to a reaffirmation of traditional sex roles, identifying traits which he labeled "instrumental" or action-oriented for men and "expressive" or nurturing for women. The former personality orientation, he said, aimed at defending and advancing a social system, while the latter sought to resolve the tensions within the group and secure family solidarity. Reflecting on the roots of this distinction in human nature, Parsons asserted that it was "the main axis of the differentiation of sex roles in all societies."[4] Similarly, the dominant figures in Freudian psychoanalysis again trumpeted individual resolution of the Oedipal and Electra complexes, and the shaping of healthy adult male and female personalities, as the sources of proper social adjustment.

Through these constructs, the theory of "natural complement," shaped most completely in the nineteenth century, again found recognition. It affirmed that there were different traits and capacities in men and women which derived from their distinct biologies. Men were larger, stronger, and more aggressive, and it was natural for them to be breadwinners, produce commodities, and perform military service. Women bore children and had a maternal, nurturing instinct that made them more sensitive and intuitive in their perceptions of human needs. The natural love relationship, accordingly, was a heterosexual union of man and woman. Together, they formed a whole being. Love between a man and a woman was the attraction of complements, each being equally powerful in his or her sphere: man in the world, and woman in the home. Psychologist Ashley Montagu, over the decades something of a philosophical chameleon, reflected this postwar consensus, arguing that "being a good wife, a good mother, in short a good homemaker, is the most important of all the occupations in the world." Jerome Kagan and Howard Moss argued that there was "a need—perhaps unique to humans—to act and to believe in ways that are congruent with previously established standards." The desire to be an "ideal male" or "ideal female," they said, naturally comprised "an essential component" of every personality. They endorsed the efforts of educators to reinforce male and female distinctiveness, the "traditional standards for sex-role characteristics."[5]

Yet following the American appearance in the early 1960s of Simone de Beauvoir's *The Second Sex* and Betty Friedan's *The Feminine Mystique* the forces of tradition fell onto the defensive. With the emergence of this newly self-confident feminism, the "recognition" of psychological androgyny grew. Its appearance reflected several impulses.

First, androgyny was necessary to fill a large gap in the feminist world view and vision of the future. In 1964, sociologist Alice Rossi summarized the feminist critique of American society and argued that sex-role behaviors needed to be redefined so that each sex could cultivate positively valued characteristics traditionally linked in the past with the other sex. In a major address five years later, Rossi added that the movement toward sex equality was restricted by the fact that a woman's "most intimate human relation is the heterosexual one of marriage." This bond to males served as "a major brake" on the development of gender solidarity among women. Rejecting the "assimilationist model of equality," which asserted that women should seek an equal place in existing male economic and political institutions, Rossi instead urged development of a "hybrid model." This approach would banish the machine and consumption orientation of "plastic-Wasp-9-5 America." In its place would stand "a radical goal which ... seeks ... a new breed of men and women and a new vision of the future." This "imaginative leap" to a fresh conception of the good society based on blended sex roles also would represent the "beginning" of a new ideology.[6]

More fuel for the fire came with an influential 1970 article in which a research group led by Inge Broverman reported that clinical psychologists held a "double standard" of mental health. Professionals tended to apply the general adult standard of health only to men, perceiving women as significantly less healthy. The authors of this paper blamed such bias on the "adjustment notion of health" dominating the psychology profession, which assumed that mental health lay with the acceptance of sex-determined behavioral norms. Such "adjustment" violated American values of equal opportunity and freedom of choice, they said.[7]

Male liberation advocate Paul Hoch also turned to androgyny as the way out of the "feminist impasse." He said that radical feminists such as Kate Millett who cast males as the oppressive, chauvinistic class, offered no real alternative for male/female reconciliation: for them, the war of women against men was inevitable, and eternal. Hoch argued that the women's movement would only be able to move forward as it began to enlist the support of male "comrades." The critical task was to destroy "the extremely heavy physical and psychological burdens the present pattern of sex roles imposes on men as well as women." Only by eliminating gender assignments of any sort could progress toward real humanization occur.[8]

At a deeper level, though, the theory of androgyny linked up with the push for total social and economic revolution. Shulamith Firestone, who performed a valuable service in 1970 by drawing out the feminist world view to its logical conclusion, was clear on the need for total upheaval. The collapse of the Communist Revolution in Russia, she said, derived from its failure to destroy utterly the family, which was the true source of psychological, economic, and political oppression. Day care and equality in pay and jobs were not enough. Capitalist tokenism was a lie and a sham, she said: "Mom is vital to the American way of life, considerably more than apple pie. She is an institution without which the system really would fall apart." Hence, "Mom" must be eliminated, to be supplanted by a "feminist socialism" that would end capitalist exploitation.

In conjunction with this, Firestone stressed the need to free women from reproduction. Hope here lay with the development of bottle-baby and cloning technologies and state nurseries. Women and children must be free to do what they want sexually, so that humanity could finally revert to "its natural 'polymorphously perverse' sexuality." In the new era, "relations with children would include as much genital sex as the child was capable of" and the elimination of the incest taboo. Finally, this true revolution would demand the total destruction of the male/female and the adult/child distinctions. As Firestone concluded:

> Revolutionary feminism is the only radical program that immediately cracks through to the emotional strata underlying "serious" politics, thus reintegrating the personal with the public, the subjective with the objective, the emotional with the rational—the female principle with the male.

Through androgyny, the revolution would find psychological victory.[9]

Anne Ferguson of the University of Massachusetts summarized and updated the "historical materialist" analysis of sexual oppression, one originating among Marxist theorists such as Friedrich Engels and members of the "Frankfurt School": Adorno, Horkheimer, Fromm, and Marcuse. Ferguson argued that sex-linked personality traits were socially, not biologically, determined. She acknowledged that in the preindustrial era, with few material resources and no means of birth control, the traditional sexual division of labor (women as mothers/nurturers; men as hunters, traders, and warriors) made sense. Yet in the modern era, technologies allowed women to control births, feed babies with artificial formulas, and combat physical strength with weapons. The sexual division of labor was no longer necessary and needed to be destroyed.

In contemporary society, Ferguson concluded, only androgynes could attain their full human potential. These superpersons, freed by an over-populated world from the need for children whatsoever, could alone experience pure "bisexual love." However, capitalist society, based on the nuclear family and women's reproductive work therein, continued to frustrate emergence of the new era. So long as the social order continued to place value on biological parenthood, most children would develop a debilitating heterosexual identity. Androgyny, Ferguson concluded, would be possible only in socialist society organized on feminist principles. Yet she noted that the transition to the androgynous, socialist order could be surprisingly easy to achieve: "If the sexual division of labor were destroyed, the mechanism that trains boys and girls to develop heterosexual sexual identities would also be destroyed . . . [and] bisexuality would then be the norm rather than the exception." Put another way, radical socialization of the means of production and collectivized child care would not be necessary as first steps. Rather, all that was needed was to secure women equal social, economic, and political power outside the home. In time, everything else would follow.[10]

Writing in *Social Forces*, sociologist Edward Tiryakian of Duke University stressed that the changes which had taken place in sexuality and sexual conduct "constitute probably the most dramatic and significant transformations of the social world in the present century." He noted that adherents to the "old school" of sociology usually saw hedonistic sexuality as a corrosive force within society. Tiryakian suggested, though, that the revolution in sexual standards and "the liberation of women (and men) from ascriptive standards," while disorienting from a traditionalist perspective, might actually "be conducive to a renovation of the social fabric." Indeed, he speculated that the human race stood poised "for a major stage of social evolution, one whose creative agents will be women as much or even more than men." The ideology of androgyny, he insisted, must be viewed as "truly revolutionary," one directed at overturning not only the sexual division of labor but also "the present prevalent form of the nuclear family which is the source of reproduction of heterosexuality." Androgyny's victory seemed imminent. In fact, Tiryakian suggested that merely two developments—the perfection of bottle-baby technologies and a Supreme Court ruling declaring it unconstitutional to teach or reinforce heterosexuality in the schools—would be sufficient to bring success. This victorious ideology, he concluded, would actually represent belated triumph for the ancient Christian Gnostic heresy, which had also aimed at creation of the androgynous personality.[11]

Some heavyweights in the fields of biology and physiology rallied behind the ideologues. Ruth Bleier, professor of neurophysiology and women's studies at the University of Wisconsin, dismissed most of the animal research done on hormonal interactions with the brain as irrelevant to human behavior. Similarly, she rejected all studies suggesting biologically innate psychological distinctions between boys and girls: "The enormous differences in socialization factors are more than adequate to explain the almost trivial differences that exist . . . without speculating about the differential evolution of female and male brains of which nothing is known." Similarly, Harvard's R.C. Lewontin and colleagues, while admitting that only women could bear children and lactate, denied that any conclusions could be drawn from those facts: "Child-care arrangements owe more to culture than to nature." More broadly, they declared: "We cannot predict the inevitability of patriarchy, or capitalism, from the cellular hormones, or the physiology of sexual reproduction." In a series of books, John Money of Johns Hopkins Medical School argued that the biological foundations of gender, while real, were infinitely variable across a wide spectrum. Concerning maternalism, for example, he cited an experiment where the injection of hormones into the preoptic area of male rat brains (simulating a natural process among female rats) led to "maternal behavior" such as nest building. Another researcher injected "antiandrogen" into unborn male rats and was able to "feminize" them, even obtaining lactation (although the foster pups died). From this, he concluded that maternalism "should . . . more accurately be designated parentalism. It is a bisexual trait."[12]

Andrea Dworkin pulled together such science and ideology into an androgynous vision of the future. The former showed, she said, "that 'man' and 'woman' are fictions, caricatures, cultural constructs. As models they are reductive, totalitarian, inappropriate to human becoming. As roles they are static, demeaning to the female, dead-ended for male and female both." Men and women had the same body structure, she continued: the clitoris is a vestigial penis; the prostate gland is most probably a vestigial womb. Humans, she speculated, were once biologically androgynous, and concluded: "We are, clearly, a multi-sexed species which has the sexuality spread across a vast fluid continuum where the elements called male and female are not discrete." Hence, all forms of sexual interaction must be part of human life. Androgyny demanded "the destruction of all conventional role-playing, of genital sexuality, of couples." The nuclear family—"the school of values in a sexist, sexually repressed society"—must also be crushed. Turning to positive models, Dworkin saw homosexuality as closer to the androgynous vision. Better still was bestiality, where "human and other-animal relationships would become more explicitly erotic." The destruction of the incest taboo was also essential to "the free-flow of natural androgynous eroticism." Children were "erotic beings, closer to androgyny than the adults who oppress them," and deserving "every right to live out their own erotic impulses." The overall goal was cultural transformation, "the development of a new kind of human being and a new kind of human community."[13]

Looking specifically to their discipline, social psychologists were eager to prove that psychological androgyny was also best. Among them, Sandra Bem took the lead. From the beginning, she was fully candid about the premises behind her work:

> My major purpose has always been a feminist one: to help free the human personality from the restricting prison of sex-role stereotyping and to develop a conception of mental health which is free from culturally imposed defini-tions of masculinity and femininity.

From this statement, Bem argued that persons freed from the desire to show sex-appropriate behavior would be more adaptive, better adjusted, and psychologically healthier. They could build up a repertoire of mas-culine and feminine behaviors, and call on them as situations or problems arose.

In order to test these assertions, Bem developed the Bem Sex-role Inven-tory (BSRI), a questionnaire designed to distinguish androgynous individ-uals from those with more sex-typed self-concepts. In essence, it asked individuals to rate themselves against a list of behaviors, some "masculine" (e.g., aggressive, ambitious, analytical, assertive, athletic, makes decisions easily, willing to take risks) and some "feminine" (e.g., affectionate, com-passionate, loves children, loyal, sensitive, tender, understanding). Bem then used a series of experiments to test the predictive capacity of the BSRI and to assess how well androgynous individuals performed. One experi-ment showed, for example, that androgynous men were quite responsive to a kitten, while feminine women were less so. Another study found that feminine and androgynous men were very responsive to a five-month-old baby, while masculine men were not. Overall, Bem concluded that the androgynous male "performs spectacularly," shunning no behavior just because the culture labeled it female. "Clearly, he is a liberated companion for the most feminist among us." Bem also pointed to the near-total failure in her experiments of the feminine woman, who reported discomfort when required to perform cross-sex behavior, yielded to pressures for conformity, and even failed to show greater nurturance of a small baby.[14]

Other psychologists followed Bem's lead. J.T. Spence and R. Helmreich developed an alternative to the BSRI, called the Personal Attributes Questionnaire, which they used to infer the degree to which a person possessed masculine, "instrumental" traits or feminine, "expressive" ones. They generated considerable press attention in the late 1970s, reporting findings that androgynous parents were superior to sex-typed mothers and fathers.[15] Additional researchers described a multiplicative model of androgyny where "increments of psychological femininity would yield larger increments of creativity among high-masculine individuals." Others described a process of sex-role transcendence, the reputed highest stage of human development, where gender became irrelevant in selecting behavior, and persons moved toward "a fluid, integrated wholeness." Still others speculated about cognitive schema, where androgynes succeeded in clearing their minds of any sex-related connotations.[16]

More evidence, of a sort, followed. A group from the University of Cincinnati reported that androgynous college students were more skillful at "interpersonal relationships" than sex-typed students. Another team from Emory University found that androgynous women performed better at college academic work than sex-typed women (although, curiously, androgyny did not appear to help men at all). A researcher at MacQuarie University in Australia reported that androgynous fathers were more nurturant and performed more direct child care than masculine fathers (even though his finding was, in some respects, little more than a self-evident tautology). After defining a "simple" cognitive system as one which uses categorical thinking, defends existing standards, and defers to prevailing moral authority and a "complex" system as one that is relativistic, free of inherited moral and cultural restraints, and devoid of categorical thinking, two New Jersey researchers reached the unremarkable conclusion that sex-typed persons were "intolerant," while androgynous persons were more "complex."[17] Capping this turn, Alexandra Kaplan argued that androgyny should be the new model of mental health. Therapy should aim at reinforcing androgynous traits in women and men. Pathology or mental illness would be defined by overly masculine men and overly feminine women. These sex-typed persons would be the ones herded into psychotherapy, where they could be "resocialized" or stripped "of the stereotypic standards our culture has imposed."[18]

Launched off this theoretical and empirical base, the theory of psychological androgyny has already had sweeping consequences in America. Within the mental health profession, for example, the dominant measure of health has shifted sharply since the late 1960s. As of 1980, 72 percent of mental health professionals—the persons responsible for counseling adults and children regarding proper adjustment—described a "healthy, mature, socially competent" adult as androgynous. Only 2 percent labeled a femi-

nine woman as healthy, mature, and competent. Psychologist Jeanne Mar-
ecek saw androgyny as the means of psychologically institutionalizing the
joint revolutions in sexuality and lifestyles, replacing masculinity and femininity as the norm for men's and women's behavior.[19]

The androgyne revolution has carried over to school textbooks. In a
recent analysis of over 100 such books in current use, Paul C. Vitz of New
York University reported that "by far the most noticeable ideological position in the readers was a feminist one." Not a single story or theme celebrated marriage or motherhood as a positive experience. Sex-role reversals
and the mockery of masculine men were common. ("For example, there is
a story of a princess who sets out to slay the dragon in her kingdom: she
invents the first gun and with it shoots and kills the dragon. The slain
dragon turns into a prince who asks the princess to marry him.") The
obvious goal is to eliminate any lingering sex roles in children, in order to
pave the way for the androgynous order.[20]

Feminists active in the mainline Protestant churches have also succeeded
in placing the androgyny concept near the apex of these churches' theologies. Such theologians identify, in particular, with the old Gnostic
heresy, the belief that God is both male and female, and that "Holy
Wisdom," the female persona of God, mediates the "fall" of humans into
bodiliness and also the escape from Creation into spiritual life. Men and
women, they say, can rise above their carnal sex roles and gain spiritual
androgyny. Some of this ilk take a different angle, denying the "androgyny"
label for its implicit assumption that maleness and femaleness once existed. As Rosemary Reuther of Garrett Theological Seminary puts it, "We
need to affirm not the confusing concept of androgyny but rather that all
humans possess a full and equivalent human nature."[21]

Among corporations, androgyny has also been the rage. In her book *The
Androgynous Manager* (published by the American Management Association), Alice Sargent argues that "an androgynous blending of behaviors is
the most effective management style in the 1980s." Existing low morale and
poor productivity in the workplace, she says, are due to overly masculine
managers. Instead, the modern executive needs to be compassionate, col-
laborative, nurturing, intuitive, spontaneous, and expressive of emotions.[22]

Finally, even the military services appear to be succumbing to the allure
of androgyny. A favorite theme among critics of the Vietnam War was its
relationship to America's crisis of masculinity. Writing in *Transaction*,
Charles Levy pointed to the heavy psychosexual content of Marine basic
training, particularly the emphasis on the cult of masculinity and fear of
homosexuality. Another writer blamed military failure on the brutal, inept
training found in boot camp. The linkage of a soldier's aggressive masculinity to success, he continued, backfired in the passive, confused, female

environment of Vietnam. In a history of American malehood, Joe Dubbert identified Vietnam as the Waterloo of the "masculine mystique." Marc Feigen Fasteau pursued the same theme in *The Male Machine*, where he delighted in identifying the phallic symbolism that marked official Washington's position (e.g., the Kennedy clan's belief that "relaxation of tensions could come only after they had proved their toughness," or the President's belief that a "pullout" from Vietnam would show him to be "soft on Communism").

Significantly, though, Fasteau took heart that the 1970–75 period had witnessed substantial numbers of women and men breaking away from traditional sex roles. These new androgynes "have the self-confidence to achieve positions of responsibility and power without feeling a personal need to respond to every challenge. Female or male, this kind of human being might well have kept us out of Vietnam." Two sociologists concluded in 1978 that military training remained perhaps the most powerful single institution for adult socialization in America. While the psychology of military training was still locked into attitudes of male virility, women as sex objects, and recruit as symbolic martyr for his family, change was rapidly coming. The influx of women into most military occupations made it doubtful that the military model of masculinity would survive. Fossils such as Marine General Robert Barrow remained, persons who argued that:

> War is a man's work. Biological convergence on the battlefield . . . would be an enormous psychological distraction for the male, who wants to think that he is fighting for that woman somewhere behind, not up there in the same foxhole with him . . . When you get right down to it, you have to protect the manliness of war.

Yet such sex-role stereotypes ran against Pentagon policy, usually bringing a reprimand. Androgyny seemed to be the more likely military future.[23]

The awful truth of the androgyny revolution, though, is that it is theoretically and scientifically unsound. Honest research over the last decade has shown conclusively that psychological androgyny is a hoax.

The theoretical failings are numerous. A research team from the University of Minnesota noted that some variations of psychological androgyny theory are logically incoherent. Given an "additive structure," for example, where androgynes are identified by their sums of masculine and feminine qualities, the androgynous label becomes redundant. "Given this predictive redundancy," they conclude, "androgyny would also appear to be conceptually redundant." Androgyny can stand as a concept only if the interaction of masculine and feminine traits produces synergistic effects, where the whole is better than the sum of its parts. The researchers then tested Bem's BRSI scale against this criterion and found that it produced "no interactions vindicating androgyny." Indeed, they warned against the appropriateness of using psychotherapy to change masculine and feminine types into androgynes, and rejected androgyny as a new model of mental health.[24]

In a complex study, Diana Baumrind of the University of California/ Berkeley showed that androgyny's constructs are not embedded in a principled, coherent working theory. In addition, the concept's crucial assumption—that sex-typed behavior detracts from psychological health—"has little cogent data to support it." Existing evidence, in fact, suggested that masculinity and femininity are not complementary; rather, they tend to be negatively correlated (e.g., a person cannot be both "aggressive" and "passive" at will, unless already mentally unhinged). She noted, furthermore, that androgyny classifications are themselves culturally determined. As an example, the Spence-Helmreich PAQ test was administered to a sample of Brazilian males. Twenty-nine percent of them turned out to be feminine, and a mere 12 percent masculine. Such tests, Baumrind affirmed, do not become a measure of gender just because scores on their component scales can, in some cultures, discriminate on the basis of sex.[25]

In her comprehensive study of psychological androgyny, Ellen Cook pointed to a basic flaw in the concept: measures of androgyny deal only with positive characteristics; they have not taken into account the negative. While research in this direction is limited, she noted several clinical studies showing androgynous persons to be dysfunctional: "Unable to integrate their masculine and feminine characteristics well, the persons were vulnerable, inhibited, and unable to direct their behavior effectively."[26] Cook also reported that some androgyny theorists were already in full intellectual retreat. Spence, for instance, recently relabeled her PAQ scale as no more than "a conventional personality test." The labels "masculinity," "femininity," and "androgyny," she added, were "murky, unanalyzed concepts."

More evidence has appeared showing the androgyne claim to superiority to be incorrect. John Ray and F.H. Lovejoy of the University of New South Wales noted that all research on androgyny with positive results was conducted among samples of college students. They suggested that the rarified atmosphere of a campus might not be exactly normal and so they tested a random sample of voters. They found high scores on androgyny to be closely related to unassertiveness, neurotic behavior, and low self-esteem. These results, they concluded, were "uniformly unfavorable to the feminist hypotheses as enunciated by Bem and her successors."[27] Sociologists Joan Hemmer and Douglas Kleiber sought to show that the children labeled "tomboys" and "sissies" were, in fact, effective little androgynes. However, they discovered that such children were actually antisocial, unable to interact effectively with their peers.[28] Two California psychologists discovered that when androgynous people scored high on creative tests (keyed, of course, to masculine attributes), it was due solely to the strength of their masculine characteristics. Androgyny was irrelevant.[29] Researchers at the University of Miami found that in measuring the ability of persons to act in a crisis, androgynes revealed no special competence. Indeed, masculinity proved to be "the most important dimension for effective performance."[30] Evelyn Bassoff and Gene Glass of the University of Colorado-Boulder, using a "meta-analysis" of 26 other studies, tested the proposition that androgynes are better adapted than their sex-typed counterparts. They uncovered, though, "a strong, positive association between masculinity and mental health." While androgynes did show higher levels of mental health than feminine types, "it was the masculine component of androgyny, rather than the integration of femininity and masculinity, that accounts for this."[31]

Cook outlined a series of studies that undermined the androgyny theory. A 1979 paper reported that while "high feminine" and "high masculine" women tended to make different life choices, neither group was less "adjusted." Other researchers discovered significant correlations between masculinity and anxiety among women feminist group members and between high androgyny scores and anxiety among working women. Cook cited numerous studies strongly suggesting that masculinity, not androgyny, was the strongest predictor of mental health. Among psychopaths, serious mental illness among males proved to be associated with low masculinity and elevated femininity scores.[32]

Diana Baumrind was more sweeping in her rejection of androgyny. Using sophisticated measures of personal and parental effectiveness recorded over a series of years, she showed that sex-typed parents performed the best [the capitalized phrases refer to qualities measured in her survey]:

> Feminine mothers are the warmest parents. They are the most Responsive and Loving/Supportive and the least irascible, that is, they Express Anger less and use less Negative and somewhat less Coercive Reinforcement than other parents. . . . While less firm than other parents, Feminine mothers are more Directive of their children's daily activities. Masculine fathers compared to other fathers use more Positive Reinforcement. . . . Compared with other parents of both sexes, they are more Firm and Require Household Help more, but are less Directive of their children's daily activities.

In contrast to these sex-typed parents, androgynes performed dismally. Androgynous fathers were responsive, but not firm, while androgynous mothers showed no special parenting traits at all "except for their tendency to use Guilt Induction."

Similarly, Baumrind found that the daughters of sex-typed parents were more mentally and operationally competent than daughters from all other homes. The sons of sex-typed fathers were more Socially Assertive. In contrast, she discovered that the children of androgynous fathers or mothers "are invariably less competent than those of sex-typed parents: Sons of Androgynous Mothers are the least Socially Responsible. . . . daughters of Androgynous fathers are less Cognitively Competent than those of sex-typed fathers." Moreover, she reported clear correlations between feminine fathers and cognitive incompetence in girls, and between masculine mothers and social irresponsibility in boys.

In sum, Baumrind concluded that traditional sex-typing was healthy for society and children. Androgyny, as a positive concept, was a complete and utter failure.[33]

The reasons for androgyny's illogic and failure have also become clear: the concept violates the natural order. While social and environmental factors have clear influences, sex-typed behavior does have a foundation in human biology.

In 1973, a paper by G. Raisman and P.M. Field showed for the first time that male and female brains (in rats) differed structurally. The difference appeared, moreover, in a region concerned with the brain's regulation of the gonadal, or sex-typed hormones. Most impressive of all, the researchers found that such hormones, circulating at birth, could change the brain.[34] As one commentator concluded, this finding "gave real credence to the possibility that the frequently observed preadolescent gender differences in aggressiveness were as biological in origin as the more easily comprehended postadolescent ones."[35] Studies of primates have reinforced this finding. One researcher, studying the effects of hormones on the prenatal development of rhesus monkeys, found that the elevated levels of testosterone in male fetuses actually "masculinizes the nervous system," predisposing it to acquire predominantly masculine patterns of behavior after birth. This biological "masculinization" occurred early in fetal development and had clearly identifiable consequences in stimulating subsequent "male" behavior such as rough-and-tumble play, threats, and play initiation.[36]

Writing in *Science*, Neil MacLusky and Frederick Naftolin of Yale's School of Medicine summarized the evidence showing that male and female patterns of behavior were largely affected by hormones produced in the gonads (testes or ovaries). In many higher vertebraes, they concluded, "an integral part of this process is the induction of permanent and essentially irreversible sex differences in central nervous function, in response to gonadal hormones secreted early in development."[37] As Thomas Fleming has noted, even cases of abnormal human sexual development point to the powerful impact of nature. Men suffering from Kleinfelter's syndrome (a genetic disorder involving an extra X female chromosome) have a lower sex drive and increased emotional dependence. Women affected by physiological androgenization, caused by a defect in the adrenal glands, develop external male genitalia and show higher levels of male behavior: rough play, aggression, and so on. Fleming concludes "that some, if not all, of the observable psychological differences between men and women are prescribed genetically and hormonally."[38]

Psychologists report similar findings. Howard Moss of the National Institutes of Mental Health studied infant behaviors in the period immediately following birth, when environmental or social factors could play little or no role. He reported that "male infants tend to function at a less well organized and less efficient level than female infants," showing irritability and less competence in responding to touch and other "social stimuli." Female newborns were better able to quiet or otherwise restore themselves to equilibrium and exhibited significantly higher attention to smiles and facial stimuli. In short, newborn girls proved to be more social.[39] Marvin Simner of Brown University investigated the reported ability of newborn babies to respond sympathetically to the cry of another infant. He discovered that newborns could distinguish between the cry of a fellow newborn and that of a five-and-a-half-month-old baby, a "synthetic" baby cry, and "white noise" of the same decibel level. Unexpectedly, though, he also found that female infants were significantly more reactive to the cry of another infant than males.[40] Researcher Dorothy Ulian of Harvard University showed that aggressive behavior in boys—play with guns, rough-and-tumble play, dramatic roles stressing danger, and heroes of gigantic proportion—was psychologically necessary, while girls acquired their feminine identities naturally. She warned that forced cross-sex play and other "sex role interventions" could psychologically cripple little boys.[41] Working with newborns, Stanford University psychiatrist Anneliese Korner discovered that females were more receptive to touch, oral stimuli, and sweet taste, and made greater use of their facial muscles. Males, on the other hand, exhibited greater muscular vigor and strength and more "spontaneous startles." She even suggested "that behavioral sex differences within the infants [may] exert a subtle influence on the parents," evoking differences in response."[42]

In short, nature will not be denied. As Yale's Helen Lewis, a committed feminist, was forced to admit to her disappointed fellow ideologues: "The difference between having an XX or an XY as the 23rd chromosome [the genetic distinction between woman and man] is tremendously powerful."[43] Hoping to find evidence of a historical convergence toward androgyny between 1973 and 1986 (using the Gough Femininity Scale), psychologist Robert Baldwin reported a negative finding: the differences between the sexes had not decreased at all. Perhaps, he observed, "it is the concept of androgyny which should be called into question."[44]

The question remains, though: Given the overwhelming medical, social, and psychological evidence affirming the naturalness and critical importance of traditional sex roles, how can we account for the success of the androgyny concept?

History knows one parallel. In 1948, Joseph Stalin's chief aide and ideologue, Andrei Zhdanov, sought means of enforcing Marxist ideological purity on the Soviet natural sciences. Zhdanov uncovered a poorly educated plant breeder named Trofim D. Lysenko, who obligingly attacked accepted doctrines of genetics, labeling them as "metaphysical-idealistic." Lysenko argued that the inheritance of environmentally acquired characteristics was possible, a "finding" of great importance to Marxist-Leninists seeking to shape "the new Soviet man." Lysenko's theory was imposed on assembled Soviet biologists, the Communist Party Central Committee having "examined and approved" his address. The leading "Mendel-Morganist" geneticists were liquidated.

In the United States, a small band of ideologues has similarly succeeded in imposing a fraudulent, dangerous ideology, masquerading as science, on broad elements of our public life. From the beginning, the ideological origins of "psychological androgyny" were clear. Even Bem, the concept's chief scientific theoretician, openly admits that her purposes were political and ideological, not scientific.

It should be noted that, after some delay, honest scientists committed to authentic research have come forward and done their job. They have exposed the errors of the androgyny theorists and affirmed the facts. While the debate still rages at that level, at least their findings are being discussed, and the truth may prevail. At a more popular level, though, the tale is different. There, it has been the "helping professions"—social workers, counselors, curriculum advisers, teachers—and the magazine media—*People*, *Psychology Today*, *Vogue*, and *Cosmopolitan*—which have elevated corrupted science to the level of public truth. These professions and magazines are responsible for incalculable levels of psychological damage to Americans, young and old, and for the corruption of many American institutions.

Notes

1. "The Androgynous Man," *New York Times Magazine* (Feb. 5, 1984); "The American Male," *U.S. News & World Report* (June 3, 1985): 44; "The New

Man's Lament," *Newsweek* (July 16, 1984): 82; Liza Dalby, "Androgyny: Yes Ma'am, a Woman Can Be More Like a Man!" *Cosmopolitan* (Jan. 1986): 198ff; Anne Rice, "Playing With Gender," *Vogue* (Nov. 1983): 434; "Best of Both Worlds," *Saturday Review* (March–April 1985): 16; and "Invasion of the Gender Blenders," *People* (April 23, 1984): 99.

2. Joseph H. Pleck, "Prisoners of Manliness," *Psychology Today* (Sept. 1981): 69–83; Howard Mason, "The Right Stuff May Be Androgyny," *Psychology Today* (June 1980): 14, 16–18; and "Androgyny Makes Better Lovers," *Psychology Today* (June 1985): 19.

3. Ferdinand Lundberg and Marynia F. Farnham, *Modern Woman: The Lost Sex* (New York: Harper & Brothers, 1947), pp. 92, 162–67, 353–76.

4. Talcott Parsons, *Social Structure and Personality* (New York: The Free Press of Glencoe, 1964), p. 44.

5. Ashley Montagu, "Triumph and Tragedy of the American Woman," *Saturday Review of Literature* (Sept. 27, 1958): 13–15; and Jerome Kagan and Howard A. Moss, *Birth to Maturity: A Study in Psychological Development* (New York: John Wiley and Sons, 1962), pp. 267–74.

6. Alice S. Rossi, "An Immodest Proposal: Equality Between the Sexes," in *The Woman in America*, ed. R.J. Lifton (Boston: Houghton Mifflin, 1964); and Rossi, "Sex Equality: The Beginnings of an Ideology [1969]," in *Beyond Sex Role Stereotypes: Readings Toward a Psychology of Androgyny*, ed. Alexandra G. Kaplan and Joan P. Bean (Boston: Little, Brown and Company, 1976), pp. 80–88.

7. Inge K. Broverman et al., "Sex-Role Stereotypes and Clinical Judgments of Mental Health," *Journal of Consulting and Clinical Psychology* 34, No. 1 (1970): 1–7.

8. Paul Hoch, *White Hero, Black Beast: Racism, Sexism and the Mask of Masculinity* (Boston: The Pluto Press, 1979), pp. 21–22, 30–31.

9. Shulamith Firestone, *The Dialectic of Sex: The Case for Feminist Revolution* (New York: William Morrow, 1970), pp. 233–40, 272.

10. Ann Ferguson, "Androgyny as an Ideal for Human Development [1974]," in *Feminism and Philosophy*, Mary Vetterling-Braggin, Frederick A. Elliston, and Jane English eds. (Totowa, NJ: Rowman and Littlefield, 1977), pp. 45–69.

11. Edward A. Tiryakian, "Sexual Anomie, Social Structure, Societal Change," *Social Forces* 59 (June 1981): 1026–53.

12. Ruth Bleier, *Science and Gender* (New York: Pergamon Press, 1984), pp. 107–09; R.C. Lewontin, Steven Rose, and Leon J. Kamin, *Not In Our Genes: Biology, Ideology, and Human Nature* (New York: Pantheon Books, 1984), pp. 155, 162; and John Money and A.A. Ehrhardt, *Man and Woman, Boy and Girl: The Differentiation and Dimorphism of Gender Identity from Conception to Maturity* (Baltimore: Johns Hopkins University Press, 1972), pp. 256–58.

13. Andrea Dworkin, *Woman Hating* (New York: E.P. Dutton, 1974), pp. 174–93.

14. See: Sandra L. Bem, "The Measurement of Psychological Androgyny," *Journal of Consulting and Clinical Psychology* 42 (1974): 155–62; and Bem, "Probing the Promise and Androgyny," in Kaplan and Bean, pp. 48–62.

15. See: J.T. Spence and R. Helmreich, "Ratings of Self and Peers on Sex Role Attributes and Their Relation to Self-Esteem and Conceptions of Masculinity and Femininity," *Journal of Personality and Social Psychology* 32, No. 1 (1971): 29–39; and Spence and Helmreich, "On Assessing 'Androgyny,'" *Sex Roles* 5, No. 7 (1979): 721–38.

16. For a summary of the various androgyny theories, see Ellen Piel Cook, *Psychological Androgyny* (New York: Pergamon Press, 1985), pp. 22–24.
17. Anne Briscoe, "Hormones and Gender," in *Genes and Gender: I* eds. Ethel Tobach and Betty Rosoff (New York: Gordian Press, 1978), pp. 31–50; Matthew Campbell, John J. Steffen, and Daniel Langmeyer, "Psychological Androgyny and Social Competence," *Psychological Reports* 48 (1981): 511–14; Alfred B. Heilbrun, Jr. and Yu Ling Han, "Cost-Effectiveness of College Achievement by Androgynous Men and Women," *Psychological Reports* 55 (1984): 977–78; Graeme Russell, "The Father Role and Its Relation to Masculinity, Femininity, and Androgyny," *Child Development* 49 (1978): 1174–84; and Naomi G. Rotter and Agnes N. O'Connell, "The Relationships Among Sex-Role Orientation, Cognitive Complexity, and Tolerance for Ambiguity," *Sex Roles* 8, No. 12 (1982): 1209–19.
18. Alexandra G. Kaplan, "Androgyny as a Model of Mental Health for Women: From Theory to Therapy," in Kaplan and Bean, pp. 353–60.
19. Diane Kravetz and Linda E. Jones, "Androgyny as a Standard of Mental Health," *American Journal of Orthopsychiatry* 51 (July 1981): 502–09; and Jeanne Maracek, "Social Change, Positive Mental Health, and Psychological Androgyny," *Psychology of Women Quarterly* 3 (Spring 1979): 241–47.
20. Paul C. Vitz, "A Study of Religion and Traditional Values in Public School Textbooks," in *Democracy and the Renewal of Public Education*, ed. Richard John Neuhaus (Grand Rapids: Wm. B. Eerdmans, 1987), pp. 138–40.
21. Rosemary Radford Reuther, *Sexism and God-Talk: Toward a Feminist Theology* (Boston: Beacon Press, 1983), pp. 100–01, 111.
22. Alice G. Sargent, "Management Opinion Column," *Administrative Management* (Oct. 1982): 82; and Sargent, "The Androgynous Manager," *Working Women* (Dec. 1981): 22.
23. From: Charles J. Levy, "ARVN as Faggots: Inverted Warfare in Vietnam," *Transaction* 8 (Oct. 1971): 18–27; R. Wayne Eisenhart, "You Can't Hack It Little Girl: A Discussion of the Covert Psychological Agenda of Modern Combat Training," *Journal of Social Issues* 31, No. 4 (1975): 13–23; Joe L. Dubbert, *A Man's Place: Masculinity in Transition* (Englewood Cliffs, NJ: Prentice-Hall, 1979), pp. 275–78; Marc Feigen Fasteau, *The Male Machine* (1974), excerpted in *The American Man*, eds. Elizabeth H. and Joseph H. Pleck (Englewood Cliffs, NJ; Prentice-Hall, 1980), pp. 379–415; and William Arkin and Lynne R. Dobrofsky, "Military Socialization and Masculinity," *Journal of Social Issues* 34, No. 1 (1975): 151–57. Barrow quotation from: Nancy C.M. Hartsock, "Masculinity, Citizenship, and the Making of War," *PS* (Spring 1984): 198–202.
24. David Lubinski, Auke Tellegen, and James N. Butcher, "The Relationship Between Androgyny and Subjective Indicators of Emotional Well-being," *Journal of Personality and Social Psychology* 40, No. 4 (1981): 722–30.
25. Diana Baumrind, "Are Androgynous Individuals More Effective Persons and Parents?" *Child Development* 53 (Jan. 1982): 45–46.
26. Cook, pp. 120–22.
27. John J. Ray and F.H. Lovejoy, "The Great Androgyny Myth: Sex Roles and Mental Health in the Community at Large," *The Journal of Social Psychology* 124 (1984): 237–46.
28. Joan D. Hemmer and Douglas A. Kleiber, "Tomboys and Sissies: Androgynous Children?" *Sex Roles* 7 (1981): 1205–11.
29. David M. Harrington and Susan M. Andersen, "Creativity, Masculinity, Femi-

ninity, and Three Models of Psychological Androgyny," *Journal of Personality and Social Psychology* 41, No. 4 (1981): 744–57.

30. Phyllis Senneker and Clyde Hendrick, "Androgyny and Helping Behavior," *Journal of Personality and Social Psychology* 45, No. 4 (1983): 916–25.

31. Evelyn Silten Bassoff and Gene V. Glass, "The Relationship Between Sex Roles and Mental Health: A Meta-Analysis of Twenty-Six Studies," *The Counseling Psychologist* 10, No. 1 (1979): 105–11.

32. Cook, pp. 114–19.

33. Baumrind, pp. 63–70.

34. G. Raisman and P.M. Field, "Sexual Dimorphism in the Neuropil of the Preoptic Area of the Rat and Its Dependence on Neonatal Androgen," *Brain Research* 54, No. 1 (1973): 1–29.

35. Melvin Konner, *The Tangled Wing: Biological Constraints on the Human Spirit* (New York: Holt, Rinehart and Winston, 1982), p. 122.

36. Charles H. Phoenix, "Prenatal Testosterone in the Nonhuman Primate and Its Consequences for Behavior," in *Sex Differences in Behavior*, eds. Richard C. Friedman, Ralph M. Richart, and Raymond Vande Wiele, (Huntington, NY: Robert E. Krieger, 1978), pp. 19–32.

37. Neil J. MacLusky and Frederick Naftolin, "Sexual Differentiation of the Central Nervous System," *Science* 211 (Mar. 20, 1981): 1294ff.

38. Thomas J. Fleming, *The Politics of Human Nature* (New Brunswick, NJ: Transaction, 1988).

39. Howard A. Moss, "Early Sex Differences and Mother-Infant Interaction," in Friedman, pp. 149–63.

40. Marvin Simner, "Newborn's Response to the Cry of Another Infant," *Developmental Psychology* 5, No. 1 (1971): 136–50.

41. Dorothy Z. Ullian, "Why Boys Will Be Boys: A Structural Perspective," *American Journal of Orthopsychiatry* 51 (July 1981): 493–501.

42. Anneliese F. Korner, "Methodological Considerations in Studying Sex Differences in the Behavioral Functioning of Newborns," in Friedman, pp. 197–202.

43. Helen Block Lewis, "Psychology and Gender," in Tobach and Rosoff, pp. 67–68.

44. Robert O. Baldwin, "Femininity-Masculinity of Blacks and Whites Over a Fourteen-Year Period," *Psychological Reports* 60 (1987): 455–58.

Part II
THE POPULATION QUESTION

4

The Malthusian Budget Deficit

Official Washington's attention remains locked on the large and apparently impervious deficit in the federal budget. Other questions on the national agenda, particularly the "divisive" social issues of abortion and family protection, continue to be pushed aside so that the White House and Congress can, with the studious attention of the accountant, concentrate their collective mind on the budget crisis.

With supreme irony, though, these very social issues left unattended are creating their own budget deficit, one that began to affect federal revenues negatively in 1985 and that quickly grows in magnitude after 1987. Alongside this gaping hole in future federal fiscal accounts, the nation's current deficit seems paltry.

This new deficit is the offspring of an ideological change that occurred during the 1960s. The fundamental conflict of ideas, then as now, has been over the simple question: Is population growth a burden or a blessing?

To understand the contemporary debate on the population issue, one need go back 200 years. The eighteenth-century political economist Adam Smith well understood that the only effective cure for mass poverty was the creation of a free, competitive economy. Population growth, he maintained, was the surest sign of such a healthy economic order. Smith did acknowledge that no animal could reproduce beyond the means of subsistence provided for it. Such was nature's law. But man had found a way to transcend nature, he showed. What Smith called "the liberal reward of labour," or rising wages, uniquely enabled human workers "to provide better for their children" and so "widen and extend those limits" which nature had set. Writing in his *Wealth of Nations*, Smith concluded: "The liberal reward of labour, therefore, as it is the effect of increasing wealth, so it is the cause of increasing population. To complain of it, is to lament over the necessary effect and cause of the greatest public prosperity." In short, Adam Smith said that a growing population was the clearest evidence that the people in a free society were cheerful and hearty. In contrast, a station-

51

ary or declining population was the surest sign of a "dull" or "melancholy" system.[1]

Yet Smith's wisdom and optimism were soon to be swept aside in the wake of the Rev. Thomas R. Malthus's famed *Essay on Population*, published in 1799. Malthus himself was a gentle man, trying simply to understand the world. Yet the tragic consequences of the shift in ideas that he spawned are almost incalculable. Where Smith had welcomed population growth as a sign that the limits of subsistence could be increased, Malthus declared that such an increase was impossible. As he put it in his well-known calculation, human population grew in a geometric ratio, while food supplies grew only in an arithmetic ratio. For mankind, he added, the necessary and inescapable results were misery and vice. The law of population, Malthus concluded, "appears, therefore, to be decisive against the possible existence of a society, all the members of which should live in ease, happiness, and comparative leisure."[2]

While Malthus modified his ideas in later editions, finally seeing hope through human abstinence from sex, and delayed marriage, his grim prediction of ever-increasing misery came to dominate economic thinking in the nineteenth century. It generated, in turn, rebuttals ranging from John Stuart Mill's early advocacy of the contraceptive society to Karl Marx's analysis of the coming proletarian revolution. In this debate, Adam Smith's original understanding of the linkage between economy and population was all but forgotten.

Even as the facts repeatedly proved Malthus wrong, the power of the Malthusian idea continued to grow and reassert itself again and again in Western history. The panic instilled by the Malthusian ratio slowly became pathological, a disease of the Western mind. Indeed, it was transformed into a kind of intellectual herpes, composed of equal parts of doubt, fear, and unreason. Like the appearance of the herpes virus, Malthusianism would strike with particular virulence, then recede back into some obscure part of our civilization's body, only to break out again in another place and time. Its most sophisticated appearance came in the mid- and late-nineteenth century, when the so-called "classical economists" devised the theory of "optimum population": calculations of the number of people for which the resources of a given territory could properly provide. It wasn't until the 1920s that a new generation of economists reduced the "optimum population" idea to rubble through keen analysis and well-deserved ridicule. The Malthusian herpes receded.

Its most recent outbreak came in the 1960s, through the great panics over "the population bomb" and "the environmental crisis." Young adults were the targets for the scare stories devised by new Malthusian disciples and propagated through groups such as the Sierra Club and Zero Population Growth. The propagandists' common message was that America's prevailing three-child family system was an ecological disaster, the cause of all our miseries. The morally superior act, they maintained, was to have no children, to become voluntarily sterile in order to save the world.

It is important to note that the return of the Malthusian disease in this manner and with this purpose was well thought-out in advance by the advocates of population control. They sought to achieve their goals by first manipulating climates of opinion; policy changes, they understood, would follow as night follows day. Such an approach proved to be an unqualified success, and deserves study as an example of gently coerced social change.

Writing in 1958, during the peak of the post-World War II baby boom, neo-Malthusian planner Richard L. Meier described the "catastrophe" that continued population growth in the West invited. Many theorists, he noted, thought that coercive controls might be necessary to eliminate such growth and the three- and four-child family system that had created it. Yet Meier argued that there were alternative ways of achieving Malthusian goals: "Satisfying lifetime roles should be established which do not require parenthood, but would, in effect, discourage it . . . [Under this system, a] fraction of the adult population could be depended upon to be sterile and this fraction must be modifiable by incentives normally available to democratic governments." The most effective strategy for increasing the number of sterile adults, Meier continued, would be to move women into jobs that required geographic mobility and so made a stable home and community life impossible: jobs such as truck driving, airline piloting, engineering, sales, and fire fighting. Easy divorce, he added, would also facilitate more sterile marriages.[3] In sum, the ideals of marriage, motherhood, and home should be purposefully eroded.

A few years later Edward Pohlman, writing in *Eugenics Quarterly*, frankly admitted the desperate need for experts and elites to manipulate family size preferences among Americans: "The population avalanche may be used to justify . . . contemplation of large-scale attempts to manipulate family size desires, even rather stealthily." The goal, he continued, must be to reverse the existing climate of opinion so that small families and childlessness would be seen as "good," in noble cooperation with the needs of the nation and world. Meanwhile, the large family of three or more children should be recast as the "flaunting" of the common good for "selfish ends." Such a covert manipulation of opinion, Pohlman concluded, could best be achieved by winning over "the most prestigeful strata" of the population and by securing "the blessing of government."[4]

And so it came to pass. First came the turn in elite opinion. The most dramatic work of new Malthusian propaganda was Paul Ehrlich's *The Population Bomb*. Published by the Sierra Club, it proved to be one of the most popular and irresponsible books of the late 1960s. The first step in Ehrlich's program of action was "to immediately establish and advertise drastic policies designed to bring our own population size under control." He continued: "Coercion? Perhaps, but coercion in a good cause. . . . We must be relentless in pushing for population control. . . . "Among his many proposals, Ehrlich urged the creation of a powerful U.S. Department of Population and Environment, which would secure the right of any woman to abortion, promote sex education in the schools, give "responsibility prizes" to childless marriages, and develop a "mass sterilization agent" to be placed in U.S. water supplies. He called for a taxation system that would penalize all families with children, but especially those "irresponsible" couples with more than two. He urged his followers to recognize the "glut, waste, pollution, and ugliness" embodied in the U.S. Gross National Product ("as gross a product as one could wish for") and to turn on "population-promoting tycoons" and "chambers of commerce" who were "especially 'black hat' on matters of population, and should be called down whenever they step out of line."[5]

Others were even more extreme, as the "our children as enemy" theme gained explicit treatment. Writing to American high-school biology teachers, Walter Howard labeled overpopulation "the erosion of civilization" and urged the mass mobilization of scientists "to help check this flood of human beings." The birth of a "surplus baby," he added, meant that another person somewhere else was "not going to be able to live a full life because of the resources consumed by the surplus baby." Bioethicist Garrett Hardin stated that "Every babe's birth diminishes me." He told a medical audience that obstetricians should discourage fertility among their patients, "in order to diminish the amount of adult stupidity, which itself is a form of social pollution, and a most dangerous one." A voluntary system of birth control, Hardin argued, could not achieve the goal of national population control: "some form of community coercion—gentle or severe, explicit or cryptic—will have to be employed."[6]

The popular media, as expected, followed the shift in elite opinion. *Look* magazine, still billed as a "family magazine," featured the article "Motherhood: Who Needs It?" in a September 1970 issue. Citing the "impending horrors of overpopulation," the *Look* article attacked what it called "madonna propaganda" and traced "almost all of our societal problems" to "the kids who have been so mindlessly brought into the world." The *Look* article placed its hope in those "younger-generation females" who embraced careers and who recognize that "it can be more loving to children not to have them."[7]

A year later, Anna and Arnold Silverman released their book, *The Case Against Having Children*. Population expansion, they argued, was "the most potentially disastrous problem facing mankind." Poverty, disease, war, crime, and famine could all be blamed on "the excesses, greed, and selfishness of people who insist on having large families" of three or more children. Particularly villainous, they charged, were suburbanites, described as "those people who swim to the suburbs to spawn." Using an argument enjoying increasing frequency, the Silvermans urged states to offer abortion-on-demand. They also urged governments to eliminate tax deductions for dependent children, so that if parents "want the luxury of a large family they are going to have to pay for it."[8]

In *Pronatalism: The Myth of Mom and Apple Pie*, ZPG's Judith Senderowitz joined with Ellen Peck to blast social attitudes and policies that encouraged reproduction or in any way exalted the role of parenthood. They mocked, in particular, "an undercurrent to . . . the way of life we know as 'the American way': the way of motherhood and the family; the nostalgia of Norman Rockwell and the homeyness of apple pie." The "fact of overpopulation," they concluded, reinforced the need to question and eliminate such profamily tendencies in American life.[9]

Then came the turn of government. In his June 1965 address before the United Nations, President Lyndon Johnson declared: "Let us in all our lands . . . including this land . . . face forthrightly the multiplying problems of our multiplying populations and seek the answers to this most profound challenge to the future of all the world. Let us act on the fact that five dollars invested in population control is worth one hundred dollars invested in economic growth." Several months later, U.S. delegate to the United Nations James Roosevelt cast American population growth as a danger to the Johnson Administration's efforts to build "a Great Society." The following year, the U.S. Department of Interior issued an overtly Malthusian document that labeled "overpopulation" the "greatest threat to quality living in this country," a danger to "America's noble goals of optimum education for all, universal abundance, enriched leisure, equal opportunity, quality, beauty, and creativity." Secretary of the Interior Stewart Udall "vigorously challenged" the myth that population growth was the key to prosperity, and the good life: "Instead, it is more likely to lead to poverty, degradation, and despair." Indeed, the department even agreed with biologist Julian Huxley that mankind threatened to become the "cancer of the planet."[10]

The key federal event undermining the existing American family system was publication of the 1972 report of the President's Commission on Population Growth and the American Future. Indeed, this widely circulated document could have been appropriately subtitled "a declaration of war on the three-child family." Among the principal tools adopted in pursuit of this goal were the promotion of free abortion and attacks on any "tradition or custom" that affirmed parenthood and family.

Seldom in the history of major government commissions has the deck of "researchers" been so stacked at the outset, the conclusions so preordained, and the facts so twisted to support those determinations. Virtually every social problem facing the nation, this report concluded, could be traced to overpopulation. From "racial antagonisms" to "wasted countrysides," all of our miseries could be blamed on the three-child family found in the nation's "spreading suburbs." As demographer Judith Blake explained in a supplemental paper, "It is clear . . . that long run population stability will require either that Americans . . . restrict themselves to micro-families or that a substantial share of the population remain childless."

Major sections of the report were devoted to bizarre comparisons between futures projected on a two-child and a three-child basis, one calculating that "the regional water deficits" under a three-child system would be precisely 110.6 billion gallons of water per day by the year 2020 compared to 52.6 billion under a two-child system. The report tossed out wildly misleading conclusions about the effect on Gross National Product of smaller families, suggesting, for example, that per capita income would be 15 percent higher by the year 2000 under a two-child system, largely through the expedient fact of having fewer mouths to feed (under this logic, though, a zero-child system resulting in human extinction would eventually make us all millionaires). The report even glossed over the problem of paying for the dependent elderly by relying on the latter's high death rates to make sure that they would not be too costly.

In sum, the commission's report—while acknowledging the nearly obvious fact that a three-child system would "cause more rapid growth in the size of the economy" and "multiply the volume of goods and services produced"—nonetheless concluded that there was "no convincing economic argument for continued national population growth." Economic growth, like other incidentals, would have to be sacrificed to the "population crisis."

The commission also exploited the alleged crisis to advocate "that present state laws restricting abortion be liberalized along the lines of the [existing] New York state statute, such abortions to be performed on request." Judging from New York's experience, the commission expected that free abortion would immediately reduce the birthrate by 8 to 10 percent, with further reductions to follow. Given the looming population crisis, wrote two legal scholars in a commission-funded research paper, "it is indeed later than we think." They added: "If voluntary birth limitation is to be given a chance in the United States, either the courts or the legislatures . . . will have to knock out our vestigial abortion law prohibitions." The U.S. Supreme Court, of course, soon obliged. Liberalized abortion thus joined economic stagnation as the price that must be paid to eliminate the three-child family from the American scene.[11]

The impact of such ideas on the "baby boom" generation just then emerging into adulthood was extraordinary. Ehrlich and company became part of the staple diet on most university and college campuses. Textbooks were speedily rewritten. Young minds were "freed" from tradition, only to be recast in the neo-Malthusian mold. Addressing her 1969 commencement at Mills College, graduate Stephanie Mills spoke for her well-indoctrinated senior class and generation. "Our days as a race on this planet are numbered," she said. "[W]e are breeding ourselves out of existence. Within the next ten years we will witness widespread famines and possible global plagues [raging] through famine-weakened populations." Mankind, Stephanie added, was "like a great unthinking, unfeeling cancer." She concluded: "I am terribly saddened by the fact that the most humane thing for me to do is to have no children at all."[12]

In short, the planners had won, first by manipulating opinion and then by turning opinion into policy. A new social ideology now reigned in America. By 1975, large families had become socially obscene; small families and the "child free" lifestyle stood as the norms guiding enlightened behavior. Dramatic statistical changes followed. As late as 1967, 55.3 percent of American women, ages 30–34, expected to have four or more children. By 1982, only 11.5 percent did. Motherhood had lost its aura.[13] Indeed, to be a nonparent had become in some circles a badge of honor, the ultimate exercise of responsibility. By way of contrast, bearing a third or fourth child stood as a political act, a minority statement of protest against the new Malthusian ascendancy.

It is now time to unmask the twisted population theories that still dominate federal policy, that justify in economic platitudes the annual abortion of 1.5 million children, and that threaten us with economic ruin. The best place to start is with a yet-to-be-recognized fact of economic and political life: the "Malthusian deficit" that is being created at this very moment by the zero-growth mentality that still dominates opinion in the United States. Where does this new deficit come from? It derives from the population requirements of current Social Security and defense policies, in collision with our abortion culture.

Turning to the first category—Social Security—it is critical to note that the early theorists of the comprehensive welfare state were clear on one point: a Social Security system cannot be maintained in a nation with a declining population. In such a land, they recognized, the growing proportion of the elderly relative to the young would eventually bring the whole system tumbling down.

The clearest thinking on this question came in Alva and Gunnar Myrdal's *Kris I Befolkiningsfragan* or *Crisis in the Population Question*. This book served as the theoretical underpinning for creation of the comprehensive Swedish welfare state. Stridently anti-Malthusian, the volume argued that the long-term stability of Sweden's welfare structure depended on the enactment of profamily, pronatalist policies that encouraged fertile married couples to bear a minimum of three or four children per family. Alva Myrdal subsequently raised the necessary minimum goal to five children per family. If small families predominated, she and her husband said, the whole social security network would be endangered through the aging of the population.[14]

It is true that Swedes today commonly ignore this formulation. It is also true that policymakers at the federal level, still holding generally to anti-birth prejudices, also ignore the hard truth. Yet the consequences of doing so are beginning to grow apparent. Former Social Security chief actuary A. Haeworth Robertson, for example, calculates that under projections based on current reproductive behavior, total payroll taxes will have to grow to over 40 percent of salaries in order for government to pay the benefits promised to current young adults.[15] Other projections of looming fiscal disaster for all the nations of Western Europe (and even Japan) could be cited. The social security edifice worldwide is being undermined by the Malthusian disease.

National defense makes the other giant claim upon the U.S. federal budget. Unlike Social Security, Medicare, and most other federal programs (aid to education, national parks, etc.), though, defense spending has no direct relationship to population size. Orders for Trident submarines and Pershing missiles, for example, are not made on the basis of whether the U.S. has 200 million or 300 million people. Rather, defense decisions for the United States are based on such matters as the offensive capabilities of potential opponents. The mandated costs are then borne by the existing population. This means that a given system of defense is purchased at a lower per capita cost by a larger population and that more taxpayers make the defense of our nation and civilization less expensive, when the costs of such defense are allocated to each household. In order to carry the defense burden, then, a growing population seems in the long run to be necessary.

Yet beginning this very year, the needed people will increasingly not be there. The number of legal abortions in the United States began its steady climb upward in 1967, at first through the loosening of state prohibitions and then, after January 1973, as a consequence of the U.S. Supreme Court's decision in *Roe* v. *Wade*. In recent years, the figure has hovered around 1.5 million legal human abortions annually. In 1985, the vanguard of these lost children would have reached age 18, ready to become full actors in the American economy. After 1987, the number of such "economic ghosts"—potential working and creating Americans lost to abortion—begins to grow rapidly.

Now it is true that if legal abortions simply replaced illegal abortions, one for one, there would be no net economic loss. However, recent research has shown that the level of illegal abortions between 1940 and 1967 was much lower than previously assumed, reaching as low as 39,000 in 1950 and averaging less than 100,000. These figures suggest that most of the lives now being eliminated would have been with us under different legal arrangements.[16] This leads to the question: What would be the impact of 1.5 million new lives on the U.S. economy? If the children lost to the saline solution, scalpel, and suction pump in any recent year had lived, what would be the difference? In making such a calculation, it is best to suspend moral and ethical judgments for a time and think like modern economists, avoiding value-laden terms like "mother love" or "compassion" and turning instead to matters such as incentives.

With these preliminaries in mind, let us proceed with a few assumptions: (1) We shall assume that for the first seventeen years of their lives, people are consumption goods, having value as emotional objects alone. In contrast to earlier times, children no longer make a significant net contribution to family income. Nor do children serve any longer as investment goods, as they once did when parents bore children in order to ensure their own personal support in their old age. Instead, children are wanted as objects to love, as perpetuators of the family name, or for other economically irrational reasons. Most of those who would have been aborted also become "wanted" either by the decision of the mother after birth to keep the child or through adoption. (2) We shall assume that persons at age 18 are transformed from consumption goods into potential producers of goods and services. (3) When projecting the individual's earnings into the future, we shall neatly cancel out two factors: (a) an expectation that real earnings will rise, on an average, by 2 percent a year; with (b) an expected average annual discount rate of 2 percent.[17] (4) In calculating the average income of persons age 18 and above, we shall use the figures on average money income provided by the U.S. Census Bureau. The mean, or average, money income for all U.S. men, age 18 and over, was $18,109 in 1983; for all U.S. women, age 18 and over, the average income was $8,780.[18] The beauty of these figures is that they include all adult persons, whether or not they are working, whether such work is full or part-time, and regardless of their race, marital status, or retirement arrangement. As such, they immensely simplify our calculation. In sum, the people that are conjured up here will be thoroughly average. (5) Assuming that mean money income for men and women has increased by 5 percent annually since 1983, we arrive at figures for 1987 of $22,111 for men; $10,672 for women. (6) Among all Americans 18 years and older, .474 were men and .526 were women. (7) A conservative "economic multiplier," measuring the stimulative impact of one person's economic activity on others is, in this case, 2.5.[19] The calculated annual impact on national income of 1.5 million economically active additional lives would then be:

$$\text{Men: } \$22,111 \times .474 \times 1,500,000 \times 2.5 = \$39,302,302,500$$
$$\text{Women: } \$10,672 \times .526 \times 1,500,000 \times 2.5 = \$21,050,520,000$$
$$\text{TOTAL additional annual national income: } = \$60,352,822,500$$

It is true that during the course of their lives, persons do to one degree or another draw upon "social funds" for support, including public education and Social Security. These drawings represent, in a social accounting sense, negative contributions. How should these costs be dealt with? In his recent look at this problem, economist Marvin DeVries calculated that an additional 1.5 million people would run up total social welfare costs (in 1983 dollars) of $240.9 billion during the first eighteen years of their lives and after retirement at age 65.[20] Assuming an increase of 20 percent since 1984, we arrive at a figure of $288.9 billion. Divided by a working lifespan of 47 years, we then have an average of $6.147 billion to be deducted annually. This leaves a net annual increase in national income of $54,205,822,500 even after these "lost children" have in effect paid the social costs for their education and retirement.

The numbers become more dramatic when we look at their cumulative impact. Since 1967, approximately 25 million American children have been legally aborted. If they had all lived, their economic impact in the single year 2012 would have been (in 1987 dollars):

$$25,000,000 \times 22,111 \times .474 \times 2.5 = \$649,510,625,000$$
$$25,000,000 \times 10,672 \times .526 \times 2.5 = \$350,842,000,000$$
$$\text{TOTAL} = \$1,000,352,625,000$$

Assuming that approximately 20 percent of income is absorbed by federal taxes of one sort or another, these never-to-exist taxpayers would have generated roughly $200 billion in tax revenues in that year alone. Such "easy" revenue, though, is already lost forever.

This figure represents "the Malthusian deficit" or, if you prefer, "the abortion deficit," which we are bequeathing to our shrinking number of children and grandchildren. Even if our contemporary politicians find the courage and common sense to solve the existing deficit problem, it may be that they do so only to fall victim during the next decades to the "Malthusian deficit" now being created.

Notes

1. Adam Smith, *The Wealth of Nations* (New York: P.F. Collier & Son, 1909), pp. 83–86.

2. Thomas R. Malthus, *Population: The First Essay* (Ann Arbor: The University of Michigan Press, 1959), pp. 5–6.
3. Richard L. Meier, "Concerning Equilibrium in Human Population," *Social Problems* 6 (Fall 1958): 163–75.
4. Edward Pohlman, "Mobilizing Social Pressures Toward Small Families," *Eugenics Quarterly* 13 (Spring 1966): 122–26.
5. Paul Ehrlich, *The Population Bomb* (New York: Ballantine, 1968), pp. 135–51, 180–81.
6. Walter E. Howard, "The Population Crisis," *The American Biology Teacher* 33 (March 1971): 149, 151; and Garrett Hardin, "Everybody's Guilty: The Ecological Dilemma," *California Medicine* 113 (Nov. 1970): 42, 45–46.
7. Betty Rollin, "Motherhood: Who Needs It?" *Look* (September 22, 1970): 15–17.
8. Anna and Arnold Silverman, *The Case Against Having Children* (New York: David McKay, 1971), pp. 96–116.
9. Ellen Peck and Judith Senderowitz, *Pronatalism: The Myth of Mom and Apple Pie* (New York: Thomas Y. Crowell, 1974), pp. 1–8.
10. *The Population Challenge . . . What It Means to America: United States Department of Interior Conservation Yearbook No. 2* (Washington, DC: U.S. Government Printing Office, 1966), pp. 3–4, 65; and James Roosevelt, "U.S. Presents Views on Population Growth and Economic Development," *The Department of State Bulletin* (January 31, 1966): 176.
11. See: *Population and the American Future: The Report of the Commission on Population Growth and the American Future* (Washington, DC: U.S. Government Printing Office, 1972), pp. 12–15, 38ff, 98, 103–04. Also, these supplemental commission research documents: Judith Blake, "Coercive Pronatalism and American Population Policy," and Harriet F. Pilpel and Peter Ames, "Legal Obstacles to Freedom of Choice in the Areas of Contraception, Abortion, and Voluntary Sterilization in the United States," in Commission on Population Growth and the American Future, *Research Reports, Volume VI, Aspects of Population Growth Policy*, ed. Robert Parke Jr. and Charles F. Westoff (Washington, DC: U.S. Government Printing Office, 1972), pp. 85–109, 59–73; and Christopher Tietze, "The Potential Impact of Legal Abortion on Population Growth in the United States," in *Research Reports, Volume I, Demographic and Social Aspects of Population Growth,* ed. Charles F. Westoff and Robert Parke Jr. (Washington, DC: U.S. Government Printing Office, 1972), pp. 581–85.
12. Stephanie Mills, "The Future is a Cruel Hoax," reprinted in Peck and Senderowitz, pp. 270–71.
13. U.S. Department of Commerce, Bureau of the Census, *Statistical Abstract of the United States*, 1984 (Washington, DC: U.S. Government Printing Office, 1983), p. 68.
14. Alva and Gunnar Myrdal, *Kris I Befolkiningsfragan*, Popular edition (Stockholm: Bonniers, 1936), particularly pp. 125–41.
15. See: A. Haeworth Robertson, *The Coming Revolution in Social Security* (Reston, VA: Reston Publishing Co., 1981), pp. 269–82; and Peter J. Ferrara, "Rebuilding Social Security: Part I, The Crisis Continues," *Heritage Foundation Backgrounder* No. 345, April 25, 1984), p. 6.
16. See: Barbara Syske, Thomas W. Hilgers, and Dennis O'Hare, "An Objective Model for Estimating Criminal Abortions and Its Implications for Public Pol-

icy," in *New Perspectives on Human Abortion*, ed. Thomas W. Hilgers, Dennis J. Horan, and David Mall (Frederick, MD: University Publications of America, 1981), pp. 164–81.

17. The discount rate measures the difference between the interest rate and the rate of inflation and is used to deflate future earnings into present value.

18. U.S. Department of Commerce, Bureau of the Census. *Statistical Abstract of the United States, 1986* (Washington, DC: U.S. Government Printing Office, 1985), p. 456.

19. This multiplier assumes a marginal propensity to consume among Americans of 0.60.

20. Marvin G. DeVries, "The Economic Impact of 1.5 Million Additional People Per Year in the United States," unpublished paper [1983], pp. 11–12.

5

Depopulation Bomb

While most literate inhabitants of the Western world lay awake at night worrying about the specter of global overpopulation, an extraordinary development occurred, one barely noticed at the time. Between 1965 and 1985, fertility rates of the industrial democracies tumbled far below the Zero-Population-Growth (ZPG), or replacement, level. In several lands, actual population decline set in, with deaths exceeding births.

Demographers measure long-term reproductive behavior by translating the annual number of new babies into a weighted average of lifetime births per woman. A figure of 2.1 just insures the replacement of successive generations in a modern nation. As of 1985, West Germany and Denmark shared a total fertility rate of 1.3, the Netherlands and Italy of 1.5, Japan of 1.7, France and the United Kingdom of 1.8. In the United States, the fertility rate tumbled from 3.6 in 1955 and 2.9 in 1965 to 1.7 in 1976, and has hovered around 1.8 through 1986.

As Ben Wattenberg has argued in his *The Birth Dearth*,[1] the geopolitical implications of this change are large. In 1950, as in 1900, the Western democracies accounted for roughly 30 percent of the world's population. Given the collapse of Western fertility, that figure has now fallen to 15 percent. Even assuming a continued decline of fertility in the Marxist and "Third Worlds" and a not-at-all-certain stability at current levels in the West, it will plunge to only 7 percent by 2025, and a mere 4.5 percent 50 years later.

While little reported in the American press, the depopulation issue has become a major domestic political question in France, Germany, and Sweden. In 1983, the French Minister for Social Affairs, Pierre Beregovoy, called for collective action by the member states of the European Economic Community to reverse falling birthrates. Sorbonne historian Pierre Chaunu talks of "a European cancer" and "a refusal of life itself." Demographer Alfred Sauvy warns that the Western world is signing its own death warrant.

The debate has now spread to the United States. *U.S. News & World Report* has described the social impact of "the baby bust" in the United States and emergence of an intensifying "politics of fertility."[2] In late 1985, The American Enterprise Institute sponsored a ground-breaking seminar on "The Consequences of Population Decline in the Western Democracies." In a joint presentation later expanded into his book, Wattenberg and Research Associate Karl Zinsmeister warned that "every major nation that is modern and free is also on a demographic track that, if not changed, will ultimately decimate it." They argued that a relatively large population, while no guarantee of great power status, appeared to be one necessary precondition. Population growth, they added, was a primary stimulus to economic expansion and innovation. Larger populations could more easily construct a modern infrastructure of industry, roads, and airlines and could also provide the tax base to support a modern defense system. Even in the realm of values and culture, they said, numbers mattered. Declining populations were also rapidly aging ones, facing loss of vigor and enormous social-welfare financing problems.[3]

Such arguments actually represent the renewal of an older debate. Between 1900 and 1940, every Western nation except the United States witnessed political attention to the depopulation threat. This earlier "population crisis" sets the context for the contemporary controversy. Significantly, it also casts the incentive structure of democratic capitalism into the very center of the debate. It is by returning to that focus, I suggest, that our options for the future can be clarified.

The roots of the original depopulation scare lay in nineteenth-century France, the first modern nation to see its "crude birthrate" fall from a preindustrial level of 30 to 45 births per thousand people to below 20 per thousand. France in 1800, with 28 million persons, was still the demographic equal of the Russian Empire. Yet fertility decline brought stagnation. Between 1870 and 1940, the French population remained stuck at the 40 million figure. In the latter year, shortly after Hitler's armies occupied Paris, Marshal Petain lamented: "Too few children, too few arms, and too few allies—those were the reasons for our defeat."

Political action had been tried in an effort to reverse the decline. The National Alliance Against Depopulation, founded in 1896, publicized the probable consequences of demographic decay. Hundreds of other French pro-natalist, pro-family organizations sprang up over the next four decades. The most successful of these was the French League of Large Families, an organization based in Roman Catholic parishes and reflecting the higher fertility found among France's religious population.

After 1900, as the fall in crude birthrates began to affect other European peoples, similar debates and pro-natalist organizations emerged. In each case, it was assumed that the decline in the birthrate would continue, and it was argued that dire geopolitical and economic consequences would result. Philosophers of the question linked the birth decline to a general spiritual and cultural crisis in the West.[4]

When shaping political responses to the fertility crisis, a majority of European pro-natalists agreed on the need to suppress neo-Malthusian propaganda advocating birth control, to prohibit the sale of contraceptives, and to strengthen prohibitions on abortion. Pro-natalist Social Democrats dissented, arguing that modern parents, having won some control over their fertility, would not relinquish it, and that any future recovery in the birthrate would have to be based on the voluntary parenthood principle. Similar differences emerged over the desirable shape of pro-natalist incentives: conservatives favored birth bonuses, child allowances, marriage loans, and maternal salaries; socialists encouraged daycare and other state services for families. Pro-natalist unanimity was found on only one point: the primary cause of the birth decline lay in the transition to an industrial society and, more specifically, in the economic incentive structure created by a classically liberal, market-oriented economy.

Within that consensus, there were different emphases. Roman Catholic theorists such as Valere Fallon argued that a market-determined wage system discouraged children by taking no account of family size. In a competitive economy, the childless bachelor and the man with a wife and five offspring at home received the same income. The family with children, accordingly, was left with a lower standard of living, which discouraged others from family formation.[5]

Social Democrats made a similar argument. A capitalist wage system, they said, took no account of family size and responsibilities. In recessions, younger workers with small children were the first to be laid off. Larger families tended to live in the worst housing. In short, modern capitalism imposed on young couples a choice between relative poverty with children or a higher living standard without them. A growing number of potential parents were simply making the rational decision to have few or no children at all.[6]

Antimodernists with fascist leanings, including the German sociologist Roderich von Ungern-Sternberg, also heaped abuse on the spirit of capitalism. The free market, they charged, had given rise to a new human mentality—"the striving spirit"—which avoided matters of the heart and encouraged heightened individualism. In striving for success in a competitive environment, "bourgeois man" recognized that those who had few or no children had a better chance of winning the socioeconomic race. Similarly, industrial production loosened social arrangements that had once given women "sensible occupations" in household management. With women so thrown into the competitive scramble, there were no rational reasons why their rise to positions of economic power and influence should be precluded. Accordingly, women turned away from the housewife and mother roles, even branding them with ridicule.[7]

In response, the defenders of market capitalism and liberal individualism argued that the crisis was only apparent, not real; that the fall in the birthrate represented an adjustment to an earlier and continuing decline in the infant mortality rate. Populations in relative equilibrium during the preindustrial era, with both high birth- and high death rates, would soon find a new equilibrium or stability at lower, modern levels.

Nonetheless, during the late 1930s, governments in democratic France, Belgium, and Sweden, National Socialist Germany, and fascist Italy were frantically attempting to construct pro-natalist policies designed to encourage larger families. Yet the war intervened before results could be assessed, and attention was diverted elsewhere.

After World War II, the depopulation issue briefly resurfaced in Great Britain and France, only to disappear quickly from the political stage. Unexpectedly, birthrates began climbing throughout the Western world in the mid–1940s. For most of Western and Central Europe, this recovery in fertility took the form of a "boomlet," peaking in 1949–50 and flattening out for a decade and a half on a stable plateau, with total fertility rates slightly above the replacement level. However, in the United States, Canada, and Australia, the fertility recovery continued to accelerate well into the 1950s, peaking in 1957–58 and remaining at a high level into the early 1960s.

The American "baby boom" derived from several mutually reinforcing factors. As ten million servicemen were demobilized in 1945–46, they quickly caught up on long-delayed weddings and births. This period also saw significant decreases in the proportion of women remaining single or childless, in the average age of marriage, and in the time between marriage and the first and succeeding births. The unanticipated economic expansion of the 1940s and 1950s provided abundant jobs for the relatively scarce young men born during the period between the two World Wars, 1919–1941, which further encouraged couples to marry and begin childbearing early. The real wages paid to men between 1946 and 1960 also rose at an impressive rate while the real wages paid women stagnated. This enabled more families to live relatively well on one income. Rapidly expanding suburbs, stimulated by carefully targeted federal subsidy, proved conducive to larger families. Undergirding these developments were reinvigorated cultural attitudes that encouraged marriage, celebrated the housewife and mother roles, and welcomed moderate-to-large families.

From our current perspective, the "baby boom" now appears to have been but the short-lived exception to the two-century-old trend of fertility decline. In the 1950s, though, it seemed to observers that a basic turning point had been reached. Pro-natalists such as Sauvy celebrated the existence of "a very new situation," symbolized by the rise in the number of Western births, by postwar documents such as the 1948 Universal Declaration of Human Rights (which labeled the family as "the natural and fundamental element in society and the state"), and by the return of educated, professional women to full-time childbearing.[8] Refined demographic calculations also suggested that the classical liberal defenders of democratic capitalism had been correct: a natural balance at or above replacement was emerging throughout Europe and North America. The completed fertility for cohorts of German women born between the 1890s and 1930s, for example, proved to be surprisingly stable: approximately two children per woman. Similar levels over extended periods were discovered for France, Sweden, and England and Wales. The cycles of decline and recovery after 1900, it turned out, had been largely caused by changes in the *timing* of births: fertility declined in periods of war and economic depression and rose in periods of peace and prosperity. The sustained prosperity of the post-World War II era seemed to betoken stable or moderately expanding populations for the future.

Giving a variation to this theme, demographer Richard Easterlin of the University of Pennsylvania developed his famous thesis of fertility change that predicted cyclical baby booms well into the next century. In the new era, he argued, the material aspirations of young adults were largely shaped by their experiences in their parents' households during adolescence. Fertility behavior (number of children) would be determined by the degree to which a young man's earnings exceeded, met, or fell below his aspirations. When male incomes were high relative to their aspirations (as during the 1940s and 50s), marriage and childbearing were encouraged. When incomes failed to meet aspirations, though, wives sought employment and childbearing was deferred or avoided. Accordingly, he predicted that the huge cohort of youth born in the prosperity of the first baby boom would probably restrict their fertility to some degree; yet their children, in turn, would have lower aspirations and, given their relatively slight numbers, would be in greater demand. Hence, these youths would produce a second "baby boom," starting in the 1990s.[9]

The Easterlin thesis emerged as the dominant interpretation of U.S. fertility trends in the post-World War II era. In the Western world generally, social scientists believed that birthrates would hover at or somewhat above the replacement level.

This held true until 1964. Then, everywhere at once, something went horribly wrong. With an uncanny coordination, birthrates throughout Europe, North America, and Australia began to fall again, and at accelerating rates. This happened in socialist and democratic capitalist countries alike. The downturn began in a period of unprecedented prosperity and economic growth and continued through the stagflation of the 1970s, into the 1980s.

Among Western nations, political reaction first came, predictably, from France. As the French birthrate plunged below the replacement level, strong pro-natalist voices reemerged. Former prime minister Michel Debre seized the issue in 1975, calling for a policy effort equivalent to war to restore the fertility rate. Historian Pierre Chaunu labeled the "new contraception and anti-birth arsenal" as "infinitely more dangerous" to the future of France than any atomic arms. The issue quickly transcended party lines. Then-president Valery Giscard d'Estaing, a Gaullist, argued in 1978 that "a society no longer able to assure the replacement of generations is a society condemned," and he argued for special policy incentives to encourage an increase in three-child families. More recently, Socialist President Francois Mitterrand has argued that "the decline in the birthrate constitutes a grave menace for the West, and we must take action." Nationwide opinion polls showed a dramatic increase in popular pronatalist sentiments after 1975 and even a jump in the "ideal family size" cited by women. In 1978–79, the French government raised the value of child allowances, particularly for third and subsequent children, and introduced a new supplemental benefit for the mothers of children age three or younger.[10]

The fertility collapse hit particularly hard in West Germany, where the number of births to the indigenous population fell from 1.06 million in 1964 to 576,468 in 1977. In the decade after 1966, the number of families with three or more children declined by two-thirds. Political reaction came in 1977, when the Christian Democratic Union tabled resolutions in the *Bundestag* that expressed "growing public concern" about the economic, social security, defense, and rural-policy implications of a declining population and urged study of the feasibility of a pro-natalist family policy. In March 1980, the *Bundestag* conducted a major debate on depopulation, with the conservative Christian parties arguing for more financial support for families, including larger child allowances and a three-year benefit package for new mothers, including a maternal salary. The Social Democrats urged expanded daycare and welfare services. The federal government did increase child allowances in 1979, particularly for third children, and extended paid maternity leaves to six months. On the *Lander* level, Bavaria, Baden-Wurttemberg, and other provinces introduced marriage loan programs providing newlyweds with low interest loans of 10,000 marks, with the principal to be forgiven through the successive birth of children.[11]

Sweden's population debate swelled during the same period. 1976 marked the first year that deaths actually exceeded native births. A year later, a book by Carl Aaberg and Allan Nordin warned the nation of the perils of depopulation. Social Democrats grew uneasy over projections that below-replacement fertility would eventually gut the financial base of the welfare state. Conservatives hoped to restore the traditional family. Disagreements over cause and cure were identical to those found in France and Germany: the right sought to reduce the incentives pushing women into the labor market and to secure recognition of home-based child care as socially useful work; the left wanted to expand daycare and encourage men to carry a greater share of the child care burden. In the 1979–81 period, the government did raise child allowances to 3,000 kronor per year for the first and second children, 3,750 for the third, and 4,500 for the fourth. They have since been raised again, particularly for third and fourth children. Day-care facilities have also been expanded and paid parental leaves from work extended.[12]

Lurking behind these developments, though, has been a common, usually unspoken fear: displacement by other peoples. The turn to pro-natalist policies, in every case, has been accompanied or preceded by a cessation of immigration. Germany ceased admitting new "guest workers" in 1974, followed shortly by Swedish and French immigration shutoffs. The reason is not hard to see. As late as 1965, the excess of births over deaths among the native German population was 334,000; among immigrant workers, 32,300. By 1975, though, the former figure had tumbled far below zero (− 235,600), compared to growth in the latter to 99,000. Similarly in France, of a growth in total population between 1950 and 1975 of eleven million, seven million was due to immigration and four million to a higher birthrate. In contrast, expansion of the French population since 1975 is attributed almost exclusively to the high birthrate of immigrant North Africans. In both cases, the reaction against immigration set in *only after* the native population slipped into incipient decline.

In short, among naturally growing modern peoples, immigrants seemed to be perceived as a healthy addition to successful, expanding social systems. Among a declining people, though, doubts about national identity appear to grow, immigrants become perceived as a threat, and liberality gives way to xenophobia and suppression.[13]

In the United States, the dominant fixtures of the professional demographic establishment argue that the new population scare is overblown; that despite fertility rates well below replacement, equilibrium will return. Easterlin, for example, continues to insist that the U.S. fertility rate will rise in the 1990s as the small "baby bust" cohort of the late 1960s and 1970s enter adulthood. Using the Easterlin model, Dennis Ahlburg of the University of Minnesota calculates a climb from 3.3 million American births in 1978 to 4.6 million in 1997. Demographer Michael Teitelbaum cites the false prophets of depopulation from the 1930s, and suggests that current alarms will also prove wayward.[14]

Yet there is strong evidence that the optimists are whistling in the dark: that we are in a new demographic era where the probable result is continued fertility decline. On a theoretical basis, it is clear that the demographers' assumption that Western societies would achieve stable populations at or near the ZPG level was never more than a pipe dream: a reflection of an understandable, if reactionary, neo-Malthusian quest for stability in a constantly changing world. As demographer Hilde Wander correctly notes, ZPG is not a development supported by some innate dynamic, as is long-term growth or long-term decline. It is rather a border case between growth and decline, liable to opposing forces, and inherently unstable.[15]

The current status of Western populations represents something altogether novel. Never before in the long history of demographic change have multiple populations stopped growing in normal times because of deficient fertility. From the 1970s on, the West has begun a "second" transition, entering an entirely new, wholly uncharted demographic terrain. Lying behind this radically different situation are three structural changes in the Western social order:

(1) *The new technologies of contraception and the legalization of abortion.* As population historians have long and correctly noted, the inhabitants of the West began to control their fertility well before modern contraceptive techniques were available. The decline in French, German, British, Swedish, and American birthrates set in during an era when *coitus interruptus* remained the primary contraceptive method for the large majority of the population. By the time the diaphragm and relatively cheap condoms were available, Western fertility rates had already tumbled to half their preindustrial level. Nonetheless, fertility control remained haphazard and the number of "unwanted" births relatively high through the mid-1960s. However, the commercial introduction of the birth control pill in 1965 and the legalization of abortion in most Western countries in the 1968–80 period resulted in a sharp decline in the percentage of unwanted births. Among married women in the United States, the percentage of unwanted births ("not wanted by mother at conception or any future time") fell from 20.5 percent in 1965 to 13 percent in 1973 and to 6.8 percent in 1982. According to one analysis, 42 percent of the fall in total fertility between 1973 and 1982 can be explained by this decline in unwanted children.[16]

(2) *The ongoing divorce of fertility from marriage.* Sweden and the

United States offer two illuminating examples of societies that are consciously severing the ancient connection between wedlock and children. In the former land, marriage is slowly disappearing as an institution. In 1966, Sweden counted 61,000 marriages; by 1972, the number had fallen to 38,000, with a slowed, albeit continued, decline thereafter. In 1960, 43.7 percent of Swedish women aged 20–24 were married; by 1978, the number had fallen to 18.8 percent. Among those aged 25–29, the fall was from 77.7 to 52.0 percent. Taking the place of marriage is unmarried cohabitation. As late as 1960, only an estimated 1 percent of couples living together were unmarried. By 1970, the figure was 7 percent. A 1978 government report put the figure at 15 percent, and more recent estimates rise near 25 percent. Cohabitating couples, it is true, continue to have babies. Yet their completed fertility appears to be less than half of that found among married couples. Sweden's 1975 census, for example, showed married women, ages 30–34, with an average of 2.0 children; among cohabitating women in the same age bracket, the figure was 0.9. Reflecting the turn to cohabitation, illegitimacy is also skyrocketing in Sweden. As late as 1960, only one out of every ten births was out of wedlock. By 1978, the figure had climbed to 36 percent; and in 1986 to almost 50 percent.[17]

In the United States, it is true, wedlock remains popular by comparison. Nonetheless, this country has also experienced significant changes. The marriage rate for 1,000 unmarried women, ages 15 to 49, has declined from 148 in 1960 to 102 in 1982. Moreover, the number of never-married young adults has climbed dramatically. Among women ages 20–24, for example, the figure doubled from 28 percent in 1960 to 56 percent in 1983; for ages 25–29, from 11 to 25 percent. Even the "remarriage rate," for women ages 14 to 44 who were previously divorced or widowed, has fallen off sharply since 1965. The number of reported cohabitating couples in the United States, while still proportionately small by Swedish standards, did climb from 523,000 in 1970 to 1,988,000 in 1984 (4 percent of all couples). Unmarried births are also enjoying a surge in popularity here, the illegitimacy ratio (illegitimate births as a percentage of live births) having quadrupled since 1957. Alice Rossi, in her 1983 presidential address to the American Sociological Association, notes that while voluntary childlessness has increased only slightly in recent decades, voluntary illegitimacy is enjoying growing popularity. She speculates that we may be moving through a time when parenting is being separated from marriage, as sex was separated from marriage in an earlier period.[18]

(3) *The creation of a new set of antinatalist economic incentives through the transition from a one-income to a two-income family norm.* All commentators on the subject of contemporary fertility decline note the important effect of the massive movement of women into the labor market. Only

a handful, though, fully explore the implications of that change. The more honest thinking on this subject comes from the pens of feminist theorists, who have focused on the revolutionary changes in male and female roles that have occurred over the last two decades.

In an article for *Feminist Studies*, sociologist Nancy Folbre lays out a comprehensive feminist theory of fertility decline. She argues that the "patriarchal family" (for nonfeminists, the traditional family), resting on the "domination" of women and the "exploitation" of female and child labor, was the historic Western family form. Such control, she says, allowed both parents to draw economic benefits from their children, whether young or grown; and it allowed men to shift a significant portion of the real cost of children (in terms of time and lost income) onto individual mothers. She argues, however, that capitalism subverted this family system, as the introduction of modern production methods led to a growing separation of home from work. In a competitive wage system, moreover, new opportunities for women to earn a wage raised "the opportunity cost" of children: the income or production foregone in order to provide maternal child care.

Folbre acknowledges that Karl Marx and Friedrich Engels had presented essentially the same argument. She adds, though, that the founders of communism "clearly neglected the possibility that patriarchal interests might be reflected in policies set by employers, trade unions, and the state which would define the terms of women's participation in the labor force." Informal sanctions on women's labor, the division of jobs into "male" and "female" categories, special protective legislation, and the clear wage differential that men enjoyed over women were the mechanisms and institutions through which the traditional family protected itself against the logic of a competitive wage system. Folbre notes that the sexual wage differential, in particular, created a powerful economic incentive for women to assume the task of child care, "simply because they cannot replace the earnings that would be lost if fathers took time off from wage work." Such a system held through the 1950s.

Yet independent of this "coercive pronatalism," Folbre continues, other economic changes were undermining the material basis of the family unit. As child labor became illegal, as families shrank in size toward a norm of only two children, and as the expansion of commodity production provided a growing number of cheap substitutes for home-produced goods and services, the valuation of women's household labor fell. Even husbands began to see the benefits of sending their wives to work, she says. As women with fewer children began to spend more time in the marketplace and less time at home, they gained more experience and training; this negated the economic (although not the social) argument for the wage differential.

Finally, many women—and some of their husbands—began demanding equal pay laws, affirmative action, and revaluation of male-female job categories on the basis of "comparable worth." At this critical point, the culturally set boundaries to industrial society, which had protected the family from the cancerous logic of radical individualism, were breached. Significantly, barely any defenders of the old order were to be found.

This collapse of a family-oriented economy, Folbre explains, is precisely what happened in Europe and the United States during the 1960–80 period. Childbearing became an activity conducted despite, rather than because of, economic self-interest. The decision to raise a child now imposes "truly phenomenal economic costs upon parents" and provides no benefits. All existing economic incentives, she concludes, point toward accelerated fertility decline.[19]

Making a similar argument in an article entitled "Will U.S. Fertility Decline Toward Zero?" Joan Huber of the University of Illinois answers *yes*: "The most probable long-run fertility trend is continued decline, not just to ZPG but toward zero." Huber argues that it was the new demand for female labor during the prosperous 1950s that undermined prevailing cultural assumptions about a woman's responsibility to care for children at home. During that decade, the rapid expansion of business and government bureaucracies increased demand for clerical workers, traditionally a female job. Similarly, the baby boom stimulated demand for teachers and nurses, also female tasks. The diminished supply of young, unmarried women workers due to the low birthrate of the 1930s and the lowered age of marriage after 1945 also conspired to expand opportunities for married women. In an era of weakened cultural institutions, the solitary decisions of employers to hire married women and of individual women or couples to send the wife/mother out to work coalesced into a revolutionary social transformation. So began the massive flow of married women into the labor force, a development which was politicized after 1960 and continues to our day.

Huber acknowledges that this trend originated "despite lack of normative support and in the face of a mass media propaganda barrage extolling the joys of family togetherness." Yet as more women began to spend more time in the labor force for more of their adult lives, powerful challenges were mounted against male and female job categories and the sexual wage differential that set the earnings of women employed full-time at about three-fifths the wages of male counterparts. Such developments, Huber says, "not only triggered a new women's movement but also set the stage for continued fertility decline." Indeed, she adds, feminist ideology in collision with the facts of biological replacement have "made the U.S. profoundly anti-natalist."

She anticipates no improvement in the future, for a variety of factors weigh against any revival of pro-natalism. First, the direct costs of child-rearing continue to rise, exceeding $175,000 for the first child. Second, the psychic costs of having children increase as parents face the awful challenges of peer groups, professional advice, and government scrutiny. Huber points to studies consistently showing mothers at home with preschoolers to be the most unhappy group in the population. Third, the economic rewards of childbearing decline as society wipes out the economic bonds of parents to children. Fourth, as women's education level and job opportunities rise, the "opportunity cost" of staying home also increases. Fifth, husbands have become primary advocates of working wives, having learned (as did husbands in the Soviet Union) that the added income, in practice, costs them almost nothing in terms of extra housework. And sixth, the dramatic rise in the divorce rate since 1965 has suppressed the desire for children, by increasing women's risks of being saddled with the children alone.

Huber concludes that the primary long-term effect of women's rising employment has been "to increase the perception that parenting couples are disadvantaged in comparison to nonparenting ones." The emerging "zero-sum squabble" over jobs and income is not between men and women; rather, it is a zero-sum contest between parents and nonparents. Barring dramatic changes, she says, children will simply and slowly disappear.[20]

Support of an econometric sort for this pessimistic view comes from the school of research known as "the new home economics." Its proponents in both Europe and the United States argue that the determining factor in fertility changes since 1950 has been the rise in the earnings capacity of women, along with other developments that have induced greater labor-force participation by young married women. Children are time-intensive, they argue, and any change that increases the "opportunity cost" of children will reduce demand for them.

From this perspective, the key change of the last four decades relative to fertility was the transition from a society in which most families had only one income-earner to a society in which most have two. In the traditional one-income family, where the wife specializes in child care and home activities, an increase in the husband's wage indirectly raises the value of her home-based time (by raising the cost of her husband's potential child-care time), thereby reducing the probability of her joining the labor force. Under these circumstances, an increase in real family income tends to *encourage* additional births. In contrast, the new home economists argue, a system in which both spouses work tends to *reduce* fertility by raising the value of leisure and working hours. These changes raise the cost of time and children in a manner that more than offsets the positive stimulus to fertility created by economic growth. Indeed, it appears that in a two-earner normative milieu, the more rapid the rate of economic growth, the more costly two-earner families find it to have children, making fertility negatively correlated to real wages. In consequence, the Western world now finds itself in a new era where *economic growth depresses fertility*.

The new home economics offers explanations of other recent changes in reproductive behavior. The rise in the average age of marriage since 1960 and the greater compression of the period during which a woman has her children (on average, starting a family later and finishing childbearing sooner) are rational acts in a society that has increased the "opportunity cost" to women leaving the workforce and has enhanced the expected degree of women's lifetime labor force attachment.

Declining marriage rates, a high level of divorce, and rapidly growing levels of cohabitation are also predicted by this model. Marriage brings the most economic gain to a couple when the uses of the spouses' time are complementary: when the husband devotes his time to paid employment and the wife to home activities. In this example, the mate with the higher earning capacity tends to allocate more time to paid employment and less to nonmarket work. Because of this division of labor, the couple is *better off* than if they operated as individuals, since household time is cheaper (in foregone earnings) when supplied by the lower-wage spouse and the time devoted to paid labor has a greater payoff when supplied by the spouse with a higher wage. This gain from marriage *increases* with growth in disparity between the spouses' potential wages. However, as the earning potentials of the average man and woman move toward equality (e.g., through a cultural-political turn toward equal pay laws, affirmative action, and "comparable worth"), the gain from marriage diminishes, and the incentive either to marry or save a marriage declines. Similarly, as the gain from marriage shrinks, risk-adverse individuals rationally seek to acquire more information about potential spouses before entering into wedlock: hence, the rising propensity to cohabit.[21]

In short, the new home economics shows that in a system where the differential between men's and women's wages is shrinking, one should expect a growing number of two-earner households, a declining number of marriages, rising levels of divorce and cohabitation, and diminished fertility. Indeed, once the initial change in normative order has occurred, the momentum of transformation grows. As University of Chicago economist Gary Becker sums up: "The increase in labor force participation and the decline of fertility eventually accelerate even when the growth in female earning power does not. Moreover, these two factors accelerate the increase in the divorce rate because the decline in the gain from marriage also accelerates."[22]

Without explaining why, economist John Ermisch does retain faith that "there is undoubtedly a floor to fertility above zero," perhaps one child per family. Yet above that floor, he insists, economic growth will tend to push fertility downward.[23]

Most available evidence supports this interpretation of the fertility decline. The correlation between fertility decline and the rise in women's wages relative to men's is very close for West Germany, Britain, and the United States. Other studies show that career-oriented women reduce their expected family size by at least one child and that higher levels of education for women even translate into higher labor force participation during and immediately after pregnancy. According to recent calculations, the "opportunity cost," or lost wages, of a woman with a Master's degree choosing to care for a child up to age 14 is roughly $300,000. Without adopting the whole materialistic argument, one can acknowledge fundamental change in the economic incentive structure: modern Western economies based on the two-earner norm structurally discourage the birth of children.[24]

If the United States stood splendidly apart from the rest of the world, this new fact of life might be acceptable: our numbers would decline, slowly at first, then with accelerated speed; our society would rapidly age, yet there would probably be sufficient reserve wealth in the nation to see us all comfortably through to our graves; last one turn out the lights, please.

Yet we do not stand apart from the world. Over the long run, our ability to maintain the industrial base essential to our national security depends on relatively large numbers.

More immediately, we are confronted by an altogether new situation relative to immigration. During the first great wave of non-British immigration to the United States (1840–1924), most arrivals came from distant lands across wide oceans and landed in a country with a native-born population that was still experiencing natural growth through relatively high fertility. The new immigration (1965–present), though, has different characteristics: (1) the largest share of the new arrivals, legal and illegal, come from the contiguous Mexico/Central America region, which has an extremely high fertility rate and some residual irredentist sentiments; and (2) they are settling in a land where the native-born population has been in long-term decline since 1973. If these two changes continue over the next several decades, it is folly to assume that there will not be major political and cultural consequences.

Indeed, it is possible that the American reaction to these trends of fertility decline and foreign immigration could turn populist and xenophobic. Nativism is a not-infrequent theme in American history, and the conditions are ripe for a new wave of passionate, possibly ugly, reaction. The future of the United States as a pluralistic democracy may depend on how we choose to handle the fertility question.

Notes

1. Ben Wattenberg, *The Birth Dearth* (New York: Pharos Books, 1987).
2. "Measuring Impact of the 'Baby Bust' on U.S. Future," *U.S. News & World Report* (December 16, 1985): 66–67.
3. Ben J. Wattenberg and Karl Zinsmeister, "A Speculation on the Geopolitical Implications of Below-Replacement Fertility in the Western Democracies." A presentation during AEI Public Policy Week, Washington, DC, December 2, 1985.
4. Perhaps the best general survey of the first depopulation scare is: D.V. Glass, *Population Policies and Movements in Europe* (Oxford: Clarendon Press, 1940).
5. Valere Fallon, S.J. *Les allocations familiales pour les classes moyennes* (Brussels: Ligue des familles nombreuses de Belgique, 1938).
6. See: Gunnar Myrdal, *Population: A Problem for Democracy* (Cambridge, MA: Harvard University Press, 1940).
7. Roderich von Ungern-Sternberg, "Die Ursachen des Geburtenruckgangs im welteuropaischen Kulturkris wahrend des 19. und 20. Jahrhunderts, *Archiv fur Bevolkerungswissenschaft und Bevolkerungspolitik.* 8 (1938): 1–19; and *Biologie und Okonomie* (Berlin: Richard Schoetz, 1936), pp. 94–98.
8. Alfred Sauvy, *General Theory of Population* (New York: Basic Books, 1969), pp. 404–06.
9. See: Richard A. Easterlin, *The American Baby Boom in Historical Perspective* (New York: National Bureau of Economic Research, 1962), and subsequent works.
10. Marie-Monique Huss, *Demography, Public Opinion, and Politics in France, 1974–80,* Occasional Paper No. 16 (London: Department of Geography, Queen Mary College, University of London, 1980), pp. 23–62; and Richard Tomlinson, "The French Population Debate," *The Public Interest* 76 (Summer 1984): 111–20.
11. C. Alison McIntosh, *Population Policy in Western Europe* (Armonk, NY: M.E. Sharpe, 1983), pp. 177–220; and Adelhard Grafin zu Castell Rudenhausen and Wolfgang Kollmann, "Past and Present Policy Reactions to Fertility Decline in Germany," in *Population Change and Social Planning*, ed. David Eversley and Wolfgang Kollmann, eds., (London: Edward Arnold, 1982), pp. 414–25.
12. McIntosh, pp. 147–73.
13. See: Julian Crandell Hollick, "Demographic Change in Europe," *The World Today* 36 (September 1980): 361–68.
14. Jean van der Tek, ed., "U.S. Population: Where We Are; Where We're Going," *Population Bulletin* 37 (June 1982): 8; Dennis Ahlburg, "Good Times, Bad Times: A Study of the Future Path of U.S. Fertility," *Social Biology* 30 (Spring 1983): 17–23, and Michael Teitelbaum and Jay M. Winter, *The Fear of Population Decline* (San Diego: Academic Press, 1985).
15. Hilde Wander, "Zero Population Growth Now: The Lessons From Europe," in *The Economic Consequences of Slowing Population Growth*, ed. Thomas J. Espenshade and William J. Serow (New York: Academic Press, 1978), pp. 41–42, 67–68.
16. William F. Pratt, et al., "Understanding U.S. Fertility: Findings From the National Survey of Family Growth, Cycle III," *Population Bulletin* 39 (December 1984): 8–9, 31.

17. Murray Gendell, "Sweden Faces Zero Population Growth," *Population Bulletin* 35 (June 1980): 11–14; and McIntosh, pp. 140–42.
18. Alice S. Rossi, "Gender and Parenthood: American Sociological Association, 1983 Presidential Address," *American Sociological Review* 49 (February 1984): 1–19; Larry L. Bumpass, *The Changing Linkage of Nuptiality and Fertility in the United States*, CDE Working Paper 79–6 (Madison, WI: Center for Demography and Ecology, University of Wisconsin, 1979), pp. 18–19; and Wendy H. Baldwin and Christine Winquist Nord, "Delayed Childbearing in the U.S.: Facts and Fictions," *Population Bulletin* 39 (November 1984): 15–17.
19. Nancy Folbre, "Of Patriarchy Born: The Political Economy of Fertility Decisions," *Feminist Studies* 9 (Summer 1983): 261–84.
20. Joan Huber, "Will U.S. Fertility Decline Toward Zero?" *The Sociological Quarterly* 21 (Autumn 1980): 481–92.
21. John Ermisch, "Investigation Into the Causes of the Postwar Fertility Swings," in Eversley and Kollman, pp. 141–55.
22. Gary S. Becker, *A Treatise on the Family* (Cambridge, MA: Harvard University Press, 1981), p. 251.
23. Ermisch, p. 154.
24. Ibid., p. 147; Linda J. Waite, "U.S. Women at Work," *Population Bulletin* 36 (May 1981): 13–14; Steven D. McLaughlin, "Differential Patterns of Female Labor-force Participation Surrounding the First Birth," *Journal of Marriage and the Family* 44 (May 1982): 414–15; and Thomas J. Espenshade, "The Value and Cost of Children," *Population Bulletin* 32 (1977): 25–27.

Part III
THE SEXUAL QUESTION

6

Pregnant Teenagers and Moral Civil War

American teenagers do one thing better than their peers in any other Western land: make babies. In 1984, the annual teenage pregnancy rate (births plus abortions per 1,000 women, ages 15–19) for the United States was 96; among whites, it was 83. This compared to 45 for England and Wales, 44 for Canada, 35 for Sweden, and a mere 14 for The Netherlands. Among teenagers 14 years old or younger, the U.S. birth rate was more than four times that of Canada, the nearest competitor in the children-having-children sweepstakes. Significantly, these American rates do not derive from more sexual activity. By age 17, for example, nearly 60 percent of Swedish girls have had intercourse, compared to only 37 percent of American girls. Yet the latter tend to get pregnant, while the former do not.

This situation stimulated a controversial 1985 report by Planned Parenthood's former research arm, the Alan Guttmacher Institute.[1] On the basis of a 37-country statistical analysis and a six-country comparative case study, the report concludes that the unique American teenage pregnancy problem is caused by the irregular and inexpert use of contraceptives by American youth, appallingly weak sex education programs, the lack of an effective national health service, and the reactionary pressures of fundamentalist religious groups.

As intended, this research study unsettled traditionalists and stimulated congressional calls for enhanced federal programs to provide free contraceptives and more and earlier sex education to the young. Yet the situation is more complex. Claims to the contrary, the Guttmacher report is not a work of science. It is an ideological tract, one reflecting a fundamental division in American society. In addition, its proposed "solutions" are not compelling logical conclusions at all. Rather, they represent a call for one side in this cultural conflict to surrender to the other. Nor is the program that the report presents startlingly new. Indeed, it is but the latest attempt to advance a moral-political agenda nearly three-quarters of a century old.

The Guttmacher report must be read and understood within these ideological and historical perspectives.

For nearly 1500 years, Western civilization managed its teenage pregnancy problem through the creation and defense of an ascetic moral code. Under its terms, marriage was ordained by God and sustained by the institutional church as the only legitimate sexual bond. The regulation of sexual mores reflected recognition of the strong linkage between human sexuality and the construction and renewal of civilization. Accordingly, human sexuality was channeled away from destructive and self-indulgent goals and toward fruitful and socially stable ends. Serious deviations from this norm were treated as perversions punishable by law. Out-of-wedlock pregnancy in the West was prevented by the most effective form of contraception ever devised: sexual abstinence or chastity outside of marriage. While by no means a perfect system, it worked reasonably well. With some modifications and strains, this code lasted in Western Europe and America through the 1950s. As one sociologist, commenting on the United States, noted as late as 1968: "the norm in this country is one of early, frequent, and random dating, with a gradual narrowing of the field, . . . delaying of coitus until after the wedding, and the strong expectation of marital fidelity."[2]

Yet individuals and organizations were already working diligently to undermine this moral system. Their tools were ideas. Their purposes: to "liberate" sexuality from religious and cultural restraints; to construct a "new" morality.

Among the intellectual "fathers" and spiritual models of this movement was English psychologist Henry Havelock Ellis, author of *Studies in the Psychology of Sex*, appearing in seven parts, 1896–1928. In this monumental work, Ellis used value-neutral scientific observation and the analytical device of cultural relativism to drive home three themes:

Everybody is not like you. In his opening chapters on "The Evolution of Modesty," Ellis argued that modesty was a universal human trait, but one that took different forms in different places. In Tierra del Fuego, for example, women wore only a minute triangle of animal skin but were so modest that they never removed it. Among the Buganda of Africa, in contrast, it was a punishable offense for a man to expose any part of his thigh. Ellis concluded that modesty was merely a function of time, place, and status. Only in Victorian England, he suggested, did it reach "pathological" levels.

Even your neighbors are different from you. Through his extensive and explicit case studies, Ellis opened the door on private sexual behavior. It was "impossible," he wrote, to find two individuals with nearly identical sexual emotions and needs. Everyone, he added, had their own little sex secrets. To choose but one example, he described the devout, church-going

American woman who "had never allowed herself to entertain sexual thoughts about men" but whose erotic desires were aroused by "the sight of a key in any bureau drawer."

There is no objective boundary between the normal and the abnormal. "The majority of sexual perversions, including even those that are the most repulsive," Ellis wrote, "are but exaggerations of instincts and emotions that are germinal in normal human emotions." As "a naturalist" rather than a judge, Ellis viewed the whole range of sexual behaviors—the heterosexual and the homosexual, the sadist, the libertine, the masochist, the fetishist, the lover of animals or corpses—with an absolute scientific objectivity. He set a standard of "objectivity" and moral neutrality that all later sex researchers and liberators would adopt.[3]

Other moral revolutionaries, all pledges to science, followed. Ellis' contemporary, Sigmund Freud, understood the role of sexual restraint in the building and maintenance of civilization. Yet his clinical reports on sexual perversion and fetishism and his elaborate descriptions of the powerful sexual desires and fantasies of children helped, however unintentionally, to advance the new moral vision. Alfred Kinsey's *Sexual Behavior in the Human Male* (1948) and *Sexual Behavior in the Human Female* (1953) presented comprehensive statistics on American sexual preferences. With clinical neutrality, Kinsey watched and described the whole range of sexual behaviors, including the induced orgasms of five-month-old babies. Many of the "myths" sustaining the Judeo-Christian moral code so succumbed to scientific realism. Finally came William Masters and Virginia Johnson, who directly observed 10,000 human sexual acts and analyzed the results in minute detail. Through their work, human sexuality was stripped of its remaining mystery and sacredness.

In America, organizations dedicated to "ethical culture," "sexual hygiene," and "sex education" had existed since the turn of the century. Yet prior to the late 1950s, their influence outside of elite circles was meager. Then they made their move. Decrying the horrors of American population growth, these groups quickly gained influence in academia, the media, and the halls of government. In 1964, former Presidents Harry Truman and Dwight Eisenhower both felt comfortable in serving as honorary cochairmen for a national campaign to shut off American population growth. That same year, the Sex Information and Education Council of the United States (SIECUS) coalesced with the stated goal of generating "public awareness, understanding, and acceptance of the multiplicity of patterns of human sexuality—to move from a restrictive concept of genital sexuality to the larger dimension in which every individual, at whatever age, boy or girl, man or woman, is seen as a whole."

By the mid-1960s, these partisans of a new moral and sexual order could smell victory and they pressed home their intellectual assault. Their arguments deserve attention as a case study on how to conduct and win a moral revolution through the manipulation of words and ideas; the same themes, moreover, appear in the Guttmacher study.

First, declare the old morality dead. "The beginning of wisdom for educators," wrote Isadore Rubin, managing editor of *Sexology* magazine, in 1965, "is the recognition of the fact that the old absolutes are gone; that there exists a vacuum of many moral beliefs about sex." The ascetic ideal was dead in America, he said; only its legalistic legacy remained. Sociologist Ira Reiss argued that abstinence was no longer the dominant standard among teens, "a fact that all of us must face, whether or not we approve of such a state of affairs." The need, all agreed, was development of a new philosophy of sex education for a democratic, pluralistic society.[4]

Second, destroy the residual influence of tradition and religion. In his call for a democratic sexual policy, Dr. Rubin made it clear that some elements of pluralistic America were not invited to participate in its shaping. Teachers, deans, and school counselors, he said, should "identify and destroy those outmoded aspects of the ascetic ideal which no longer represent the ideals of the vast majority of American ethical leaders . . . and which no longer contribute either to individual happiness and growth or to family and social welfare." Sex educator Esther Middlewood welcomed American churches to the new liberating task only if they presented "a program which is sufficiently well founded on facts about current practices, current moral concepts, and sociological and psychological knowledge;" e.g., only if they had abandoned efforts to teach the old ascetic dogma and joined the revolution. Surprisingly, many churches readily abandoned Christian principles. The United Methodist Church and the United Church of Christ were soon receiving special praise from the experts for their progressive sex curricula. Even the Roman Catholic Church, long the chief enemy of the new sexuality, wavered. Ethicist Daniel Callahan, writing in the Catholic journal *Commonweal*, pointed to Catholicism's cultural isolation on the matter of human sexuality and argued that a "better" strategy "would be for the church, in its teaching authority and in its members, to immerse itself in the present."[5]

Third, make everything relative by recasting the traditional as the abnormal. Professor Reiss concluded that the choice of a premarital sexual standard in modern America was "a personal one, and no amount of facts or trends can 'prove' the superiority of one standard to another." Editor Rubin surveyed the vast anthropological data and said there had been no universals in sex values, with the possible exception of a prohibition on incest. If anything, he said, Western society had been deviant in its obsession with premarital chastity. Sociologist F. Ivan Nye drew a distinction between "intrinsic," unchanging values, and "instrumental" or utilitarian values. Under the ascetic ideal of the past, he noted, values such as obedience to parents and maintenance of a strong family had been treated as intrinsic and necessary. Yet as a consequence of social change, Nye charged, obedience to parents had become "meaningless," while a prosperous welfare state had actually made the value of "strengthening the family"—with the exaction of "its pound of flesh from family members in terms of sacrificed individual goals, interests, recreation, and social relations outside the family"—negative.[6]

Fourth, declare religious opinion unacceptable in any public moral debate, allowing only science to take part. Nye argued that all forms of social structure should be viewed as instrumental, open to infinite variations. "Thus freed from the dead hand of traditional practice," social scientists and policymakers could "objectively weigh the changes that from time to time need to be made if the family and other social institutions are to function more effectively." Core values were admittedly necessary to society, Rubin added, yet these must bear no relation to "religious values, prejudice, or irrational fears." Rather, borrowing from the ideas of philosopher John Dewey, he defined the new democratic and scientific values that should be inculcated: faith in the free play of critical intelligence; respect for the equality and dignity of each individual; the right of self-determination; and the need for cooperative effort for the common good.[7]

Fifth, advocate "choice." In a pluralistic, democratic society, the moral revolutionaries said, the indoctrination of youth into the traditional ascetic sexual code could not be allowed. Adolescent sex should be controlled only to protect the health of the young, and not to defend adult prejudices. The "motives" of behavior, not "actions" themselves, were the appropriate foci of concern. The question to ask regarding premarital sexual behavior was not: "Is it moral?"; rather, it was: "do the sexual partners care for each other?" In the current "transitional period of morality," youth must be exposed to the whole range of possible patterns of sexual behavior. Rubin suggested training young people in six competing value systems, ranging from "traditional repressive asceticism" to the "sexual anarchy" of Rene Guyon. He concluded: "If . . . we give [youth] the skill and attitudes, the knowledge and the understanding that enable them to make their own intelligent choice among competing moral codes, we have given them the only possible equipment to face the future."[8]

Sixth, advance the "contraceptive" solution as the sole answer to our social problem. With traditional moral barriers crumbling and with sex open and free, only the problem of out-of-wedlock pregnancy remained. Traditionalists defending chastity, Professor Nye noted, advanced the following scenario: fewer moral restraints on sex outside of marriage mean more extramarital intercourse mean more premarital pregnancies and related social problems. "Notably lacking from this chain," he added, "is any more effective use of contraceptive devices by the unmarried."[9] In the new moral order, freely available contraceptives and instruction on how to use them would provide the solution.

Finally, seize control of the schools and begin indoctrination of the young in the "new" code. Education in the schools, not training in the homes or churches, must be the goal, the moral revolutionaries said. Research showed that "democratic morality" could be taught at very young ages. Where this method superseded the traditional dogmatic, judgmental approach, the child becomes "less punitive, less anxious, more tolerant, more democratic, more responsible, more secure, has fewer conflicts, and shows better school adjustment."[10] In short, such a child had been successfully converted to the new moral order; he had been socialized.

Between 1960 and 1980, moral revolutions of this sort succeeded in most parts of Western Europe. The sexual codes inherited from the Christian past and sustained, most recently, by the middle class, crumbled with surprising rapidity. Chastity became a joke-word. Premarital experimentation by teenagers was recast as normal, expected behavior. Contraception and, if necessary, abortion would be relied on to handle potential negative consequences such as pregnancy.

Yet in a major deviation from the European pattern, this moral revolution didn't quite succeed in America. True, many battles were won, particularly on the policy level. The federal government caved in to elite pressure and elevated Planned Parenthood into a quasi-federal agency. Public school systems began adopting sex education curricula based on the scientific model and presuming teenage sexual activity. The national media fostered the same sense of revolution, and taboo after taboo fell on the television networks.

At the popular level, though, curious things were happening. It is true that in some areas of the country, tolerance of premarital sexual relations appeared to grow. A study by B.K. Singh of Texas Christian University found that 59 percent of Americans in 1978 thought premarital sex to be "not wrong at all" or "wrong only sometimes," compared to 49.4 percent in 1972. However, when these numbers were broken down by region and religion, startling divergences appeared. The highest levels and greatest expansion of approval for premarital sex between these years were in the Northeast United States, the Pacific coast, and the Mountain states. In contrast, approval of premarital sex actually *declined* in the South and Midwest. While the percentage of Catholics approving premarital sex jumped from 48.7 to a startling 62.8 percent, the increase among Protestants was only 4.7 percent. More dramatically, among all persons of "high" religious attendance, there was no change in attitude (actually, a statistically insignificant decline from 36.5 to 36 percent).[11] Translating these statistics into impressionistic terms, we can almost see the early mobilization of evangelical and fundamentalist Protestants against the "new morality" attempting to secure cultural and political control of America.

The difference between Europe and America is that the Western religions—Christianity and Judaism—are culturally alive in the United States in a way that they are not on the other side of the Atlantic. "That the Americans are exceptional in their attitude to religion is obvious to all, and never more so than today," reported British historian Paul Johnson in the inaugural Erasmus Lecture.[12] Among large numbers of Americans, religious dogma is still taken seriously and the indoctrination of children into the moral code of the Judeo-Christian tradition is still considered a parental obligation. In short, the United States may be the last place in the developed world where the Judeo-Christian ascetic code still has a significant number of adherents. Accordingly, in an era of conflict between this inherited moral code and the new one, America's religious exceptionalism would predictably produce exceptional results.

Indeed, this is exactly what the Guttmacher Institute researchers had unwittingly discovered and reported. American political and religious leaders, they said, "appear divided" over what course to take: discouraging sexual activity among young unmarried people or promoting contraceptive use. In consequence, "American teenagers seem to have inherited the worst of all possible worlds regarding their exposure to messages about sex." Movies, rock music, the radio, and television tell them that sex is romantic and exciting. Premarital sex and cohabitation are visible ways of life among the adults they see and know. Yet, at the same time, young people get the message "good girls should say no."[13]

These observations are correct. The United States is a nation divided between two moralities. Unlike Europe, the great leap to the new morality of sexual freedom fell short. The partisans of the "old" morality of sexual asceticism were numerous enough and organized quickly enough to deny the advocates of change a full victory. As a result, American teenagers are suspended between these poles. Given generally complete dominance of the mechanisms of social control, either morality does—in radically different ways—prevent teenage pregnancy. Yet locked in stalemate, neither one works very well, for each moral system necessarily undermines the other. The price of coexistence is a high and increasing level of teenage pregnancy.

The Guttmacher report, of course, advanced the standard "new morality" solution to the deadlock: American teens have the lowest level of contraceptive practice among the six developed nations studied, so give them free contraceptives and government-funded abortions. Those American youth who do employ contraceptives use birth control pills less frequently than their European and Canadian counterparts do, so abolish the "daunting" pelvic examination that medical protocol in the United States still requires before the pill can be prescribed. Agencies with full contraceptive services are found only sporadically in the United States, so create a national health service giving everyone access to contraceptive services. Parental desires to control the sex lives of their children are still strong in America, so adopt the Swedish law where all doctors (not just the federally funded variety) are specifically forbidden to inform parents about a child's request for birth control services. Sex education in the United States is sporadic, a local option, so seek a national sex education curriculum. "Fundamentalist groups in America are prominent and highly vocal," so adopt the Dutch administrative model which avoids messy questions of democratic governance by turning over emotionally charged issues to governmental experts who could "make birth control services available to teenagers without exacerbating divisions in the society." Americans still view sex as both romantic and sinful, so promote the "matter-of-fact attitudes" found in Europe. There is nothing new here; just the same cultural battle cries heard over the last twenty years.

Interestingly, though, the Guttmacher researchers this time tip their hat a bit too far, and reveal a broader agenda usually kept hidden in presentations such as this.

On the question of unemployment, for example, they note that the other five countries in the study all provide more assistance than the United States for youth training, unemployment benefits, and other forms of support. All of the other countries grant more extensive welfare benefits, including national health insurance, food supplements, and housing and child allowances. "Poverty to the degree that [it] exists in the United States is essentially unknown in Europe," they state. "Western European governments are committed to the philosophy of the welfare state." Moreover, the researchers stress that the larger 37-country study "found that more equitable distribution of household income is associated with lower teenage fertility—at least among the young teenagers." The message here is that democratic socialism "works."

The Guttmacher report's fondness for the socialist solution explains the special and admiring attention given to Sweden. There, egalitarian income policies and the world's most comprehensive welfare state have combined with universal sex education, special youth sex clinics, free, widely available, and fully confidential contraceptive and abortion services, the frank treatment of sex, and the widespread advertising of contraceptives to produce the desired effect: "Sweden is the only one of the countries observed to have shown a rapid decline in teenage abortion rates in recent years."

Indeed, it seems true: socialism and the "new morality" work well together in the war against pregnancy.

There are, though, serious logical problems to be found within the Guttmacher study. In particular, the presumption that pregnancy is a disease leads to several major interpretive errors. First, it ignores the fact that over half of the births to teenage mothers in America are marital births, compared to only 18.6 percent in Sweden. In many parts of America—rural areas and the South, for example—marriage at 18 or 19 is still considered normal and the births that result are welcomed.

Second, even unwanted teenage pregnancies may not be a disease so much as a symptom of a disease. American youths' problems are not limited to those peculiar to pregnancy. The United States holds the unenviable distinction of having the highest rate of adolescent homicide in the developed world. Adolescent drug use is also higher in the U.S. than anywhere else in the developed world. Like the teenage pregnancy rate, these two symptoms of disorder have been on the upswing in our country for the last two decades. Homicide, drug use, and out-of-wedlock pregnancy are all symptoms of serious emotional troubles and widespread cultural alienation. These phenomena derive, in part, from the conflict of the two moralities now found in America. For that reason, there are no simple clinical ways to treat these deeper disorders. It is clear, though, that treatments aimed at merely one symptom are not cures at all.[14]

Third, the Guttmacher report notes, but quickly retreats from, a familiar fact, one with disturbing implications: all of the six countries closely studied "have fertility levels below that required for replacement." If the statistical correlations of the type used by the Guttmacher researchers mean anything, casual sex and a rigid antipregnancy policy seem to be directly related to the accelerating disappearance of children and nations.

Accordingly, the terms of the teenage pregnancy debate in America can be clarified. To begin with, it is not a conflict between "science" on the one hand and "religion" on the other. The scientific method was never meant to be used to settle moral questions. "Right" and "wrong" are categories alien to the authentic scientific process. Rather, the misuse of science by the partisans of the "new" morality must be seen as an ideological ploy.

Moreover, the call for abandoning social concern about "actions" and concentrating simply on motives represents another political maneuver, a subtle call for full surrender by the traditionalists at the outset. As Paul Landis has correctly noted, "Social systems have to assume that it is 'acts,' not merely thoughts and motives ... , that are consequential."[15] Social order in a free society rests on the regulation of behavior, not on the unknowable machinations of the human mind.

Finally, the problem is not amenable to a social libertarian solution: let everyone be free to act as he or she pleases. On fundamental questions of moral and social order, the bond of the individual to society is necessarily close. Individual choices have social consequences as, for example, when a divorce reverberates through a neighborhood. Similarly, broad social changes affect individuals, as when the mass media enter the home. Successful free societies are those where inherited moral codes preserve social order and allow material growth with a minimum of state coercion. "Free to choose," while effective economic doctrine, brings ruin when applied to basic moral principle. As Western moral theologians understood long before Freud, human sexuality is bound in complex ways to the maintenance of civilization. Accordingly, the divorce of sexuality from family formation and social responsibility must result in the disintegration of what remains of the Western heritage. Impressionistic observation and demographic statistics suggest that this is already occurring in Western Europe.

Notes

1. Elise F. Jones, et al., "Teenage Pregnancy in Developed Countries: Determinants and Policy Implications," *Family Planning Perspectives* 17 (March/April 1985): 53–62.
2. Harold T. Christensen, "The Impact of Culture and Values," in *The Individual, Sex, & Society: A SIECUS Handbook for Teachers and Counselors*, ed. Carlfred B. Broderick and Jessie Bernard (Baltimore: The Johns Hopkins Press, 1969), p. 160.
3. From Edward M. Brecher, *The Sex Researchers* (Boston: Little, Brown and Co., 1969), pp. 3–49.
4. Isadore Rubin, "Transition in Sex Values—Implications for the Education of Adolescents," *Journal of Marriage and the Family* 27 (May 1965): 185–87; and Ira L. Reiss, "Premarital Sexual Standards," in Broderick and Bernard, p. 109.
5. Rubin, "Transition in Sex Values," p. 189; Esther Middlewood, "Sex Education in the Community," in Broderick and Bernard, pp. 91–92; and Daniel Callahan, "Authority and the Theologian," *The Commonweal* (June 5, 1964): 323.
6. Reiss, p. 115; Rubin, p. 188; F. Ivan Nye, "Values, Family and a Changing Society," *Journal of Marriage and the Family* 29 (May 1967): 244–45.
7. Nye, p. 248; Rubin, p. 188.
8. Rubin, p. 187.
9. Nye, p. 245.
10. R.E. Munss, "Mental Health Implications of a Preventive Psychiatry Program in the Light of Research Findings," *Journal of Marriage and Family Living* 22 (May 1960): 155.
11. B.K. Singh, "Trends in Attitudes Toward Premarital Sexual Relations," *Journal of Marriage and the Family* 42 (May 1980): 387–93.
12. Paul Johnson, *The Almost-Chosen People: Why America is Different* (Rockford, IL: The Rockford Institute, 1985), p. 3.

13. Jones, p. 61.
14. My thanks to Professor Edward Wynne of the University of Illinois-Chicago and editor of *Character II* for his useful insights here.
15. Paul H. Landis, "Review of Lester Kirkendall's *Premarital Intercourse and Interpersonal Relations*," *Journal of Marriage and Family Living* 24 (Feb. 1962): 97.

7

The Sensual School

To an increasing degree, the solution of choice for the adolescent pregnancy problem is the school-based clinic. Local, state, and federal officials ponder the experiments found in a number of large American cities, where family-planning units disguised as "comprehensive health service programs" have been operating, with apparent positive results.

The program established in 1973 at St. Paul, Minnesota's Mechanic Arts High School is the prototype. Using facilities within a high school, yet set up legally as an independent entity, the school-based clinic is not covered by school law, which virtually eliminates any public or parental accountability. Such clinics offer adolescents pregnancy testing, psychosexual interviews, contraceptive counseling and distribution, prenatal and postpartum care, treatment for venereal diseases, and abortion counseling, all within the general "health" framework. Clinic planners openly admit that the comprehensive character (physicals for sports teams, weight-loss clinics, etc.) is primarily a smokescreen for ensuring privacy while delivering contraceptives to the children. As one advocate explains, virtually all new clinic patients—whatever their reason for contact and whether male or female—are asked if they are or plan to be sexually active. If the answer to either query is "yes," they are "encouraged to practice contraception." Most clinics have elaborate displays of contraceptive methods and devices, to help the youngsters choose their method. Some clinics fill prescriptions on the spot. Others also offer referrals to abortion centers. The clinics, of course, stress complete confidentiality. The youth are assured that their parents will not be notified. Indeed, historic patterns of family control are precisely reversed: "Program staff generally encourage parents to visit the clinic and, *with the permission of the child*, often speak with them about their children's [sic] problem."[1]

In its cover story on "Children Having Children," *Time* magazine highlights school-based clinics as the one institutional ray of hope for an otherwise worsening problem. At Mechanic Arts High, for example, the

93

birthrate among female students fell from 59 per thousand in 1977 to 26 per thousand in 1984.[2] The professional literature is even more adamant about the need for clinics nationwide. In his book *Unplanned Parenthood*, Frank Furstenberg, Jr., concludes that the necessary "intervention strategies" of contraceptive education, pregnancy testing, and abortion counseling make schools the logical place for teenage family planning programs. Sociologist Susan Phipps-Yonas criticizes existing school sex education programs as too little and too late. Sex courses must begin earlier, she says, and be supplemented by contraceptive clinics on the premises. Another social scientist, Hyman Rodman, concludes that teenagers "typically engage in sexual activity whether or not they have access to contraceptives." Consequently, it "does not make sense to place obstacles in the way of their seeking contraceptives."[3]

Such affirmations add to the policy drumbeats in favor of government funding of the clinics. In many parts of the country, though, parental groups are fighting tooth-and-nail against the innovation. They see the clinics as an insidious challenge to parental rights, an attempt by "professionals" to usurp control over their children's moral and sexual education.

In fact, school-based clinics and teenage sexual enlightenment represent the logical culmination of the twentieth century's birth control movement, the last frontier of the contraceptive revolution. Opponents seeking to isolate and attack the clinics outside this broader perspective are merely flailing at a moving, impervious target. Understanding the historic dynamics of, and the ideas behind, the contraceptive revolution is prelude to sorting out our social, cultural, and policy options for the future.

In retrospect, it is clear that the rational control of births, or family planning, was and is a universal consequence of the modernization process. The anthropological evidence suggests that contraceptive practice or "planning" in some form is to be found in most human societies. Democratic capitalist societies, though, appear to accentuate this activity. In them, children lose the economic value they held in peasant cultures and become instead relatively expensive objects of consumption. Industrial production begins to supplant home-produced commodities. As modern economic pressures make smaller families more desirable, modern medical science also makes contraception easier. Meanwhile, the use of the market as a measure of personal worth and the accompanying legal emancipation of women further encourage a turn away from family creation. As one frustrated American physician observed at the turn of the century:

> The family idea is, indeed, drifting into individualism. . . . Now [woman] has weaned herself from the hearth stone, and her chief end is self. Pray, what has brought about these changes? By the invention of the sewing-machine, by the

introduction of ready-made clothing, and by that damnable sin—the avoidance of offspring, our women are no longer compelled to stay at home—the home-tether is broken.[4]

This century's birth control movement represented one cultural attempt to come to terms with these changes, to bring modern reason to the reproductive process. In a confusing turn, though, the movement went through several distinct ideological phases—radical, eugenic, profamily, and renewed radical—where idea systems with political content altered the goals of the movement. These successive phases continue to obfuscate the debate.[5]

Radical Phase, 1914-39

As early as 1871, author Catharine Beecher warned that the "woman movement" was causing "all the antagonisms that are warring on the family state," including "free love, free divorce . . . [and] the worldliness which tempts men and women to avoid large families, often by sinful methods, thus making the ignorant masses the chief supply of the future ruling majorities." In the decade after 1900, these concerns welled up into a political issue, sometimes called the "race suicide" scare. Birth control was the target. President Theodore Roosevelt seized the family question, labeling Americans who avoided having children as "criminals against the race . . . the object of contemptuous abhorence by healthy people." Addressing the National Congress of Mothers in 1905, Roosevelt condemned the "viciousness, coldness, shallow-heartedness" of women who refused to do "their duty," especially the growing number of college-educated women, over half of whom remained unmarried. Birth control, he said, was sinful and denied to the nation the necessary growing population and stock of large, stable families. The one-child family "spells death," he wrote, "the end of all hope."[6]

Under this attack, American feminists abandoned their lingering rhetorical commitment to family and moved toward more radical positions. Radical sexual attitudes, brought over from Europe, grew prominent. English "free love" advocate Edward Carpenter linked the feminist, birth control, and anticapitalist messages together, condemning men, "to whom it seems quite natural that our marriage and social institutions should lumber along over the bodies of women, as our commercial institutions grind over the bodies of the poor."[7] Radical bohemians engaged in sexual experimentation made a tentative political alliance with militant socialists. The prewar American Socialist Party drew together feminists, birth controllers, and workers into "a simultaneous attack on capitalism" from many fronts. Anarchist Emma Goldman became the model new-style activist. The syndicalist, violence-prone International Workers of the World (IWW) also made sexual radicalism a plank of their program, with one 1915 IWW petition declaring in then-scandalous language that "a woman has the right to control her own body," that "unfit children ought not to be born into the world," that "scientific knowledge of sex-physiology can never be classified as impure or obscene," and that the masses "have no right to add sufferers to the already too many competing for bread."

Margaret Sanger, the eventual leader of the American birth control movement, was shaped by this environment. Appointed as an IWW labor organizer in 1912, she turned her energies to the contraception issue in 1913, a move reinforced by several trips to Europe and a love affair with English sexologist Havelock Ellis. Her 1914 periodical, *The Woman Rebel*, focused on the birth control issue, where she blasted the moderate "bourgeois feminist" who "currie[d] favors of capitalists and politicians in order to gain power." Her campaign turned to direct action in 1916, when she violated state law by establishing a birth control clinic in Brooklyn, which—with much publicity—was closed by police after nine days of operation.

By 1920, though, the birth control movement had largely shed its radical reputation. World War I, like all modern wars, accelerated the challenges to the existing social order. For instance, the Navy and War Departments, fearful of venereal disease, began programs of sex training and the distribution of condoms to soldiers and sailors. Navy officials even took Sanger's infamous pamphlet, *Family Limitation*—which the post office had banned as obscene—and distributed it (with her name removed) to the troops. Attitudes were apparently widely altered: in prewar Baltimore, one survey showed, approximately two million condoms were sold annually; in the postwar era, over six million.

Moreover, the 1920s witnessed the taming of sexual radicalism as the rapidly changing advertising industry absorbed the sex revolution and turned what had been a challenge to capitalism into simply another splendid business opportunity. Sex became the *leit motif* in promoting an array of new consumer goods. The automobile also weakened one of the last physical barriers to premarital sex: lack of privacy. Reflecting these changes, Robert and Helen Lynd's famed study of Muncie, Indiana, in the mid-1920s reported that 4,000 copies of "sex-adventure" magazines poured monthly into that little city, featuring articles such as "The Primitive Lover" and "Indolent Kisses."[8]

As prelude to a new phase in the movement's history, Sanger also abandoned the radical perspective. Her sexual tutor, Havelock Ellis, had no sympathy for the working class, and he introduced her to a respectable version of the birth control ethic. By 1922, she dismissed Marxism as "masculine" reasoning and embraced birth control as a single, all-consuming passion.

Sanger also began courting the wealthy and influential and found a ready audience. By 1920, most "race suicide" theorists had reached the conclusion that birth control was unstoppable: the prosperous and "fit," it appeared, could not be dissuaded from its use. A revolution was occurring in fertility patterns, and it seemed clear that the middle classes would not consent to raise their fertility. The only eugenic option left was to "democratize" birth control, bringing it as quickly as possible to the poor.

In this new phase, capitalism ceased to be the enemy and a new opponent was recruited. As Sanger put it: "It was now a battle of a republic against the machinations of the Roman Catholic Church." Hostile to mass society and believing, with atheist Robert Ingersoll, that "ignorance, poverty, and vice are populating the world," the eugenicists flocked to the birth control cause, joining with Sanger in 1922 to create the Birth Control Federation of America (BCFA).

As her apologists have stressed, Sanger's private motivations in this period were not primarily "eugenic" in nature. She considered sex to be a mystical, almost religious, event that needed to be freed from the threat of pregnancy in order to be whole and beautiful. She was also a fervent, if somewhat unorthodox, feminist concerned with women's rights. However, she enthusiastically embraced eugenic ideas in this era, pleased to have such a highly prestigious scientific movement behind her campaign.

Accordingly, Sanger argued that the poor had large families only out of ignorance. Give them access to birth control information and devices, and they would "spontaneously" limit their families. "Birth control," she said in 1920, "is nothing more or less than the facilitation of the process of weeding out the unfit, or preventing the birth of defectives or of those who will become defective." Two years later, Sanger said that using the techniques of "modern stockbreeders" would keep society from "fostering the good-for-nothing at the expense of the good." She explained that immigrants from southern and eastern Europe were ignorant of hygiene, made the cities wretched, and threatened to replace native workers. When Sanger raised funds to create the Population Association of America in 1931, its first president was Henry Pratt Fairchild, author of *The Melting-Pot Mistake* (1926) and the leading academic racist of the interwar period.

With eugenic concerns at the forefront, this period also witnessed the establishment of BCFA clinics in dozens of American cities. A last feeble legal challenge to the clinics, mounted at the urging of Roman Catholic officials in 1929, proved to be a public relations coup for the BCFA. The existence of the clinics was never again seriously challenged.

By the late 1930s, though, eugenicists were losing enthusiasm for the birth control cause. There was growing evidence that Sanger's "spontaneity theory" was not correct; the "unfit" were not clamoring for birth control. Rather, it appeared that the poorer elements of the population were simply not interested in controlling their births, which meant that the spread of contraceptive practice continued to have a "dysgenic" effect, merely discouraging the "best stock" from reproducing.[9] Many eugenicists drifted away.

1940–60: The Pro-Family Phase

Starting around 1940, the birth control movement gave new emphasis to the family. Symbolic of this, the BCFA, on the advice of a public relations counselor, changed its name to the Planned Parenthood Federation of America (PPFA).

Several developments lay behind this new emphasis. The 1930–39 period had witnessed the increased professionalization of the movement, as Sanger's policy of working through physicians began to pay off. The number of birth control clinics reached 549 in 1939; by 1942, 803. As the business grew, physicians resolved to bring it under their control. In 1937, the American Medical Association approved for the first time a qualified endorsement of birth control. By 1947, a survey showed that two-thirds of all physicians approved of birth control for married women and provided advice and the necessary prescriptions.[10]

During this period, Sanger entered semiretirement. Under new leadership, the birth control movement forged a fresh synthesis of themes. From the eugenics phase, Planned Parenthood carried over "the encouragement of sound parenthood." Terminology changed, however, and "class," "income level," and "health" replaced "good stock" as measures of quality. The birth control movement also gave new emphasis to "planning." As one poster from the era read: "Modern Life is Based on Control and Science. . . . We control machines. We endeavor to control disease and death. Let us control the size of our family to insure health and happiness." Common emphases were "planning" for the effective use of the "human resources," the "overproduction of people" among families that could not afford them, and "haphazard childbirth," which wasted resources.

Most dramatically, Planned Parenthood shifted in a decidedly profamily direction, an altogether new emphasis for the birth control campaign. The family, rather than the woman within it, became the unit of reproductive control. Social peace and harmony, resting on contented families, was the birth control goal. The PPFA program saw mutual sexual enjoyment as the new cement of modern marriage, the source for renewed family stability after the turmoil of earlier decades. Women's sexual repression was the problem to be overcome, albeit only within the confines of the family. Talk of "women's rights" vanished from PPFA literature; it now presented very traditional male and female roles. Aid and advice was restricted to married women, as PPFA assumed a norm of premarital chastity and turned the unmarried away. Abortion was considered to be fetus-murder.

The special psychology of the World War II period reinforced these new themes, with a form of quality-oriented pronatalism. As the major wartime PPFA pamphlet explained:

> "PLANNING FOR VICTORY"
> The American people today need no further evidence on the necessity for quality in manpower and materials to win the war. It sees, at last, that victory cannot be won without *planning*. . . . Planned Parenthood, with your understanding and support can, in 1943, be made to mean that more healthy children will be born to maintain the kind of peace for which we fight.

Sanger herself came out of retirement and called for "national security through birth control." PPFA's new emphasis on marriage, family, social planning, and national security carried over into the Cold War era, and birth control—now called "family planning"—found a welcome place as a favored charity in the child-centered suburbs of the 1950s.

Even with this new respectability, it is important to note that "family planning" remained a distinctly private phenomenon, a matter of personal choice and voluntary action. No government money or encouragement was involved. Indeed, anti-birth control laws remained on the books at both the federal and state levels (although few were enforced). When asked in December 1959 about a proposal to fund a population control program, President Dwight Eisenhower spoke for the large American majority when he replied: "I cannot imagine anything more emphatically a subject that is not a proper political or governmental activity or function or responsibility. . . . This government will not, as long as I am here, have a positive political doctrine in its program that has to do with the problem of birth control. That's not our business."

1960-1986: Re-Radicalization Phase

Four years later, Eisenhower—like many other Americans—had changed his mind and had begun urging Americans to recognize both that population growth threatened world peace and that birth control was a legitimate federal concern. This dramatic shift was the result of the great "population scare" of the 1960s. Relative to the birth control movement, this triumph of neo-Malthusianism had several consequences. First,

Planned Parenthood quietly shed the profamily label, as the population crisis let childless adults off the hook. To refuse to marry or to bear children were no longer antisocial acts. Second, the "crisis" environment seemed to justify drastic actions. Unmarried women could no longer be denied services. Sexually active teenagers also became an important new category of clients. Abortion was recast as a necessary option for an overpopulated world. Third, the "population crisis" coincided with rapid expansion of "entitlements" at the federal level, and birth control became another "service" to be provided by the growing American welfare state.[11]

As the population panic peaked in the late 1960s, another ideology emerged further to energize and redirect the birth control movement: the new feminism. Through books such as *Our Bodies, Our Selves* (1971), this long-dormant campaign declared war on "the inhumane legal restrictions, the imperfections of available contraceptives, the poor sex education, the highly priced and poorly administered health care that keep too many women from having this crucial control over their bodies."[12]

The "right" to family planning, a novel construction, was so born, and almost irresistible political pressures began breaking down the public/private distinction that had long kept the federal government out of the birth control business. In 1970, Congress enacted The Family Planning Services and Population Research Act (Title X of the Public Health Service Act), with the goal of giving low-income women access to effective contraception. The 1972 Report of the President's Commission on Population Growth and the American Future, recommended providing contraceptives to teenagers.

President Richard Nixon tried to halt the juggernaut, responding that "I do not support the unrestricted distribution of family planning services and devices to minors. Such measures would do nothing to preserve and strengthen close family relationships." However, cries for more action grew. Medicaid soon offered family planning services to federal recipients. Title XX of the Social Security Act provided block grants to states for, among other activities, family planning. The Adolescent Pregnancy Act of 1979 provided funds "to expand and improve the availability of, and access to, needed comprehensive community services which assist in preventing unwanted initial and repeat pregnancies among adolescents." By 1980, the federal government could claim a comprehensive national fertility-control program.

In sum, the birth control movement could point to extraordinary achievements. Once scorned as immoral and antithetical to the American political tradition, it had now triumphed at the political, cultural, and social levels. "Family planning" was nearly universal; even conservative Catholics were resorting to the Billings method, involving methodical testing of mucous and body temperature, perhaps the most complex and "rational" form of fertility control. Abortion had been legalized (using the method pioneered by Margaret Sanger's legal advisor in the 1930s: "The law process is a simple one," he had said, "it is a matter of educating judges to the mores of the day"). Population control was national policy, and the marital birthrate was cut in half between 1957 and 1977. More sex; fewer babies; the decay of marriage; the weakening of all other traditional re-straints on sexuality; a gently declining population: Margaret Sanger's ini-tial dream—distorted over the decades by eugenic and profamily phases—had been all but secured.

Except among the teenagers. To be sure, they had gone far along the prescribed path. Illegitimacy, for example, had been relieved of any "pa-triarchy-imposed" stigma. Even Catholic leaders had ceased using the term.[13] Marriage, too, had all but disappeared among those under the age of twenty.

The problem, though, was that such clear steps toward the liberation of women and the sex act had not taken quite the right twist among adoles-cents. They were still getting pregnant and were keeping their babies. Fifty-four percent of births to teens in 1983 were outside of marriage, compared to 15 percent in 1960. While the 1975-80 period witnessed a 6.5 percent decline in rate of conception among "sexually active teens," the number of them increased sufficiently to drive up the overall teenage pregnancy rate. Although black teenagers still bore out-of-wedlock babies at a much higher rate than Whites, the rise in the number of illegitimate births since 1970 has been particularly dramatic among the latter.

These changes occurred despite the fact that the number of teenagers using family planning services climbed 300 percent for Blacks between 1969 and 1980 and 1,700 percent among Whites. In the latter year, 2.5 million adolescents received contraceptive services from PPFA clinics, pri-vate physicians, and other sources. Nonetheless, the teenage pregnancy crisis only seemed to worsen.

From this, PPFA officials have concluded that the existing network of clinics and federal and state birth control programs are insufficient to the task. PPFA President Faye Wattleton lays the blame for failure on parents, most of whom, she says, fail to discuss birth control with their children. Her organization's polling data also show that "the solution to this devas-tating problem lies in increasing access to sex education in the schools . . . and making contraceptives available, even if it means providing them free, and establishing school-linked clinics."[14] The Alan Guttmacher Institute's 1981 report, *Teenage Pregnancy: The Problem That Hasn't Gone Away*, recommends programs to identify and encourage early contraceptive use among sexually active teens, with Title X, Medicaid, and Title XX all viewed as sources for augmented federal funding.

In calling for this new program of early intervention, the PPFA cites evidence that its existing activities produce results. According to one literature survey, most studies "have found a negative correlation between teen enrollment in family planning programs and birthrates."[15] In the most sophisticated analysis to date, Jacqueline Forrest of the Guttmacher Institute acknowledges the glaring error in these previous measures of effectiveness: they looked only at birthrates, ignoring pregnancies that ended in miscarriage and abortion. Using a complicated series of assumptions, she calculates the number of pregnancies averted by family planning programs during the 1970s to be 5,434,000, including 2,257,000 births, 2,485,000 abortions, and 692,000 miscarriages. In 1979 alone, Forrest says, 792,000 pregnancies were averted among the 4,486,000 women enrolled in the programs. If these pregnancies had occurred, they would have raised the number of births by 8 percent and the number of abortions by 25 percent. Such numbers do imply dramatic success in meeting stated goals.[16]

Such confidence extends to a blanket dismissal of the opposition's arguments. Sociologist Ruth Kornfield reports that the initiation of adolescent sexual involvement is due to "changes in values or social mores," and not to the availability of contraceptives at family planning clinics.[17] As school-clinic advocate Kristin Moore of The Urban Institute bluntly puts it, "There is no evidence that supports the contention that the availability of family planning services to teenagers encourages sexual activity."[18]

As a matter of fact, though, the latter statement is not true. Furthermore, new evidence suggests that the impact of family planning programs among teenagers is far from salutary.

On the first point, several decidedly neutral studies do show that adolescent enrollment in a birth control clinic *does* increase sexual activity. Three researchers working with 192 subjects at a Los Angeles youth medical clinic found that girls taking oral contraceptives under clinic guidance for six to eight months had an average of 13.4 acts of intercourse per month. This compared to 8.8 for girls just beginning the program.[19] Similarly, a project in Illinois found that during the year in which teenagers first used clinic-prescribed contraception, their monthly frequency of coitus increased from an average of 4.3 to 6.8.[20]

On the second point, a 1986 study by Joseph Olsen and Stan Weed of the Institute for Research and Evaluation concludes that "greater teenage involvement in family planning programs appears to be associated with higher, rather than lower, teenage pregnancy rates." Like Forrest, they note that most previous studies of clinic effectiveness only measured change in birthrate. But they also criticize Forrest for measuring the clinics' effects on abortion by merely extrapolating from the estimated effect on fertility. Instead, Olsen and Weed take relatively hard 1979 numbers on teenage abortions, calculated on a state-by-state basis, and use Guttmacher In-

stitute assumptions to estimate the number of miscarriages among teenagers. They also take into account differences attributable to poverty rate,
the proportions married, urban, and White, population mobility, and—
most importantly—prior teenage fertility rate. As anticipated, they discovered that there were 30 fewer live births for every 1,000 new teenage
family planning clients. However, they also found a *net increase* of 120
pregnancies per 1,000 clients. In short, enrollment in a family planning
program appeared to *raise* a teenager's chances of becoming pregnant and
of having an abortion.[21]

Who's right? Dr. Forrest of the Planned Parenthood combine? Or Drs.
Olsen and Weed? In fact, both are, and these seemingly conflicting findings
cast light on the true situation in which we Americans find ourselves.

It might best be understood as a sexual spiral, where a growing national
toleration of premarital sex[22] and a breakdown of traditional restraints
have resulted in ever more teenagers indulging in sexual activity. As the
data shows, their introduction to and use of contraceptives encourage more
frequent sexual contact. Simple immaturity, along with intense emotional
drives to please boyfriends or bear a child ensure some level of "contraceptive failure" and resulting pregnancy. In short, a spiral of more sexually active teenagers, more contraception, more sexual encounters per
teenager, and some level of contraceptive failure would produce *both* a
rising level of *averted* pregnancies and a rising level of *real* pregnancies, at
least during the transition phase.

As noted earlier, the United States is engaged in a great moral struggle,
where traditional means of controlling teenage sexuality—parental regulation of dating and courtship, religious condemnation of sex outside of
marriage, informal community controls such as the shame attached to an
illegitimate birth—are being supplanted by a new social model. In this new
scheme, children are cast as wholly independent moral actors, sexual activity is considered independent of marriage, and community use of stigma
or shame is relabeled as illegal "discrimination." The post–1960 birth control movement has clearly aligned itself with this latter model.

The processes by which the "new morality" undermines the "old" are
fairly obvious. School-based-clinic advocates, for example, are adamant on
one point: adolescents have a "right to privacy" which overrides parental
control. If the children want contraceptives, parents must not be informed
without their offsprings' consent. Indeed, at the national level, this same
"right" has served as the legal device through which the federal courts have
tossed out the laws in all fifty states that once governed birth control and
abortion. At the family or neighborhood level, this same "right" has
worked to destroy the traditional means of scrutiny by which parents or
other elders governed the fertility of the young. With traditional controls so

shattered, *only* the welfare state—in the guise of state-funded family planning clinics—remains to fulfill the role, albeit through radically different means.

On occasions, direct evidence reveals how the new morality of the birth control clinic destroys the old morality of family, church, and neighborhood. In a study of adolescent California girls, researchers compared young women's beliefs and behaviors before and after entering a youth clinic program and obtaining oral contraceptives. They found that 39.6 percent of the girls just entering the program disagreed with the statement "I enjoy participating in religious activities." Among those who had been involved for six to eight months, 56.2 percent disagreed.[23] The change is in the direction one would anticipate: adapting one's behavior to the new moral order must result in greater dissatisfaction with the old.

The true conflict, then, is not over birth control. Rather, it is over the morality and the social norms governing family life, neighborhood, and community: the question of how we shall order our lives together as citizens in a free republic.

Notes

1. From: Joy Dryfoos, "School-Based Health Clinics: New Approach to Preventing Adolescent Pregnancy?" *Family Planning Perspectives* 17 (March/April 1985): 70–75; emphasis added.
2. "Children Having Children," *Time* (Dec. 9, 1985): 78–90.
3. Frank F. Furstenberg Jr., *Unplanned Parenthood* (New York: The Free Press, 1976), pp. 224–26; Susan Phipps-Yonas, "Teenage Pregnancy and Motherhood," *American Journal of Orthopsychiatry* 50 (July 1980): 421; and Hyman Rodman, "Controlling Adolescent Fertility," *Society* 23:1 (Nov./Dec. 1985): 35–37.
4. William Goodell, "The Dangers and the Duty of the Hour." Quoted in: Linda Gordon, *Woman's Body, Woman's Right: A Social History of Birth Control in America* (New York: Grossman Publishers, 1976), p. 157.
5. The following historical discussion draws primarily from three sources: Gordon, *Woman's Body, Woman's Right*; James Reed, *From Private Vice to Public Virtue: The Birth Control Movement and American Society Since 1830* (New York: Basic Books, 1978); and David M. Kennedy, *Birth Control in America: The Career of Margaret Sanger* (New Haven and London: Yale University Press, 1970).
6. See: *The Works of Theodore Roosevelt*, ed. Hermann Hagedorn (New York: Scribner's Sons, 1926), Vol. 13, pp. 320–21, 497; Vol. 20, p. ix; Vol. 21, pp. 142–46, 168.
7. Edward Carpenter, *Love's Coming-of-Age* (New York: Modern Library, 1911), p. 37.
8. Robert S. and Helen M. Lynd, *Middletown* (New York: Harcourt, Brace, 1929), pp. 241–42, 258–69.
9. See: Kennedy, p. 120.

10. See: Joyce M. Ray and F.G. Gosling, "American Physicians and Birth Control, 1936–47," *Journal of Social History* 18 (1984/85): 399–411.
11. See: James Reed, "Public Policy on Human Reproduction and the Historian," *Journal of Social History* 18 (1984/85): 392–94.
12. The Boston Women's Health Book Collective, *Our Bodies, Our Selves* (New York: Simon and Schuster, 1971), p. 13.
13. *Time* (Dec. 9, 1985): 80.
14. "Sex Education: Best Way to Curb Teen Pregnancy," *Jet* (Nov. 25, 1985): 26.
15. Kristin A. Moore and Martha R. Burt, *Private Crisis, Public Cost: Policy Perspectives on Teenage Childbearing* (Washington, DC: The Urban Institute, 1982), pp. 71–73.
16. Jacqueline Darroch Forrest, "The Impact of U.S. Family Planning Programs on Births, Abortions and Miscarriages, 1970–79," *Social Science and Medicine* 18, No. 6 (1984): 461–65.
17. Ruth Kornfield, "Who's To Blame: Adolescent Sexual Activity," *Journal of Adolescence* 8, No. 1 (1985): 17–31.
18. Moore and Burt, p. 74.
19. Lorie Garris, Allan Steckler, and John R. McIntire, "The Relationship Between Oral Contraceptives and Adolescent Sexual Behavior," *The Journal of Sex Research* 12 (May 1976): 138.
20. Paul A. Reichelt, "Changes in Sexual Behavior Among Unmarried Teenage Women Utilizing Oral Contraception," *Journal of Population* 1 (Spring 1978): 61.
21. Joseph A. Olsen and Stan E. Weed, "Effects of Family Planning Programs on Adolescent Birth and Pregnancy Rates," *Family Perspectives* 20, No. 3 (1986): 153–72.
22. See: Norval D. Glenn and Charles N. Weaver, "Attitudes Toward Premarital, Extramarital, and Homosexual Relations in the U.S. in the 1970s," *The Journal of Sex Research* 15 (May 1979): 111.
23. Garris, et al, p. 142.

Part IV
THE ECONOMIC QUESTION

8

Work and Family in Collision

In an unprecedented, potentially dangerous move, some American corporate philosophers are attempting to redefine the workplace as the central institution of human existence. They have cast the firm as a necessary substitute for religion and family, the place where humans will find purpose and meaning.

Perry Pascarella, executive editor of *Industry Week*, reasons that the majority of Americans no longer feel "the hands-on guidance of the church." Given the confusing panoply of American denominations, moreover, "there is . . . no central message—no cohesive social gospel" that might give people moral guidance and unity. In similar fashion, the family, the primary vehicle in the past for nurturing character and life skills, "has been seriously weakened in modern America." Pascarella concludes that corporations must step into the breach, tend more to human values, and offer workers new ways to help them "integrate their lives."[1]

At a less coherent, albeit more influential level, futurist John Naisbitt presents the same message. The traditional family is failing, he says. Many women now choose to have no children at all, only 26 percent believing in 1983 that motherhood was "an important part" of being a woman. Among those who do choose to bear a child, he notes, most work right up to delivery, take a few months off, and quickly return to work. Accordingly, Naisbitt concludes that child care is becoming a corporate rather than a family responsibility, part of the broader trend recasting the corporation as the value-shaping, life-affirming center of human life.[2]

While neither writer seems aware of it, such visions in fact harken back to the work of the great French sociologist Emile Durkheim. Writing in the late nineteenth century, he too saw religion and family as weakening, with neither institution any longer able to give meaning and purpose to life. It was within the "occupational group or corporation" that he found the possibility for social reconstruction. While Durkheim did not exactly have General Motors in mind, he did see the productive economic unit as the sole option left for real community. The corporation followed workers wherever they went, "enveloping them, calling them to their duties, supporting them at need." In short, the corporation had all the elements necessary "to give the individual a setting, to draw him out of his state of moral isolation; and faced by the actual inadequacy of the other groups, it alone can fulfill this indispensable office."[3]

Such musings give historical and philosophical content to the growing pressures on American corporations to assume greater responsibility for pregnancy, child care, parenting, preschool education, and psychological counseling. Reagan administration Secretary of Labor William Brock noted that most business and governmental policies were geared to a vision of the home as a private sphere, separate from the workplace, with the husband as breadwinner and the wife as homemaker. Such a family structure, he countered, now encompassed less than 10 percent of American households: "It's just incredible that we have seen the feminization of the work force with no more adaptation than we have had."[4]

Brock's number was not quite right (the figure is more like 14 percent), and even the correct figure ignores the fact that a majority of married-couple households still *pass* through this traditional phase at some point in their institutional life. Nonetheless, it is true the corporate community faces rapid reorientation in a "family" direction. Parental leave, for example, has in recent months become a major issue on the national agenda. Since 1978, the number of corporate child-care programs has grown geometrically. Approximately 2,500 American companies now provide some form of child-care assistance; 150 of them offer on- or near-site daycare centers. A few companies even provide sick-child care.

It appears true that ninety years after Durkheim's analysis, American corporations are moving in, semiconsciously, to meet fundamental human needs where religion and family have failed. The significance of this shift in family structure and responsibility is large. In every society, the family has served as the central crucible for character formation, the locale for training in values and behavior, the place where human energy is produced and socialized. As Seymour Martin Lipset has put it, the family is "the integrator par excellence." Accordingly, the profound interest which corporations have in effective family functioning is undoubted. The wisdom of assuming the parental burden, whether by choice or force of circumstance, is more in question. If this strategy succeeds, the corporate world would emerge stronger than ever, with enhanced employee loyalty and meaningful influence over the socialization and character of future generations. If it fails, though, the corporate system may find that, in abandoning the traditional family unit, it has sacrificed the social foundation necessary for its own survival.

At the national level, this tension between the workplace and family life lies at the very heart of the emerging "family policy" debate. The feminist and socialist left understands this fact and has developed a political agenda that uses unwitting corporations and liberal ideology as vehicles for the achievement of socialist goals; once the latter has been achieved, they make clear, liberal capitalism can be jettisoned. Conservatives, meanwhile, tend to look wistfully to the past, unwilling to face the enormity of recent change and unable to shape a cultural and political agenda that might restore a viable family system for a free society.

Where lies the truth? As noted earlier, the Western family-wage (or, alternately, "living-wage") economy, created with great difficulty in the eighteenth and nineteenth centuries, has collapsed over the last thirty-five years. This structure, which had rested on a complex sexual division of labor, served to protect the family unit from the logical consequences of radical individualism. The mechanisms employed—including the crafting of the "separate spheres" of home and work, the creation of "men's" and "women's" jobs, the skewing of compensation in favor of heads-of-households, and the normative expectation that men and women would marry and raise children—were the products of decades of trial and error. However imperfect, they allowed capitalism to blossom and prosper while preserving the basis for social life and human reproduction.

The political right, infected of late by an ostrich-like form of libertarianism, has all but forgotten the family-wage concept. The left, though, thoroughly understands the magnitude of their victory here. The radical anthropologist Claude Levi-Strauss, for example, has stressed the logic that lay behind the sexual division of labor. It was this mechanism, he said, that formed the basis for all society. It made males and females into different, complementary beings who needed each other to be whole. This gave compelling reasons to their unity in marriage, which established reproduction as a social process. This "reciprocal state of dependency between the sexes" also assured heterosexual marriage and the moral foundation of society.[5] According to a more recent feminist cross-cultural analysis, "All societies allocate at least some tasks by sex, a practice that . . . makes men and women dependent on one another." This "works against sexual arrangements other than those containing at least one woman and one man," and so protects the traditional moral order.[6]

The defenders of capitalism once understood the same lesson, even attributing the sexual division of labor to Divine Plan. In 1835, English industrialist Andrew Ure wrote:

> Factory females have . . . in general much lower wages than males, and they
> have been pitied on this account with perhaps an injudicious sympathy, since

the low price of their labor here tends to make household duties the most profitable as well as agreeable occupation, and prevents them from being tempted by the will to abandon the care of their offspring at home. Thus Providence effects its purposes with a wisdom and efficacy which should repress the short-sighted presumption of human devices.[7]

The dominant wing of the feminist movement in the late nineteenth century also stood firmly behind the family-wage ideal. Advocates linked the "social feminist" emphasis on the importance of motherhood and the family with the historic trade union emphasis on the dignity and independence of the male breadwinner. As the slogan of the Women's Trade Union League, the primary organization of working women, put it: "The eight-hour day; a living wage; to guard the home."[8] Writing in 1930, historian Ivy Pinchbeck still celebrated the progressive nature of the assumption that men's wages should be paid on "a family basis," arguing that this "prepared the way for the more modern conception that in the rearing of children and in homemaking, the married woman makes an adequate economic contribution."[9]

The mid-twentieth century, though, saw the doctrine fall into disrepute. In part, this derived from technological change. The development of labor-saving household devices such as vacuum cleaners, electric washers, and refrigerators and the advance of new food processing and storage technologies reduced the amount of time needed to maintain a home. As the home production of commodities gave way to the market provision of goods and services, there was an undoubted decline in the perceived value of housework and in the homemaker's bargaining power within the family. In a similar way, the decline in average household size and subsequent loss of economies of scale reduced the economic advantages of the traditional household.

The emergence of the home economics movement and other attempts to professionalize housework and motherhood delayed this trend during the first half of the twentieth century. So, too, did the unique psychological and social environment of the 1950–59 decade—a period, according to one writer, that "was unusual in ways it would not then be possible to know." On the surface, this era appeared to witness a strengthening of the traditional family unit: the marriage rate climbed as the divorce rate receded; the birthrate boomed, and the large family seemed to be back in fashion. Yet at another level, the disruptive technological advances cited above were gaining momentum. Even as the popular media of the period reinforced the message that child care was the most important job a woman could undertake, the movement of women into the paid labor force began to accelerate.

Moreover, educational and corporate leaders along with the federal government quietly departed from historic policy and began encouraging the greater use of female labor. The 1955 Conference on the Effective Use of Womanpower, organized by Columbia University and informally supported by the Eisenhower Administration, probably represented the turning point. Speakers at this meeting called for a new agenda for women's work, including flexible hours, increased formal education and training, the discouragement of early marriage, and the movement of women into scientific and technical jobs. As one feminist historian has concluded, the event "reflected a major turnabout in official thinking. Except in periods of national emergency, women's home-centeredness had been taken for granted by policymakers, the Labor Department, the Women's Bureau, and most women. . . . But slowly a new mentality was dawning."[10]

Today, the revolution is nearly over. The working or two-wage-earner family—the bane of the family-wage economy—is now the most common family form in society: 57 percent of intact families today have two wage-earners, with about two-thirds of these women working full-time. Even single-parent, women-headed families outnumber the traditional, father-headed variety: 15 percent to 14 percent. Only among American families with one or more children under the age of six do we still find a significant number of nonworking mothers, slightly under half. Even here, though, the trend appears to be inexorably toward their employment.

Why is this happening? The socialist left has offered clear explanations, rooted in the historical dialectic. Karl Marx's fundamental work, *Capital* (1867), emphasized the impact of capitalistic production on the family. Machinery, he wrote, "squeezes itself" into the old manufacturing industries based on skilled labor, first for one process and then for another. "Thus the solid crystal of their organization, based on the old division of labour, becomes dissolved, and makes way for constant changes." In its wake, he explained, a new division of labor emerged, one based "whenever possible, on the employment of women, of children of all ages, and of unskilled labourers, in a word, on cheap labour." The pressure of competition drove the capitalist to find the least expensive workers that he could, which, according to Marx, translated into the "shameless," "unconscionable" exploitation of entire families. Marx emphasized that family life under such conditions progressively degenerated: "The wretched half-starved parents think of nothing but getting as much as possible out of their children. The latter, as soon as they are grown up, do not care a farthing . . . for their parents, and leave them." The impact of labor on the morals of children also drew his ire. He favorably quoted an 1866 government report on the girls employed in the tile industry, which condemned the "evil" of a system that turned young girls into "rough, foul-mouthed boys, before Nature has taught them that they are women."

Many modern commentators, otherwise friendly to Marxism, try to dismiss such passages as quaint Victorianisms, matters without significance to the main body of Marxist doctrine. They are wrong, for it is clear that this proletarization of the industrial family was a necessary feature of the historical transformation that formed the core of Marxist theory. It was only by drawing ever more family members into the labor force at ever shrinking real wages, Marx said, that capitalists could squeeze more "surplus value" (profit used as capital) out of human labor. Moreover, it was the growing misery of the working family and its increasingly unnatural, distorted structure that would finally drive the proletariat to revolution. Put another way, Marx both decried and welcomed the proletarization process, this "contradiction" of capitalism, as a necessary and inevitable step in the historical process leading to communism. As he explained: "However terrible and disgusting the dissolution, under the capitalist system, of the old family ties may appear, nevertheless, modern industry, by assigning as it does an important part in the process of production, outside the domestic sphere, to women, to young persons, and to children of both sexes, created a new economic foundation for a higher form of the family and of the relation between the sexes."[11]

The German Marxist August Bebel, in *Women Under Socialism* (1883), elaborated on the point. He portrayed the female sex as the group most victimized by capitalism, both brutalized in the workplace and abused at home. He was confident, though, that the course of history was set toward the disappearance of the oppressive private household. As he wrote: "The trend . . . is not to banish women back to the house and the hearth, as our 'domestic life' fanatics prescribe. . . . On the contrary the whole trend of society is to lead women out of the narrow sphere of strictly domestic life to a full participation in the public life of the people." In his *Origin of the Family, Private Property, and the State* (1884), Friedrich Engels offered a detailed explanation of the linkages between capitalism, private property, and the position of women. The bourgeois family, he argued, contained "in miniature" all the contradictions that characterized the larger capitalist society, contradictions that would eventually bring the system crashing down. In essence, Engels argued that it was impossible for women to become free without socialism; similarly, socialism could succeed only by freeing women from the home.

In the interwar years, philosopher Max Horkheimer expanded on the reasons for the inevitable disappearance of the bourgeois family. Like many Marxist philosophers, Horkheimer almost rhapsodized about middle-class institutions, secure in the knowledge that history had slated them for elimination. He noted that the bourgeois, father-headed family transmitted the kind of human character that social life under capitalism required, and gave to the young "the indispensable adaptability" for conduct on which the existence of bourgeois capitalism rested. For the middle class, faith in a single God and submission to paternal authority represented the necessary, eternal principles of social order, the source of progress toward virtue. In the bourgeois era, family proved to be the place where the individual found retreat from the marketplace; the one area of life where "relationships were not mediated through the market and the individual members . . . not competing with each other." Within the family, shared life took particular form in sexual love and maternal care. The growth and happiness of "the other" were emphasized in such an environment. The bourgeois family also served as the shelter for parental affection, for the protective love of a wife toward her husband, and for the bonding of generations. Indeed, Horkheimer concluded, defense of the traditional family unit always characterized the unity of the bourgeois identity.

Yet with the expansion of monopoly capitalism, Horkheimer said, the antifamily contradiction implicit in capitalism's hunger for cheap labor would grow. Demand for women's labor, in particular, would overwhelm religious and familial scruples and bring the social order tumbling down. Already, family life was "breaking up over the greatest part of the Western world." As its material base vanished, the remnant family survived only as a relic which political movements sought, with increasing desperation, to shore up: "The admittedly indispensable family is becoming a . . . problem of technological manipulation by government." Yet history would soon claim its prize, he said, and put the bourgeois family, along with capitalism, to rest.[12]

In his recent study *Late Capitalism* (first published in the German in 1972), Marxist economist Ernest Mandel also turns to the family crisis to explain both the reasons for the dazzling success of Western economies in the post-World War II years and why they must soon enter a period of collapse. He looks, in particular, at the emergence of "service" economies in the West, characterized by the rapid growth in personal services. Mandel denies that such economies represent a "post-industrial" system, as some theorists have argued. Rather, he says, they embody for the first time in history "generalized universal industrialization," where mechanization, standardization, and the specialization of labor, once largely confined to the production of commodities, are penetrating into all areas of life. Mandel argues that this is seen particularly among "proletarian" families which are progressively displaced as units of both production and consumption. "The growing market for pre-cooked meals and tinned food, ready-made clothes and vacuum cleaners," he notes, "corresponds to the rapid decline of [the production of] immediate-use values within the family, previously cared for by the worker's wife, mother, or daughter." In short, "the material basis of the individual family" is progressively dissolving.

This development, Mandel says, corresponds to another tendency of "late capitalism": the growing occupational activity of married women. Capitalism, in classic Marxist doctrine, realizes profit and accumulates capital by appropriating the "surplus value" that workers produce when they transform raw materials into usable products: "hence the permanent compulsion to limit wages, and to keep them below the level necessary to cover all the new needs of consumption generated by capitalist production itself." Mandel concludes that the ever-growing discrepancy between the needs of family consumption and the wages of the male worker inevitably leads to the increased employment of married women and children.

In sum, Mandel argues that while capitalism has "an obvious interest" in integrating the traditional nuclear family into bourgeois society, "its long term development tends to disintegrate this type of family by incorporating married women into the wage-labour force and by transforming duties performed by women in the household into capitalistically produced commodities." In the short run, he said, this capitalization of the home economy would be a boon to the whole system, allowing the investment of surplus capital in the growing service sector. Over the long run, though, it would result in the "growing alienation and deformation of workers," the essential precondition for crisis and revolution.[13]

The more recent development of socialist/feminist philosophy in America has generally followed the Horkheimer/Mandel line. In her influential analysis of the origins of the modern family wage,[14] historian Heidi Hartmann claims to identify the uses that capitalists have made of the sexual division of labor: "If they can supersede experienced men with cheaper women, so much the better; if they can weaken labor by threatening to do so, that's good, too; or, if failing that, they can use those status differences to reward men, and buy their allegiance to capitalism with patriarchial benefits, that's okay too." It was the latter strategy, she says, that eventually won out with the provision of a family- or living-wage to male heads-of-household as the central pillar of "patriarchal capitalism."[15]

Other feminist writers argue that capitalist patriarchal society cannot deliver on its "liberal" promises of equality and equal rights for women "without destabilizing itself." They emphasize the "contradiction" found in advanced capitalism, where structural changes, bound to inflation, have "required" married women to enter the labor force. Work formerly done in the home has shifted to the marketplace, while many responsibilities incumbent in the family unit have been taken over by the state. In consequence, "the capitalist need for women workers" in nursing homes, fast-food restaurants, and state welfare agencies has spread to other sectors of the economy and so mounted an internal challenge to job segregation by sex, the very basis for family life. The rise of the two-earner family to normative status, they say, symbolizes the decay of the family order protecting capitalism.

Following Lenin's advice, sociologist Zillah Eisenstein urges feminists to accentuate the contradictions. They "need to marshal the liberal demands for individual self-determination, freedom of choice, individual autonomy, and equality before the law" to indict patriarchal social and economic arrangements. The resulting family crisis, she says, could then be used to indict capitalism, and so complete the struggle.[16]

Surely, though, such a socialist-feminist fantasy can't happen here? The fact *is* that it is happening here: slowly, quietly, often invisibly. There are many roads to socialism, and we Americans have apparently followed the gradualist, feminist one. For us, indeed, the Swedish model should loom large, representing as it does a more overt, more honest version of the American journey to the postbourgeois, postcapitalist order.

The origins of Sweden's debate over gender and work date back to the 1930–40 period, yet lay dormant from 1940 until 1956 as Sweden, too, experienced the Indian summer of bourgeois domesticity. Published that latter year was *Women's Two Roles* by Alva Myrdal and Viola Klein. According to the authors, married women must of necessity continue to bear primary responsibility for child rearing. Public policy, they concluded, should aim at offering women an eased transition through three phases of life: education and work, followed by fifteen to twenty years of full-time child rearing, followed by a return to the labor market.[17]

In 1961, though, this "progressive" view was challenged in an influential essay by Liberal Party leader Eva Moberg. So long as women filled two roles while men filled one, she said, sexual equality could not be achieved. Parental responsibilities must be shared equally, and men's roles altered to include housekeeping and child-rearing tasks. This "radical" view quickly won acceptance among political and professional elites and by 1968 was official governmental policy.[18]

The commitment to the elimination of gender roles meshed well with the goals of Sweden's labor planners. During the 1950–59 period, heavy demand for additional labor in Sweden's factories was met by importing foreign workers, principally from Finland and Southeastern Europe. By 1965, policymakers began to recognize housewives as Sweden's largest untapped labor supply, one more easily integrated into the labor force than immigrant workers. If government economic policies were to be implemented, they concluded, it was necessary that ever more women should begin to work.

Over the next ten years, labor market policy aimed primarily at achieving "full employment" for women. The government directly funded the placement of women in traditionally male industrial jobs and offered "equality grants" to employers who trained men and women in jobs dominated by the opposite sex. In 1969, Sweden's state schools were specifically directed "to counteract the traditional attitudes to sex roles and stimulate pupils to question the differences between men and women with respect to influence, work assignments and wages that exist in many sectors of society." The government's instructions to the 1971 Commission on a New Marriage Law made explicit the state's social and economic priorities: "There is no reason to refrain from using legislation on marriage and the family as one of the instruments in the struggle to shape a society in which every adult takes responsibility for himself without being economically dependent on another and where equality between the sexes is a reality."

Capping such changes was a basic 1971 reform of the nation's income tax. In prior years, the system had treated households as unified taxable units, where the earnings of husband and wife were added together and, due to the progressive tax schedule, taxed at a significantly higher rate than if they filed individually. Since 1971, though, husbands and wives are taxed separately on salary and wage earnings.[19] In combination with rate hikes, this reform sharply raised the after-tax income of two-wage-earner families, while reducing the after-tax income of single-wage-earner families.

The revolutionary sweep of this seemingly modest change should not be discounted. In effect, the Social Democratic government here sacrificed one of its most hallowed principles—the taxation of households on a progressive basis—in order to reward wives for entering the workplace. Phrased ideologically, feminism triumphed over traditional socialism. As the influential Swedish feminist Annika Baude has noted, this single change in the income tax was probably *the critical turning point* "in the struggle for the liberation of women in Sweden." Indeed, the changes wrought were immediate and dramatic. There was now a large economic benefit to be gained from a wife's salary, and "married men started to look with much more favour than before on the idea of their wives taking jobs." With the tax law's economic incentive to marriage eliminated, moreover, that institution fell out of favor.[20]

While the results of the Swedish experiment outlined here might appear familiar to Americans, the policy content probably seems out-of-kilter. The U.S. political process is open to the rhetoric of equality, equal opportunity, even equal results, yet the family context of Sweden's debate seems strangely alien. Why?

The primary reason lies in one of the sociopolitical assumptions that has long defined the American Republic: the family is not a political subject, at least at the federal level. Rather, the view has held that the family represents a distinctively private sphere, cordoned off from public life and the uncertain, rough, and competitive civic realm. Family life is a "private venture for personal satisfaction," a common response to Americans' individualized pursuit of happiness. This understanding is rooted in the Lockean conception of a government of free individuals, and it contrasts sharply with European political traditions built on visions of traditional community (Roman Catholic) or class solidarity (Social Democratic), both of which are more open to attention to the family.

Moreover, American economic theory has failed the family. Neoclassical economic dogma and its Keynesian variation—the interpretations long dominant in the United States—simply provide inadequate frameworks for analyzing the sexual division of labor and other economic phenomena relevant to the family. A family-wage economy had emerged in the United States in the latter nineteenth and early twentieth centuries. The American labor market had stratified according to sex, and judges and legislatures had sought, usually with success, to defend a special place for the family in the face of continuing efforts to extend Lockean individualism into the domestic realm.[21] As long as this cultural consensus held, the family was economically protected in America. By the 1950s, though, the hard lessons learned during the decades of industrialization had been forgotten. As the private demand for the labor of married women grew, no one bothered to calculate the social consequences. Passage of equal pay and civil rights laws in the early 1960s generated the same nonresponse: race was the hot issue, and the extension of liberal individualism into the domestic sphere occurred with scarcely a yawn.

An example of America's absent-minded waltz down the same path as Sweden can be seen in the U.S. tax treatment of marriage. Between 1948 and 1969, the federal income-tax system maintained two tax tables, one for married couples filing jointly and a second for single taxpayers or married taxpayers choosing to file separately. In tandem, this structure produced a "marriage bonus" (or "bachelor's penalty," depending on your point of view), where the tax on a single person could be as much as 40 percent greater than the tax of a married taxpayer with the same income (and, of course, dependent spouse) filing a joint return.

When the House Ways and Means Committee turned to the question of tax reform in early 1969, chairman Wilbur Mills expressed some interest in extending "head-of-household" tax treatment to single persons above some specified age, seeking to help "bachelors and spinsters as well as widows and widowers."[22] When the committee reported its bill, it proposed that tax rates for single persons age 35 or over and for widows and widowers be set halfway between those available to married couples and singles. Clearly, the "marriage bonus" was to be maintained for those of prime marrying age, and the House approved this measure. Yet when the Nixon Administration brought its tax reform proposals to the senate in September, it proposed to eliminate the age requirement altogether. Rather, it called for a tax rate cut for singles across the board, so that their additional tax liability would never be more than 20 percent above that of couples filing jointly. Married couples would also be prohibited from filing separately. The administration's version eventually became law. The "marriage bonus" survived, albeit in significantly weakened form.

Yet this bundle of reforms had an unintended consequence: creation of the so-called "marriage penalty." It turned out that many working couples, now unable to file separately, were paying more in annual income taxes than two single persons with the same incomes. As a man's and a woman's income neared equality, this "marriage penalty" grew. For example, a couple with total earnings of $50,000 in 1979 (one $30,000, the other $20,000) paid a "marriage tax" of $2,439.

The issue was tailor-made for moral posturing. One Maryland couple drew a great deal of attention for its sequence of December divorces/January remarriages, designed to foil the tax collector. Representative Millicent Fenwick said that "we ought not to force people to fraud or cohabitation." Federal Judge Cynthia Hall labeled the policy "a sin subsidy, an annual cash penalty on virtue." The Indiana Legislature passed a resolution urging reform in order to "encourage the preservation of marriage." Even the New Right jumped on board, one group arguing (only half-correctly) that "present tax law requires married couples filing joint returns to pay higher taxes than single people living together."[23] All but forgotten, conveniently or otherwise, was that the "marriage penalty" emerged only out of the attempt in 1969 to preserve some residual tax recognition for the one-income, two-mouth (at least) family.

The real issue, of course, was not marriage. Rather, it was whether the federal government was prepared to shift its taxation policies away from the one-income norm in favor of the two-income working family. As a pair of change advocates explained: "Many decisions on social policies by American political leaders need to adjust to the reality that the two-earner family is the norm."[24] When it turned to the issue in 1981, Congress chose to preserve the illusion of the traditional family, while granting the real relief to the two-income couple. It rejected a plan to require everyone to file separately (the clean Swedish solution), opting instead for one allowing a couple to exclude from taxation 10 percent of the wages of the lower-earning spouse, to a maximum of $3,000. The "marriage penalty" (or, from an alternate, one-earner perspective, the "marriage bonus") was sharply cut (albeit not wholly eliminated) and one of the few meaningful policy-related supports to the historic American family wage quietly put to rest. The Tax Reform Act of 1986 represented a "wash" as the two-earner exemption was traded in for lower rates, which tended to benefit the two-earner household and so cement the diminution of the mother-at-home.

What have been the consequences of allowing the historic American family wage simply to disappear without creating some alternative? Critics on the rational left, such as Columbia University's Alfred Kahn and Sheila Kamerman, are entirely correct in condemning the United States for its shabby treatment of families with children. Using a cross-national analysis of nine modern industrial countries, they found that in terms of relieving parents of some of the costs of rearing children, "the United States does less than any other country." Moreover, even in American families with only *one* average salary, "tax and transfer benefits make little difference in income whether there are four, two, or no children."[25] While debate on the subject still rages, there is also strong evidence suggesting that the economic benefits of two-income families are skewed: highly educated, well-paid wives tend to be married to highly educated, well-paid husbands, while low-income women tend to be wedded to low-income men. In consequence, inter-family income inequality appears to be growing, with the rich becoming relatively richer, and the poor poorer.[26] Moreover, numerous studies continue to show a strong negative correlation between the labor force participation rate of young married women and lifetime fertility.[27]

Some analysts see a deeper dilemma. Sociologist Judith Lorber argues that the decline of the sexual division of labor has undercut the very basis for family life. The functional interdependence of men and women formerly reinforced heterosexual union. While the sentiment of love often embellished this functional bond, love—particularly romantic love—could not by itself maintain a stable marriage. Accordingly, as employment gives women independence from marriage and men derive diminished benefits from wives, heterosexual unions will become more fragile and women less available to rear children. The result will not be some "new family form"; rather, it will be a steadily diminished place in society for any family with children.[28]

Making a similar argument, sociologists Janet and Larry Hunt draw a distinction between a "job," held primarily to earn a living, and a "career," defined as an all-encompassing, rigorous life pattern to which everything else is subordinated. They note that career and family involvement have never been easily combined in the same person, for the simple reason that the family-oriented worker is in daily competition with persons who are without spouse and children, and hence able to give all to their work.

Until recently, they note, the two-person career was the norm. Under this model, a husband and a wife usually collaborated in advancing the man's career: she relieved him of most home and child-care burdens, managed the family's social life, performed symbolic volunteer work, and so on: he made the full commitment to advancement and success. Other normative expectations reinforced this orientation, including a general suspicion of confirmed bachelors and social pressures on existing two-career families to conform their lives as much as possible to the majority pattern, including the presence of children. The Hunts note that while not without strains and inequities, this pattern at least "provided a structural basis for families," where the social reproduction of the species was ensured.

This was not true, though, among the emerging dual-career families of the post-1965 period. By then, conventions were crumbling, and the dual-career couple emerged as true revolutionaries, "antifamily" to their core. The Hunts argue that there is nothing that the state or corporations now can do to right the balance, for the "very idea that women as well as men could embrace careers and, at the same time, become more humane and responsive to families is a contradiction." Employers might try to provide child care during working hours, flexible schedules, leave to care for sick children, and so on. But so long as there are workers who do not value these benefits and who will apply themselves to occupational and professional advancement, the gains won by parents will serve only to highlight their greater cost to their employers and their more modest work orientations.

Relative to work, women can now be "sociological men," while men can be "sociological women." Accordingly, in place of gender, the great divide in the workplace has become parental status. For a society that has demolished any normative obligation to marriage and children, the result will be *a widening gap* in standard of living between parents and nonparents. As the Hunts explain:

> Those without children can monopolize the highest-paying jobs and combine their resources (through marriage and other alliances) to drive up the price of everything from housing to health care to transportation. Those with children will tend to have lower incomes, in addition to absorbing the expenses of children, and will fall further and further behind their child-free counterparts.

Put another way, families with children will not be able to compete effectively in a market stimulated by the spending and investing power of "child-free" adults.[29]

In facing up to this new situation, American politics has fallen flat. The "profamily" banner is now raised up by both the left and right, yet little of meaning has been accomplished for families. Proposed liberal policies, such as daycare subsidies and parental leave, would merely accelerate the decomposition of the private home. Meanwhile, many conservatives long for a restoration of the patriarchal or traditional family norm which would reinforce the father as breadwinner and the mother at home with her children. Yet they have no political will to tackle the federal laws that have solidly codified a different model: the Equal Pay Act of 1963 and Title VII of the Civil Rights Act of 1964. As critics of the New Right have pointed out, much of the movement's ideology is essentially liberal, in its adoption of the values of individualism and equality of opportunity. Even conservative opponents of the Equal Rights Amendment tended to argue "equality yes, the amendment no." Conservatism is stuck on a distinctively American dilemma: how to reconcile a generally shared American commitment to equal opportunity and individual freedom with a family system that is premised on major distinctions or "discriminations" on the basis of gender. Such theoretical confusion has led to policy paralysis.[30]

Political feminism actually suffers from less confusion. On the question of homemakers' pensions, for example, feminists have rightly concluded that the normative arrangements which once justified the Social Security coverage of homemakers only through their husbands no longer exist. Back in 1977, the National Organization for Women (NOW) established a National Homemakers' Rights Committee to promote the interests of mothers and to defend the woman's right to stay home (in part, it is true, to combat "workfare" schemes). NOW's representatives emphasized the economic contribution made by homemakers and the right of women to remain at home with their children.

The feminist left, of course, has a vastly broader agenda, one internally consistent and supported by a large body of scholarship. It is an agenda that confronts the core questions that modern family policy must address: "the social construction and control of . . . sexuality and the mix of women's domestic and market labor, especially . . . when young children are present."[31] It is an agenda that also claims to bear historical inevitability: the traditional family, and the wage system which sustained it, is gone forever; a new structure must be created by the state. In its essence, this family agenda involves the socialization of child rearing. It would create child allowances as part of the Social Security system; maternal and child health care as the first stage of a national health insurance scheme; direct governmental subsidization of daycare as a right; and the transformation of corporations into quasi-public agencies for the socialization of children.

In short, it is precisely the "new economic foundation for a higher form of the family and of the relation between the sexes" that Karl Marx described in *Capital*, over a century ago.

Notes

1. Perry Pascarella, "The Corporation Steps in Where Family, Church, and Schools Have Failed," *Industry Week* (June 25, 1984): 34–35; and Pascarella, *The New Achievers* (New York: The Free Press, 1984).
2. John Naisbitt and Patricia Aburdene, *Reinventing the Corporation* (New York: Warner Books, 1985), pp. 90, 209–22.
3. Emile Durkheim, *Suicide: A Study in Sociology*, trans. John A. Spaulding and

George Simpson (New York: The Free Press of Glencoe, 1951 [1897]), pp. 376–81.

4. Quoted in: "A Mother's Choice," *Newsweek* (March 31, 1986): 47.
5. Claude Levi-Strauss, "The Family," in *Man, Culture and Society*, ed. Harry L. Shapiro (New York: Oxford University Press, 1971), pp. 348–49.
6. Barrie Thorne, "Feminist Rethinking of the Family," in *Rethinking the Family: Some Feminist Questions*, ed. Barrie Thorne (New York and London: Longman, 1982), p. 9.
7. Andrew Ure, *The Philosophy of Manufacturers* (London: C. Knight, 1835), p. 475.
8. See: Ali Zaretsky, "The Place of the Family in the Origins of the Welfare State," in Thorne, pp. 212, 216–17.
9. Ivy Pinchbeck, *Women Workers and the Industrial Revolution, 1750-1850* (London: Frank Cass & Co., 1930), pp. 312–13.
10. Alice Kessler-Harris, *Out to Work: A History of Wage Earning Women in the United States* (New York: Oxford University Press, 1982), p. 308.
11. Karl Marx: *Capital: A Critique of Popular Economy*, ed. Friedrich Engels, trans. Samuel Moore and Edward Aveling (New York: The Modern Library, 1906 [1867]), pp. 504–20.
12. Max Horkheimer, *Critical Theory: Selected Essays* (New York: Herder and Herder, 1968), pp. 47–128.
13. Ernest Mandel, *Late Capitalism* (Thetford, Norfolk, G.B.: Lowe and Brydome, 1975), pp. 387, 391–92, 401–03.
14. The influence of her work as one of "the most important contemporary feminist accounts" is noted in Zaretsky, p. 191.
15. Heidi Hartmann, "Capitalism, Patriarchy, and Job Segregation by Sex," *Signs: Journal of Women in Culture and Society* 1 (1976 Supplement): 137–69.
16. Zillah R. Eisenstein, "The Sexual Politics of the New Right: Understanding the 'Crisis of Liberalism' for the 1980s," *Signs: Journal of Women in Culture and Society* 7, No. 3 (1982): 567–88; Thorne, p. 20; and Julie A. Matthaei, "Consequences of the Rise of the Two-Earner Family: The Breakdown of the Sexual Division of Labor," *American Economic Review: Proceedings of the American Economics Association* 70, No. 2 (1980): 198–202.
17. Viola Klein and Alva Myrdal, *Women's Two Roles: Home and Work* (London: Routledge and Kegan Paul, 1956).
18. Carolyn Teich Adams and Kathryn Teich Winston, *Mothers at Work: Public Policies in the United States, Sweden, and China* (New York and London: Longman, 1980), pp. 224ff.
19. Nonwage income from capital gains and property is still added together.
20. Annika Baude, "Public Policy and Changing Family Patterns in Sweden, 1930–1977," in *Sex Roles and Social Policy: A Complex Social Science Equation*, ed. Jean Lipman-Blumen and Jessie Bernard (New York: SAGE Studies in International Sociology, 1979), pp. 145-72.
21. See: Zaretsky, pp. 200–01.
22. "Taxes: How to Ease the Squeeze," *Newsweek* (Feb. 24, 1969): 66.
23. See *National Christian Action Coalition Alert* (July 1981): 2.
24. James A. Duran and Elizabeth Duran, "The Federal Sin Subsidy," *America* (Jan. 24, 1981): 58.
25. Alfred J. Kahn and Sheila B. Kamerman, "Income Maintenance, Wages, and Family Income," *Public Welfare* 41 (Fall 1983): 23–30.

26. Zahid Shariff, "Intra-Family Equality and Income Distribution," *American Journal of Economics and Sociology* 38 (Jan. 1979): 49–59.
27. See, for example: James DeFronzo, "Female Labor Force Participation and Fertility in 48 States: Cross-Sectional and Change Analyses for the 1960–70 Decade," *Sociology and Social Research* 64 (Jan. 1980): 263–78.
28. Judith Lorber, "Beyond Equality of the Sexes: The Question of Children," in *Marriage and Family in a Changing Society*, ed. James M. Henslin (New York: The Free Press, 1980), pp. 522–33.
29. Janet G. Hunt and Larry Hunt, "The Dualities of Career and Families: New Integrations or New Polarizations?" *Social Problems* 29 (June 1982): 499–510.
30. Eisenstein, pp. 574–75.
31. Borrowed from: Barbara J. Nelson, "Family Politics and Policy in the United States and Western Europe," *Comparative Politics* 17 (April 1985): 351–71.

9

Working Mothers at Home

"An idea whose time has come," Colorado Representative Pat Schroeder calls it. A true "profamily issue," says a representative of the United States Catholic Conference. A matter of simple justice, the National Organization for Women insists.

The issue is parental leave, a proposed federal law that would require employers to grant extended leaves of absence to female and male employees for purposes of childbirth or child care. Advocates note that the fastest-growing segment of the workforce is found among mothers with children under the age of three. Eighty percent of all employed women become pregnant at some point in their working lives, and over half of them will be back to work within a year after childbirth. America, they say, must adjust to these sweeping changes.

Most recent students of family policy, it is true, lambast the United States for its institutional backwardness on the maternity question. For example, panels of business executives, labor leaders, and child-care specialists at Yale University and the Economic Policy Council have lamented American nonrecognition of parenthood and recommended that job-protected leaves of six months, with partial pay, be made available to all new parents.

Sociologists Sheila Kamerman and Alfred Kahn have noted that seventy nations, including every major industrial nation except the United States, provide paid maternity or parental leaves through national legislation. Sweden, for example, grants twelve months of leave, at 90 percent of the insured wage. Canada covers 60 percent of the insured wage for a maximum of seventeen weeks. Yet in the U.S., Kamerman and Kahn note, a "real revolution in family life styles" symbolized by the working mother has produced no major policy changes. Under the terms of the Pregnancy Disability Amendment of 1978, firms with disability benefits are only required to treat pregnancy as they treat any other disability. Kamerman and Kahn complain that, in this mode, pregnancy and birth are defined as

127

illnesses, rather than maternity, while employees at firms without disability policies lose coverage altogether. American attitudes have been "strangely unaccommodating" to maternal policies, they conclude. The "larger meaning of maternity as motherhood has been ignored."[1]

Writing in *American Psychologist*, two Yale scholars complain that the United States gives "no recognition" to the fact that a healthy parent may have a psychological need for some time off with a new baby or that both parent and infant could benefit "from a six-month get-acquainted period." They cry out: "How have we come to such an impasse, where mothers and fathers must be in the workforce, psychologically safe daycare is prohibitively expensive, and yet there is no funding to help either parent stay home for even a few months to take care of a baby?"[2]

The popular press has fallen behind the call for action. *U.S. News & World Report* says that "companies preach family values, but in most cases their practices do little to ease work-family strains." *Glamour* complains that "there is no national policy to protect women's interests." *Ms.* notes bitterly that few companies have facilities that allow mothers to pump and store breastmilk. *Working Woman* adds that companies also abuse adopting parents and concludes: "Are we pushing women out of the work force and back home because there are no systems out there to help them with their families?"[3]

Congress has listened and responded, and the "Family and Medical Leave Act of 1987" has been garnering new support. The House of Representatives' Committee on Education and Labor approved a similar measure in 1986, and action by the full House is anticipated this time around. Parental leave has also become an important domestic issue in early jockeying for the 1988 presidential nominations.

The bill cites the growing number of single-parent and two-career households in America and the importance "for the development of the child and the family unit that fathers and mothers be able to participate in early child rearing." It says that many working parents are forced to choose between job security and parenting and declares its purpose to be the balancing of "the demands of the workplace with the needs of families." The measure would require all companies with 15 or more employees to allow men and women up to 18 weeks of unpaid leave from their work after the birth or adoption of a child, or in order to care for a sick child or parent. Employees exercising this new right must be guaranteed their old, or equivalent, or better job on their return, as well as full benefit coverage during the leave and seniority privileges. The measure would also create a Commission on Paid Parental and Medical Leave to study and recommend steps toward creating a comprehensive "system of salary replacement" like those found in other industrialized countries.

Opposition to the bill has come primarily from the U.S. Chamber of Commerce and small business groups. They argue that government should not mandate one approach to benefits for all companies. Most large companies already provide maternity leave, they note. Ninety-five percent of the Fortune 1500 companies offer an average of eight weeks of disability, including cash benefits and job protection. A majority of firms either now provide or are considering paid personal days for child care and family matters as an additional benefit. The financial impact of this measure, they conclude, would primarily strike small firms without the resources to hire and train part-time replacements for the leave period.

These groups have rallied around a substitute measure, proposed by Republican Representative Marge Roukema of New Jersey. While agreeing with the liberal majority that the "time is now at hand to develop a pro-working-family leave policy," she has proposed alternate language that would reduce the leave period, increase the number of exempted employers, and scuttle the commission on paid leave.

Her effort has so far failed, though, as proponents of the more comprehensive measure have successfully held the profamily ground. Indeed, in the pregnancy bill debate, liberals are beginning to rediscover the power of the family and motherhood labels as levers for social reform, while the conservative opposition has been left with arguments based on utility and efficiency.

Unfortunately, emotions surrounding home, hearth, and babies have obscured the larger questions. Indeed, close analysis of the parental leave concept reveals great mental confusion masking a strongly ideological agenda.

This almost pathological illogic is apparent in the volume frequently cited as best presenting the social and intellectual case for the plan. In *Maternity Policies and Working Women*, Kamerman, Kahn, and Paul Kingston mobilize all the arguments noted above for a federal law, but are strangely ambivalent about the actual need for parental care. They note with some satisfaction, for example, that the fertility rate for American women has fallen dramatically. Wives aged 18 to 34, for example, have borne an average of only 1.5 children, with employed women moving toward a one-child norm. This trend toward depopulation, they happily note, "makes the costs of providing maternity benefits both more predictable and less costly."

The authors also strain to emphasize that parents are not actually all that important. The research, they say, "does not suggest that mothers cannot safely be members of the labor force or plan on use of child care programs." Day care, even from the earliest period after birth, is perfectly fine for mother and baby, so long as it is freely chosen. In line with this, Kamerman and friends decry the wearisome American emphasis on "matters other than maternity benefit," such as "the possible negative effects on children caused by absence of working mothers from the home," the negative impact of two-earner households on the living standard of one-earner families, or "the alleged effects of maternal employment on family stress and family break-up." These are nonissues, they say, distracting the nation from the critical need for social reconstruction.

At the same time, the researchers use carefully chosen words to transform what they have first labeled a nonnecessity and a pure matter of choice into a right so compelling as to require the full backing of federal law. They begin: "When individual resources or social policy can make it possible, it is a good strategy to ensure a joint child-parent start for a period of at least three to nine months, even though parental circumstances might then require labor force participation of both parents, or a single parent, and alternative child care arrangements." A few pages later, this extremely cautious affirmation of a "bonding" period for mother—or father—and baby is translated into semihysterical assaults on the American system, as in: "Don't we value children and understand optimal conditions for child development in the early months of life?" Somewhat later, the same bonding period is redefined as the very heart of the American polity, as they conclude: "Maternity policy is integral to our nation's core values and ideology."[4]

The mind-twisting message that the mother-at-home is not important and the federal government must therefore force all employers to grant parental leaves pervades the popular women's press, too. Glamour, for example, stresses the absolute moral imperative for parental leave as national policy. Yet the magazine also encourages new mothers to get back to work as quickly as possible, warning darkly that "babies are hard to resist once they're at this stage of one to six months, and mothers can sometimes find it difficult to 'break away' if they delay too long." It adds that no matter when mothers go back to work, "there is no evidence that exclusive mothering is good for babies." Glamour also reports on the personal triumph of one Washington, DC, radio newscaster who did manage to leave her newborn and "loved it": "On the first day back, my sitter brought the baby in so I could nurse him. I was working and saw a stroller out of the corner of my eye. I thought, 'Who's that baby?' I was so into a work mode that I forgot for four hours that I had a baby."[5]

What accounts for such disjointed thought? Simply put, we see here the frantic efforts of ideologues to piece back together a social order at least capable of its own partial reproduction, after the dissolution of the natural bonds and economic structure of the old American family system.

Parental leave was never before an American issue because, until about

1965, the nation's family and economic systems meshed relatively well. Men were expected to marry and to work, to be "good providers," to set a good table, to pay the mortgage, to buy the shoes, to contribute to the church, and to keep their children warmly clothed. Women were expected to marry and to care full-time for the resulting offspring. If they worked before marriage, they received pay calculated on an "individual" basis and were expected to resign on the wedding day or, later, on becoming pregnant. In 1930, for example, 77 percent of American school systems still refused to hire married women, while 63 percent automatically dismissed teachers on their marriage. As late as 1965, a hefty 87 percent of American housewives saw "breadwinning" as the husband's primary role. In 1980, though, the Census Bureau provided a benchmark of change, deciding that year that it would no longer automatically denominate the male as a family's head of household.[6]

Of course, that social and moral order constructed so as to reinforce marriage and the birth of children has now vanished. Millions of Americans still live by its tenets, but they find themselves strangers in a strange land.

The triumph lies with the first stage of the feminist revolution. In this phase, the strategy was to secure equal treatment in matters of hiring, firing, promotion, and pay. Children were not mentioned; they were labeled irrelevant; even the briefest hint that women might be bound to children in a special, time-specific way (e.g., birth or breastfeeding) would give "reactionary homemakers" and "male chauvinists" a solid argument with which to defend the old order. As Wendy Chavkin explains in *Ms.*, "Many feminists were afraid that if they drew attention to pregnancy-related needs they would imperil newly gained jobs." Hence, in this phase of change, they embraced a model holding that women were no different from men and that women's needs were legitimate only when viewed as analogous to male experiences. When the pregnancy and work issue arose, NOW and other feminist groups resorted to the "sickness" analogy and eventually won legal recognition of pregnancy as a covered disability, no different from cancer or a broken leg.

The result was great success in tearing down the economic supports of the old family system and the nearly complete victory of the equality principle in matters of work. Predictably, the primary casualties were the children: those small ones already born but increasingly left to fend for themselves in group care, and those never-to-be-born as the workplace displaced the home and children in many women's lives.

However, except among the lunatic fringe, feminist theorists remained aware that children could not be ignored forever; that some new structure must be built to provide at least some level of human reproduction. As

Elise Boulding puts it, children are "enduring features" of the human land-scape, and as women face a conflict between their "breeder" and "provider" roles, the whole society suffers. Karl Marx understood only part of the problem, she says, thinking that state control of production and distribution would be solution enough: he did not understand the conflicts of sex roles. Rather, the true "second phase" of the feminist revolution holds two imperatives: (1) the costs and burdens of combining employment with motherhood must be shifted from the family unit to "the broader community" (read "the state"); and (2) men and women must share child nurturing and homemaking tasks equally. Anything less would mean social turmoil and decay. As Boulding explains: "Human liberation depends on sharing breeder-feeder roles between women and men, as well as on having state-administered support services." Equality in the workplace, in short, demands fairly complete social, psychological, and economic reconstruction.[7]

Translated into policy, these are no small expectations, and parental leave lies at the core of necessary change. Chavkin says that such a feminist family policy program "must demand": job modifications to accommodate the physical changes of pregnancy; temporary transfers to safer jobs, when needed; paid leave to attend prenatal classes and visit doctors; paid leave for the late stages of pregnancy, childbirth, and (for both parents) child care after birth; facilities for breastfeeding (including on-site infant care so women can breastfeed during work breaks); low-cost, high-quality daycare; and paid leave for both parents to care for sick children.

Other lists of demands go further and eventually embrace the full welfare state agenda. Kamerman and her co-authors argue that "the relationship between a national health policy and maternity policy seems very close." Child allowances and other state benefits would also be necessary.[8] Another writer endorses generous "drawing rights" on society (read a "government allowance") for single parents of either sex who undertake the care of small children alone.[9] Sociologist Jessie Bernard cites the need for radical gender role changes among all unenlightened men, women, and children, processes that she compares to those used in "deprogramming a cult member."[10]

Boulding, though, offers the fullest vision of human transformation to the new order in which parental leave plays a central role. Through gross distortions of the real anthropological evidence, she points to the primitive hunting band as the "most egalitarian of all types of human societies." It was a social order that successfully managed zero population growth through abortion and infanticide, one with abundant leisure where there was "no accumulation of resources to serve as a power base for individuals of either sex," and where women shared decision-making equally with men. Americans now stand on the verge of restoring a similar egalitarian order, built on the ruins of discredited patriarchy, she says. This "new vision of human potential" absolutely depends on the state assuming the burdens of child care and on "the exposure of men to breeder-feeder roles." This means that the full welfare state must be constructed, and prevailing male attitudes, shaped over seven thousand years of patriarchal rule, must be shattered, so that humankind might enter "a process of mutual liberation on behalf of that gentler and more creative generation to come—our children's children."[11]

Such a vision embracing a pristine ancient order, followed by centuries or millennia of repression, followed by revolution, followed by the construction of a new society, and culminating in the creation of a new human type, "gentler and more creative," should be familiar to students of the history of ideas. It is the same vision that motivated Robespierre in 1795, Lenin in 1917, Hitler in 1933, and Mao Tse-tung in 1949. Only the details have been changed. In this spirit, it seems significant that Chavkin praises Fidel Castro's Cuban Family Code as one of the few policy models that actually enables "people to manage both family and job responsibilities" and promotes the "equitable sharing of . . . responsibilities between the sexes."[12]

Admittedly, only a handful of contemporary proponents of a parental leave policy have this vision in mind. Only movement theorists understand the broader picture, and are aware that the germ of a welfare-state solution to an ideological problem is inherent in a system of salary replacement for parents. Most proponents are simply responding to what is, indeed, a real crisis in the relationship between the workplace and the home. They are casting about for a solution—any solution—to the social disorders that have followed the collapse of America's old family-wage economy. They sense intuitively that family life is good and that raising children is the raison d'etre of the human species. And they understand that our current cultural-economic structure does make family life and competent child-rearing problematic.

Even as a utilitarian response, though, is "parental leave" the way to go? When one actually looks at the differential or discriminatory impact of the currently favored plan, the answer is no. As in all state-mandated benefits, there would be winners and losers, and the losers under the parental-leave plan would be fairly numerous.

Who would bear the negative costs for this attempt at social reconstruction? There appear to be four groups:

Small businesses. Large companies with employees numbering in the thousands find it relatively easy to use similarly trained personnel to cover a four-month vacancy caused by a parental leave. Small companies have much less flexibility and would usually face problems in filling a skilled vacancy with short-term help. The real, if somewhat invisible, costs of providing leave would also have to come out of some other pocket, possibly through a reduction in other benefits or in a greater reluctance to hire new employees.

Lower income families. An unpaid leave of absence is tailored primarily to the needs of highly paid professional women who can more easily afford a period of time without income. The working poor and families at the lower end of the income scale have less choice here and receive a "benefit" they cannot afford, while probably losing other benefits that employers might have offered.

Traditional families. Behind all the hype about the massive flow of mothers into the labor force lurks one little-noticed fact: nearly half of mothers with children age three and younger are not in the labor force. About the same proportion do not return to work after their first child's birth; they become a clear majority of mothers after the second and third births. Often at considerable personal and professional sacrifice, these women continue to perform the socially valuable task of nurturing small children on a full-time basis. The "opportunity cost" (foregone income) of this choice is, on average, nearly $16,000 a year. It is unclear why this financial sacrifice for family-supportive ends should receive no recognition from the government, while working mothers demand benefits for which others (small businesses, the poor, the traditional) will pay, directly or indirectly. One possible response is that leaves should be transformed into a government maternity grant, paid to all mothers, whether working or not. While plausible, this response shows how partial measures, in face of the equity problem, quickly descend down the welfare state's slippery slope.

Children. Common sense tells us that an ideological vision, however fine in theory, cannot turn women into fathers or men into mothers. Social research, fortunately, confirms the same point and suggests that efforts to create the envisioned "new human type" are futile and can only damage the children. A team of research psychologists headed by Michael Lamb set out in 1980 to determine whether "nontraditional" Swedish fathers, who, under various state pressures, had taken parental leave to care full time for their infant children, were as effective as stay-at-home mothers and more effective than "traditional" fathers who worked. Measuring qualitative actions such as discipline, play, and affection, the team hypothesized that a reversal in sex roles and the assumption of "the primary caretaker role" by the father would result in an effectively nurturing, unisex parent.

To their surprise, though, they found that mothers—whether working or at home—proved more likely to hold, tend, vocalize to, smile at, and display affection toward their infants than did fathers, whether traditional or "caretaking." Moreover, they discovered that while traditional mothers engaged in more effective play with infants than working mothers, the opposite effect occurred among men: traditional "working" fathers engaged in better play with their infants than "nontraditional" fathers. In other words, men did not change even after being the full-time caretaking parent; in some ways, in fact, they became less effective.

In sum, women remained better mothers; men remained better fathers; and social engineering had failed. The researchers reluctantly concluded that biological gender was apparently "a more important influence on parental behavior than caretaking role or sex role." They did, though, hold out hope that truly "radical changes in gender-related prescriptions and expectations" might still make a difference.[13] In the interim, though, it was clear that infants made by the social engineers to suffer the full-time caretaking of their fathers were paying the price of stunted psychological and emotional development.

Clearly, it is time to stop trying to repair a symptom of a problem and focus instead on the problem itself: the collapse of the historic family-wage economy in the United States and our failure to acknowledge or correct the situation. By 1976, only 40 percent of American jobs paid enough to support a family of five in minimal comfort, not so long ago the standard measure of a fair wage. Today, the figure is close to 25 percent. Particularly in the lower and low-middle sectors of the income scale, there is truth to the assertion that two incomes are needed just to get along. We know, for example, that perceived "income inadequacy" is tied heavily to employment in the "service sector," where the large majority of new female workers is concentrated.[14] The inflationary economy of the 1969–1983 period also masked a general stagnation of real household income, so that a family's standard-of-living could be maintained only by sending a second (or third) earner into the workforce and/or by reducing household size through the avoidance of children.

Economist Reuben Gronau of Hebrew University has demonstrated at the household level how the illusion of prosperity has masked this economic decay of the family. He has calculated that in 1973 the average value of home production by American wives exceeded 70 percent of the family's money income, after taxes, and was almost equal to that income when the family had young children. Moreover, when a young mother entered the paid labor market, the value of lost home production *far exceeded* the gain in money earnings, when at least one preschool child was involved. His findings indicate that a family with children has not really improved its real standard of living when Mom goes to work. Indeed, its standing may have actually declined, although that decline is hidden by the nonmonetized nature of lost home production. For the economy as a whole, as fast-food restaurants displace mother's kitchen and daycare centers supplant the home, the result is merely apparent economic growth, the expansion of the service sector. In fact, the result may be, at best, a wash, as we simply substitute measured for unmeasured economic activity.[15]

Finally, as George Gilder has recently pointed out, it is a great mistake to view "working women" as a uniform mass of full-time laborers. In 1984, only 37 percent of all women ages 20 to 64 held full-time, year-round jobs (including teaching). The large majority were either homemakers or holding seasonal or part-time work. Even managerial, professional, and executive women—by a 51 to 19 percent margin—still prefer seasonal or part-time, to full-time work, if they can find it.[16] A parental leave policy constructed to help meet an ideological vision of dubious, if not absurd, dimensions and catering primarily to the needs of the richest segment of the target population does almost nothing to accommodate this great complexity. Rather, its real intent is to impose a new and twisted model of human nature on American life through coercive social engineering.

Notes

1. Sheila B. Kamerman, Alfred J. Kahn, and Paul Kingston, *Maternity Policies and Working Women* (New York: Columbia University Press, 1983), pp. 5, 7, 24.
2. Edward Zigler and Susan Muenchow, "Infant Day Care and Infant-Care Leaves: A Policy Vacuum," *American Psychologist* 38 (Jan. 1983): 91–94.
3. "Expectant Moms, Office Dilemma," *U.S. News & World Report* (March 10, 1986): 53; "Should Congress Set a National Maternity Leave Policy?" *Glamour* (Sept. 1985): 232; Wendy Chavkin, "Parental Leave—What There Is and What There Should Be," *Ms.* (Sept. 1984): 116; and Charlene Canape, "The Forgotten Parents: When Working Women Adopt," *Working Woman* (June 1985): 136.
4. Kamerman, et al., pp. 8, 13–14, 25–26.
5. Andrea Boroff Eagan, "Long vs. Short Maternity Leaves," *Glamour* (March 1986): 214ff.
6. See: Jessie Bernard, "The Good Provider Role: Its Rise and Fall," *American Psychologist* 36 (Jan. 1981): 1–12.
7. Chavkin, pp. 115, 117; and Elise Boulding, "Familial Constraints on Women's Work Roles," *Signs: Journal of Women in Culture and Society* 1 (Spring 1976): 115.
8. Kamerman, et al., p. 156.
9. Boulding, p. 116.
10. Bernard, p. 11.
11. Boulding, pp. 116–117.
12. Chavkin, p. 117.
13. Michael E. Lamb, Ann M. Frodi, Carl-Philip Hwang, Majt Frodi, and Jamie Steinberg, "Mother- and Father-Infant Interaction Involving Play and Holding in Traditional and Nontraditional Swedish Families," *Developmental Psychology* 18, No. 2 (1982): 215–21.

14. Patricia Voydanoff and Robert F. Kelly, "Determinants of Work-Related Family Problems Among Employed Parents," *Journal of Marriage and the Family* 46 (Nov. 1984): 890.
15. See: Reuben Gronau, "Home Production: A Forgotten Industry," *Review of Economics and Statistics* 62 (Aug. 1980): 408–16.
16. George Gilder, "Women in the Work Force," *The Atlantic* (Sept. 1986): 20ff.

10

The Moral Politics of the Minimum Wage and Work-at-Home

The relationship of the family to the economic order has been a matter of central concern to the American Republic for over a century. Indeed, many contemporary policy issues now debated on a "family" basis have long histories.

As examples, two labor questions on the docket of the 100th Congress have deep "family" components. First, a choir of voices is lamenting the erosion in the real value of the minimum wage, and is calling for an immediate 20–50 percent jump in its value and its indexing to inflation as a means of defending the family. Second, the controversy over home-based work, which welled up in 1980 and resulted in a recent Department of Labor decision to lift a 42-year-old ban on outerwear knitted in homes, seems sure to continue.

The critical issues in both debates, one hundred years ago as today, have been motherhood and the place of the family in industrial society. Yet a remarkable shift occurred sometime in the late 1960s or early 1970s that has fundamentally altered and confused the dialogue.

Decades ago, it was the "progressive," left-liberal, pro-union side that, with some legitimacy, claimed to be defending the home and the motherhood principle. For their part, conservative, probusiness elements tended to avoid such social questions, arguing instead for freedom of contract and other legal, classically liberal principles. More recently, though, the liberal left has abandoned all traditional social and moral content focused on the family, while business interests have found themselves the unexpected heirs to an alliance with the profamily cause. The magnitude of the change, its political and cultural implications, and its fragility are difficult to overestimate. Indeed, its continuation or collapse may largely determine the course of domestic American politics over the next several decades. The

139

history and current dynamics of the minimum wage and homework controversy offer insight into the choices that are faced.

The tension between the family and the emerging industrial order was clearly drawn in the long controversy over homework. Defined as unsupervised employment of a productive (not distributive) nature, commonly paid for by the piece and performed in the worker's dwelling, homework continued to thrive in some product areas long after the rise of the factory. Persons engaged in the practice varied widely in their circumstances: from farm wives and middle-class mothers to the handicapped, widowed, and new immigrants crowded into New York City tenements. By 1885, though, the derogatory term "sweating" became something of a synonym for the process. "Unduly" low wage rates, excessive hours, unsanitary dwellings, and child labor were all considered hallmarks of the "sweated" industries. As one writer put it, "home work is a combination of every possible evil." Estimates of the numbers of workers involved varied widely, yet the figure of 150,000–300,000 was used both in 1890 and in 1930 and probably represents a fair approximation.[1]

As historian Eileen Boris has shown, though, the real issue in the homework debate in the three decades either side of 1900 was the use of public policy to influence the social relationships of gender, "with the state as a battleground for the social construction of the female life cycle as well as for the division of labor."[2] In this early controversy, partisans of homework defended the labor rights of women; opponents of the practice wrapped themselves in the family.

The employer-backed Homework Protection League did note certain "social reasons" for the existence of homework. For many married women, advocates said, family, children, and housework led to the choice of homework over factory labor. Yet, they noted, this was primarily true among immigrant Italians and Jews, groups which had "almost Oriental" traditions of the place of women in the family setting. More commonly, the Homework Protection League used the arguments of classical liberalism: freedom of contract; right to work; individual autonomy; limited government. Indeed, League advocates also proved quite comfortable with the rhetoric of feminist individualism. Homework, they said, was a means for women in certain conditions to escape "economic parasitism" on men, with its "resultant social, economic and moral slavery." Others stressed that "women are also people" and had a right to paid labor in any setting they chose.[3]

In contrast, the progressive opponents of homework stressed their commitment to motherhood and home with a firm, consistent voice. According to Amy Hewes, Supervisor of Investigation for the State of Massachusetts, homework was not a reurn to the bucolic days of rural weaving, baking, and candle making. Rather it represented a distinctive phase of modern industrialism, involving the subdivision of labor, uncertainty of contract, the imposition on workers of overhead, waste, and transportation costs, the irregularity of employment, and the evils of child labor and long hours. Homework must be abolished, Hewes emphasized in her 1915 report. Indeed, she said, such an act would reinforce women's domesticity, for by so driving up the price of wearing apparel, all women would be forced to produce more clothing for their own consumption.

Other critics of homework made similar points. The system undercut male wages in factories, making impossible a decent, family-sustaining income in affected industries. More damningly, they agreed, homework degraded motherhood, forcing a woman "to exploit her own children and to neglect her home and her children." The little ones were allowed to run the streets; husbands grew careless and drifted into bars. When married women were forced to augment the family income, it was "greatly to the physical and moral disadvantage of the children."[4]

Before the early 1930s, efforts at the regulation of homework with stated profamily purposes occurred primarily at the state level. The New York legislature passed a law in 1892 prohibiting homework, except in case of an immediate family living in the same apartment. A 1904 law imposed still stiffer restrictions on work in tenement houses, exempting persons living in single-family dwellings in smaller cities, towns, and villages. In 1913, that exemption was abolished. By 1939, seventeen states had similar laws which regulated, licensed, or prohibited homeworkers.

The minimum wage movement emerged during the same era. The temporal connection, it should be emphasized, was not a coincidence.

The idea of setting a minimum wage for labor had a long pedigree, reaching back to the certainty and uniformity of the medieval era, when the preservation of the social unit took precedence. As Barbara Armstrong, one of the intellectual architects of the New Deal, explained in 1932: "The medieval scheme of life within its social units 'insured the essentials' to its members far better than does its modern prototype."[5] Progressive reformers also took a cue from Pope Leo XIII's 1891 encyclical, *Rerum Novarum*, which had declared the just industrial wage to be one "sufficiently large to enable [the worker] to provide comfortably for himself, his wife, and his children." As a prominent Catholic theologian subsequently explained: "Until a larger social justice reigns, minimum wage laws must enable every male worker to support a family in Christian decency."[6]

The first political application of the principle, though, came in that relatively non-Catholic country, Australia. Motivated, certainly in part, by the solidarity spawned among those "down under," Australian state governments responded quickly to the proposed social regulation of wages. An

1884 parliamentary investigation of factories had reported many instances of long hours coupled to low wages. The worst conditions, the commissioners had found, were combined with homework or "outworking," which was targeted for elimination. In 1893, the Anti-Sweating League pressured Victoria's parliament into considering a bill that would establish boards in "the sweated industries" for the fixing of minimum rates. While no bill was passed, reports from the Chief Factory Inspector in 1894 and 1895 recorded cases of women working eighty-five hours a week, particularly in the "outworking" trades. Under these mounting pressures, the Victorian parliament approved the "Factories and Shops Act of 1896," which created elective boards in six industries (e.g., men's clothing, shirt making, and baking), with the power to fix minimum wage rates. Over the next two decades, wage boards spread to other industries and eventually to trades not connected in any manner with factories, as well as to Queensland, Tasmania, and the other Australian states.

At the heart of the Australian approach lay the idea of a "living wage." This concept held, in the words of one English writer, "that every workman, shall have a wage which will maintain him in the highest state of industrial efficiency, which will enable him to provide his family with all the material things which are needed for their health and physical well-being, enough to enable him to qualify to discharge his duties as citizen." An Australian justice saw the "living wage" as resting on the worker's "requirements as a man in a civilized community." In a 1905 decision, a second justice defined the living wage as one sufficient to enable the worker "to lead a human life, to marry and bring up a family, and maintain them and himself with, at any rate, some small degree of comfort."

Maintenance of the family was clearly the central concern, and distinctions based on gender necessarily followed. The wage boards assumed that men would be supporting a wife and children, while women would be working either to supplement family income or to support only themselves. Accordingly, different minimums for each group were set. Victoria's Boat and Shoe Board, for example, declared that seven shillings and six pence per day should be the minimum rate for adult men; for women, three shillings and four pence. The wage boards and appeals courts also wrestled with the family size that should be considered the basis for calculating need. In a precedent-setting 1907 decision known thereafter as "the Harvester Judgment," Commonwealth Justice Henry Bourne Higgins chose a family of "approximately five" and a corresponding daily wage of seven shillings as meeting "the normal needs of the average employee, regarded as a human being living in a civilized community." While a few states subsequently sought to use a family of four as the standard, the model of husband, wife, and three children was reaffirmed by a Royal Commission in 1919 as forming the desired basis for calculation.

Australian advocates of the living wage ideal understood that application of the plan might result in the bankruptcy of some industries. This was a price, though, they said they were willing to pay, labeling industries unable to meet the standard as "parasitic." As a union official explained: "If an industry cannot be conducted on an economic basis paying to its workers a living wage, then that industry is a charge on the community and should not be carried on at all."

Of course, these attempts at setting wages by calculated need soon ran into a host of problems. Micromanagement of household budgets remained a standing temptation. One 1918 union petition, for example, called for a living wage that included precise sums designated for, among other things, "union fees and one newspaper"; the replacement of "broken crockery-ware"; the fulfillment of "the obligations of charity and amusements"; the purchase of "children's toys, stamps and stationery"; and, of course, "tobacco and drink."

More importantly, calculations of the size of "normal" families proved extremely wasteful, since few of them exactly corresponded to the arithmetic average, particularly when the resulting figure was a fraction. Indeed, paying an average wage to all male workers meant overpaying or underpaying the majority. For example, bachelors made out extremely well, while families with six dependent children fell far short of a true "living wage." On a system-wide basis, moreover, the family-of-five standard resulted in a gross "overpayment" to labor. On the basis of 1,000,000 adult male laborers in early-twentieth-century Australia, 3,000,000 children were provided for by the basic wage. In fact, the country had only 900,000 dependent children. Industry was forced to pay for 2,100,000 dependents who did not exist, a situation causing widespread consternation among employers.

Some defenders of the system were untroubled. The president of the South Australian Living Wage Board for Printers simply declared in 1920 that "it is better for an allowance to be made for children who are nonexistent than that no allowance should be made for children who are or will be existent." Yet a 1919 commission, headed by A.B. Piddington, reached a different conclusion. In light of serious efficiency problems, the body recommended that the living wage system be fundamentally altered. A basic wage should be paid to a male worker sufficient to support himself and his wife. This wage should then be supplemented with a weekly allowance of twelve shillings per child, paid from a centralized child endowment fund. At first, the Piddington plan was rejected and the "Harvester Judgment" reaffirmed by the wage courts. Yet by the late 1920s, the Australian states began moving toward the family endowment approach, with New South Wales taking the lead.[7]

Other nations within the Commonwealth crafted "living wage" arrangements that paid prime attention to the family nature of work. In New Zealand, the Court of Basic Rates wrestled with the same problems of determining basic need, and finally settled in 1926 for a male wage sufficient for man and wife, supplemented by a child allowance paid out of general tax revenues.[8] In Great Britain, the concept attracted no less a champion than Fabian socialist Sidney Webb. He contrasted the need to provide for "competent male adult workers at a full Standard Rate" with the "persistent desire" of employers to use "boy labor, girl labor, married women's labor, the labor of old men, of the feeble-minded, [and] of the decrepit and brokendown invalids." Work in the latter categories, he emphasized, was "parasitic" on the community, since these persons could draw on support from others: "The employer of adult women . . . pays them a wage insufficient to keep them in full efficiency, irrespective of what they receive from their parents, husbands, or lovers." Accordingly, it was necessary to set minimum wages for men and women, in order to defend the community against this economic parasitism of "the marginal woman" and prevent the biological "degradation" of the nation.[9] Stimulated by such arguments and by pressures from the Anti-Sweating League, Britain's parliament passed the Trade Boards Act in 1909, setting up wage boards in selected industries with the power to set minimum rates and with the central goal of reducing or eliminating homework.

The minimum wage took unique shape under American conditions. Yet, as in Australia and Great Britain, the central questions were again gender differences, the elimination of homework, and the assurance of a living wage to families with children.

According to a leading commentator, the "living wage" principle borrowed from Australia "played a large part" in the determining of wages in the United States in the early decades of this century.[10] Another influence was Roman Catholic theory on the moral needs for a "family wage." Father John Ryan's books, *A Living Wage* (1907) and *The Legal Minimum Wage* (1919), bore particular significance, especially in their argument that the payment of a living wage to heads of families was the sole practical political alternative to socialism.[11]

The minimum wage movement in America grew out of the anti-homework campaign. The Consumer's League of the City of New York, organized in 1890, was the pioneer of these antisweating societies. Its early activities were "educational" in nature, which involved the setting of standards for a "fair house"—including a $6 per week minimum wage for adult homeworkers and $3.50 for working children—and intense propaganda to encourage consumers to buy only "fair house" goods. The New York League joined with similar bodies in other states to found the National Consumers League in 1899. Ten years later, the League abandoned the "fair house" strategy, turning instead to a program for securing legislative minimum wages. In that year (1909), bills were introduced in Nebraska and several other states that would have created a flat minimum wage of $9 per week. In these early bills, there was "substantial agreement" that a "living wage" should be the standard for determining wage rates.[12] Economist Harleigh Hartman cited "virtual unanimity of opinion" as to what constituted this minimum wage for men. It included food of decent quality to maintain a family of two adults and three children "in health and efficiency," sanitary living quarters for such a family, warm clothing, the heat and light necessary for comfort, and a reserve for medical attention, insurance, old age, recreation, and protection against unemployment.[13]

Yet by 1911, the movement had altered its goals and sought to secure a minimum wage applicable only to women and children. This shift was due to several factors. To begin with, the American labor movement was extremely hostile to government-set wages for men. As the American Federation of Labor declared in 1913: "Through organization the wages of men can and will be maintained at a higher minimum than they would be if fixed by legal enactment."[14] At the same time, the unions looked upon women workers as a hopeless problem. It was believed that minimum wage legislation "would exclude from industry that great body of inexperienced temporary women workers who are partly supported from sources other than their wages, and who, therefore, demoralize the entire wage system."[15]

Second, there was a general conviction among legal scholars that minimum wage legislation covering both sexes would violate the "due process" clause of the Fourteenth Amendment to the Constitution. These same scholars argued, though, that women could be protected in labor matters through the police powers of the state. Since miserable wages degraded women's health and since women must bear the children of their generation, it was reasoned that the state had a compelling interest in regulating female labor.[16]

Massachusetts enacted the first minimum wage statute in 1912, establishing a commission and subordinate wage boards to set minimum rates for minors and adult women. Over the next few years, Wisconsin, Minnesota, Oregon, California, and a half dozen other states passed similar measures. All emphasized, directly or implicitly, that the female minimum wage should be calculated on an "individual" rather than a "family" basis, and that it should be of adequate amount to protect the health and morals of the women involved.[17]

Family, motherhood, and morality: these were the primary arguments advanced for the minimum wage, and they enjoyed widespread affirmation. The National Industrial Conference Board declared that minimum wage legislation "can only be justified by the social necessity of protecting the family. The woman is the mother and trainer of children. She is the ridge pole of the family structure. ... The male has been the head of the family and principal breadwinner since the dawn of civilization. ... Women and children of the families of able-bodied male workers have no legitimate place in industry." The Kansas Industrial Welfare Commission, in its 1917 report, cited "the harmful results to future generations when the mothers of the race are caused to work," as the central justification for a legal minimum wage. The health commissioner of the District of Columbia saw wage regulation as essential to "the full development of young girls ... because after all it is on marriage and the bearing of offspring that the race relies for its continuance." Congressman Augustine Lonergan of Connecticut warned that "national strength will disappear if the health and moral welfare of the women of our land is not safeguarded [through] wages ... that will guarantee good living conditions." Felix Frankfurter, then counsel for the Oregon Industrial Welfare Commission, emphasized in a 1916 legal brief that low female wages led to "the abyss of prostitution" and "a list of promiscuous immorality." The chairman of the Washington State Industrial Welfare Commission defended the practice of setting female wages at a lower rate than for men, noting that "wage rate determinations ... are based on the estimated cost of living of a self-supporting woman. No other basis could be just." More broadly, the National War Labor Board established in World War I set out the principles that should guide the settlement of industrial disputes: "The right of all workers ... to a living wage is hereby declared"; and "minimum rates of pay ... which will insure the subsistence of the worker and his family in health and reasonable comfort."[18]

Early state court decisions denied challenges to the minimum wage statutes, with matters of family and gender animating their reasoning. The Minnesota Supreme Court, for example, declared: "We think it clear there is such an inequality or difference between men and women in the ... ability to secure a just wage ... that the legislature may by law compensate for the difference."[19] In Washington state, the supreme court affirmed that "[t]he unit, as applied to the problem of living, is the family, not the individual," while minimum wage legislation was necessary to sustain society's claim to civilization.[20]

Nonetheless, the U.S. Supreme Court, in its 1923 *Adkins* decisions, struck down state minimum wage laws as a violation of the Fifth Amendment. Using the pure logic of classical liberalism, the Court ruled that in making labor contracts, both employer and employee had an equal right to obtain from each other the best terms they could through private bargaining. While conceding the "ethical right" of every worker to a living wage, the Court majority denied that every employer must be bound to supply it. Selling labor was no different from selling goods; minimum wage laws were but price-fixing schemes. Significantly, the Court dismissed the argument that the differences between the sexes justified the regulation of women's labor:

> In view of the great—not to say revolutionary—changes which have taken place [recently] in the contractual, political and civil status of women, culminating in the Nineteenth Amendment, it is not unreasonable to say that these differences have now come almost, if not quite, to the vanishing point.

Women, quite simply, were now on their own: cut loose from both the living unit of the family and the special protections and treatments once offered by the state. In the same vein, the Court ruled that it was arbitrary to assume that decent wages for women produced decent morals: such a relationship could not be shown.

The dissenting opinions of Chief Justice William H. Taft and Associate Justice Oliver Wendell Holmes also focused on the gender question as a primary point of dispute. As Holmes put it: "I will need more than the Nineteenth Amendment to convince me that there are no differences between men and women or that legislation cannot take those differences into account."[21]

For about a decade, the homework and minimum wage issues lay dormant, only to be revived as a common problem in the legislative vortex of the New Deal. This time, again, they were cast within the framework of gender, family, and moral questions.

The central actors at this stage were a group of women sometimes labeled "social feminists" or "the New Deal Women": Secretary of Labor Frances Perkins; Women's Bureau head Mary Anderson; Clara Beyer, head of the Labor Department's Children's Bureau; and Mary Dewson, chief of the women's division of the Democratic National Committee. In contrast to the aging, self-proclaimed feminists of the National Women's Party, most members of this group had experienced marriage. Those with children had left the paid labor force while their offspring were young. These women believed, with Eleanor Roosevelt, that "women are different from men." From National Consumers' League Secretary Florence Kelley, they had learned that "sex is a biological fact" and that, while political rights were not properly determined by gender, "social and domestic relations and industrial activities are." With legal scholar Barbara Armstrong, they agreed "[t]here can be no dispute that it is today assumed that a male worker's wage should be a family wage rather than an individual wage." Their careers had been devoted to improving working conditions for all, but particularly for women and children, viewed as the most at risk. Mary Anderson summarized their basic social and political agendas in one sentence: "The only thing to do about homework is to abolish it and to arrange for higher wages for the breadwinner in a family so that his wife and children do not have to supplement the family income by doing homework, or, if there is no regular breadwinner, to provide pensions or relief."[22]

A family wage for dad; mom at home with the kids; mothers' pensions and child allowances for widows and orphans; this was the New Deal social vision. Without discounting its troubling socialist ideological precepts and negative psychological consequences, the New Deal needs to be seen as almost coercively traditional in its social orientation. And there is little doubt that this "populist conservatism" helped account for the program's wide popularity.

The first attempt by the New Deal Women at reviving the "living wage" concept was through the National Industrial Recovery Act (NIRA). Theorists had long emphasized that piecework, commonly performed in the home, must yield to the living wage,[23] and this is precisely the strategy the Roosevelt administration followed. The NIRA required industries to adopt "codes of fair competition." Large manufacturers and labor leaders were particularly articulate in denouncing homework as unfair competition, and they joined with the social feminists in attempting to end the practice. Of the 556 codes eventually adopted, 118 included homework provisions; 101 prohibited homework altogether. At the same time, many of the codes maintained wage differentials between men and women. Due to the weakness and confusion of the enforcement machinery, though, most homeworkers remained active through May 1935, when the U.S. Supreme Court struck down the NIRA as unconstitutional.[24]

The second attempt came in the wake of a 1937 U.S. Supreme Court decision overturning the *Adkins* precedent, and reopening the way for the direct establishment of a state minimum wage. The NIRA experience had convinced the New Deal Women that only legal prohibition could end "the evils of homework." Accordingly, the new Fair Labor Standards Act (FLSA) of 1938, which mandated a federal "ceiling on hours" and "floor to wages," granted the Department of Labor a mechanism to prohibit the practice. Section 8 of the Act provided "that wage orders issued shall contain such terms and conditions as the Administrator finds necessary to carry out the purpose of such orders . . . and to safeguard the minimum wage rates established therein." Accordingly, in the early 1940s, the secretary of labor issued a series of orders banning homework in women's apparel—and related industries. In combination with the mothers' pension provisions of the new Social Security Act, the vision of the social feminists had triumphed: a minimum "living wage" for the father was secured; homework was abolished; women in unprecedented numbers were at home; motherhood was saved.

In the three decades that followed (roughly to 1970), the system held together. The "living wage" structure codified in the New Deal programs did work to temporarily strengthen the cultural association of women with motherhood and home. Keyed to the needs of a male breadwinner with wife and children, the minimum wage enjoyed regular increases. And, given its defining assumptions, the system produced, in relatively painless fashion, democratic, egalitarian results. Several studies, for example, have suggested that "earnings discrimination against women" (a negative way of looking at the "living wage") does make social classes and races more equal: the concentration of men in the better paying jobs benefits Blacks and poorer males, but not better paid, more skilled, or highly educated white males. Conversely, the breakdown of job and wage stratification by gender primarily benefits white males and already wealthy females.[25]

Yet about fifteen years ago, the whole system collapsed, and the New Deal synthesis has been transformed into a kind of parody of its once authentic profamily ambitions. Some writers pleased with the new arrangement have attempted to lay blame for the change on "the unstable economy of the 1970s and 1980s."[26] In fact, the collapse of the "living wage" order occurred because its central assumptions—men must be the primary breadwinners, women should focus on home and children, the family should be treated as the "living unit" of society—all fell into various levels of disrepute among key elite groups—the media, the clergy, the professoriate. In wake of this breakdown in the sexual division of labor, the logic of the New Deal system simply disappeared, and a host of new questions arose. Does the AFDC system still retain a moral justification following its transformation from a "child's endowment" for widows and orphans into a guaranteed state allowance for the mothers of illegitimate children? With a husband and a wife both expected to be in the labor force, does a minimum wage for one worker keyed to a "living standard" for a family of four still make sense? With some mothers struggling desperately to stay home with their small children in a "non-living-wage" economy, is the "profamily" ban on homework still justified?

Indeed, in wake of this change, current debates on homework and the minimum wage have essentially been reversed. Concerning the former, the 1970–80 period did witness rapid growth in the number of firms and homes again experimenting with homework. Alvin Toffler's much ballyhooed "electronic cottage" has become something of a reality. At least thirty-five corporations now have home-based work programs for their professional and clerical employees. The period also witnessed apparent growth in the number of persons working in more traditional homework trades: knitting, sewing, handcrafts. The U.S. Chamber of Commerce estimates that 10–12 million persons may now be laboring exclusively in their homes.[27]

The homework debate heated up in 1980–81 in the infamous "Vermont knitters" case. The broad facts are fairly well-known: the Labor Department, under the authority of the FLSA, closed in on a group of rural Vermont women knitting children's outerwear for sale by a young entrepreneur. Their fate soon became a *cause celebre* for defenders of the free market. After four years of hearings and rule making, the Reagan Administration rescinded the ban on homework in knitted outerwear.

More interesting was the shift in the policy debate. In a remarkable change, the opponents of homework on the liberal-left completely abandoned appeals to family, home, and motherhood. Rather, homework was now cast primarily as antifeminist! Sandra Albrecht of the University of Kansas argued that home-based work "might force" women to assume the responsibilities of child-rearing in addition to a job and so serve as "a throwback to the 1950s when women were isolated at home." Kathleen Christensen of the City University of New York fretted that homework "might lead to safeguarding the executive suite as the workplace for men. Today's working woman could find herself barefoot, pregnant, working at the word processor in the kitchen." Socialist writer Betty Berch labeled "homebound wives" as "involuntarily unemployed," trapped in a sexist society. Eileen Boris of Harvard University complained that "the Right's desire to confine women to the home is converging with capital's drive for a cheaper and more flexible labor system as part of a . . . dismantling of the welfare state." Homework, she said, denied women the ability to upgrade their skills and economic well-being, "further enmeshing them in relations of dependency" with men. The only answer, all agreed, was the standard feminist solution to all social problems: socialize the childbearing burden through state daycare.[28]

In contrast, defenders of homework avoided much of the rhetoric of classical liberalism, and wrapped themselves instead in the garb of family and motherhood. The knitters' employer, C.B. Vaughan, explained that "we work together to enable the mothers of small children to stay at home." The Iowa Senate passed a resolution supporting the knitters, arguing that "no rational legislative objective is served by effectively forcing mothers out of the home and into the factory." Vermont's secretary of labor asserted that Vermonters preferred mother care to daycare because they valued "the family as a building block in our society." As a Massachusetts homeowner explained during a hearing: "Children need a home life, and by being able to knit in my home I am able to stay home and nurture my own children [and] not rely on others for their child care. . . . Many of us do not want to be on welfare and food stamps and Medicaid. Some of us don't want full-time careers and 'latch-key' children. We just want to help out, but not at the expense of our children." As a feminist writer bitterly and correctly complained, "[d]espite their own merging of home and workplace, [the homeworkers] cling to that ideological dichotomy of family and market so central to the social relations of capitalism and patriarchy."[29]

Renewed debate over the minimum wage reflects a similar confusion, or loss of focus. There is little doubt that the real value of the minimum wage has eroded considerably in recent years. In 1969, an hourly minimum wage of $1.60 provided, for a person working full-time, an income at 110 percent of the poverty level (a kind of modern gauge of an American "living wage") for a family of three. By 1979, an hourly wage of $2.90 met but 100 percent of the poverty line. For 1987, the minimum wage of $3.35 fell below 75 percent of the poverty line for a family of three, and under 60 percent for the intact two-child home.

The situation has generated numerous calls for an increase in the minimum wage. Bills introduced since 1978, backed by the AFL-CIO, have sought to index the minimum wage at 60 percent of the average manufacturing wage. In 1987, Marian Wright Edelman, president of the Children's Defense Fund, called for an immediate upgrade of the minimum wage to $4.25 per hour, and its indexing to inflation. As she declared: "We must restore the concept of a family-supporting floor to wages."[30]

Yet on what basis? In setting minimum wages, the family question cannot be avoided.[31] If the two-earner family has become the norm (as most progressive voices incessantly argue), then the inflation-caused erosion of the minimum wage is an appropriate adjustment to that change. Sixty percent of the poverty level plus 60 percent of the poverty level equals 120 percent for a family of four, a respectable social minimum. If female-headed families are to be protected as one "lifestyle choice" among all the others (again, as virtually everyone on the liberal-left argues), then supplemental AFDC is the appropriate response to the newly individualized "living wage." Indeed, an increase in the minimum wage could today be justified only on a traditional, patriarchal family basis, and could only be seriously considered in this time if accompanied by a kind of reverse "affirmative action" with a comprehensive, New Deal-like push of women either back home or into lower-paying "women's" jobs. Needless to say, these are not items on the existing liberal agenda.

More bluntly put, the New Deal made moral sense and worked socially only when it was structured on the basis of the traditional family unit, only when it scrupulously set the home apart from the workplace as a "private" sphere, and only on the basis of clear distinctions between the genders. Ironically, it is those very principles that the purported heirs of Franklin Roosevelt betrayed fifteen to twenty years ago.

In recent policy debates, liberal philosopher-politicians such as Representative Patricia Schroeder and Senator Daniel Moynihan have delighted in berating social conservatives for living in the past, and for defending institutions such as the traditional family long after their time had passed. The same charges, it appears, can more correctly be directed at the tired, confused defenders of the decrepit, morally hollow New Deal kingdom.

A clearer vision is needed. First, we must recognize that the advocates of the minimum wage and the opponents of homework have currently and totally abandoned the profamily sentiments that once animated their causes. Indeed, while some residual rhetoric still remains, their real agenda has now been precisely reversed. The family must be devalued, they say, if justice is to reign. Children must be separated from their mothers, if equality is to be won. The welfare state must be used to promote, rather than discourage, gender equality. There must be social solutions to child care.[32]

Second, social conservatives—the defenders of family, of motherhood, of the differences between the sexes, of the private sphere of the family— have taken refuge in a political coalition sustained by, at best, an uneasy balance. Some of their erstwhile allies, schooled to distrust appeals to social order, cast suspicious glares at their strange public preferences for family life and children, rooted in metaphysical or natural law assumptions. Nonetheless, social conservatives and libertarians have made common cause in seeking to dismantle the archaic institutions of a vanished age that have now become oppressive. A "profamily" form of welfare state is a theoretical possibility, yet such a condition is probably impossible to achieve, given the real politics and the bureaucratic inertia of late-twentieth-century America. Relative to homework, this means that its defense has emerged as a conservative cause. With the collapse of a family-based minimum wage, homework has become a necessary option for women who love and care for their children. Similarly, the minimum wage concept has lost its moral bearings. Without a gender differential built into it either directly or culturally, the ideal becomes purely a matter of greed where negative, antigrowth incentives restrain enterprise and inhibit initiative without any compensating social gain.

Notes

1. Ruth Enalda Shawcross, *Industrial Homework: An Analysis of Homework Regulation, Here and Abroad* (New York: Industrial Affairs Publishing Co., 1939), pp. 1–15; and Alice Henry, *Women and the Labor Movement* (New York: George H. Doran Co., 1923), p. 183.

2. Eileen Boris, "Regulating Industrial Homework: The Triumph of 'Sacred Motherhood,'" *The Journal of American History* 71 (March 1985): 748.
3. See: Boris, pp. 725–55; Shallcross, pp. 25–31; and Amy Hewes, *Industrial Home Work* (Boston: Women's Educational and Industrial Union, 1915), p. vii.
4. Hewes, pp. viii–xiii; Boris, pp. 754–58; and Edward Cadbury and M. Cecil Matheson, *Women's Work and Wages* (London: T. Fisher, 1906), pp. 20–22.
5. Barbara Nachtrieb Armstrong, *Insuring the Essentials: Minimum Wage Plus Social Insurance—A Living Wage Program* (New York: The Macmillan Company, 1932), p. 19.
6. Leo XIII, *Rerum Novarum* (1891) in *Two Basic Social Encyclicals* (Washington, DC: The Catholic University of America Press, 1943), pp. 55–59; and Joseph Husslein, *Democratic Industry* (Boston: J. Kennedy & Sons, 1919), p. ix.
7. On Australian living wage experiments, see: George Anderson, *Fixation of Wages in Australia* (Melbourne, Australia: Melbourne University Press, 1929), pp. 188–217; E.M. Burns, *Wages and the State: A Comparative Study of the Problems of State Wage Regulation* (London: P.S. King & Son, 1926), pp. 299–331; and Armstrong, pp. 18, 40–42, 125–29.
8. Armstrong, pp. 137–38; and Burns, pp. 306–07.
9. Sidney Webb, *The Economic Theory of a Legal Minimum Wage* (New York: National Consumers' League, 1912), pp. 14–21.
10. Burns, p. 299.
11. On Ryan's influence, see: James Boyle, *The Minimum Wage and Syndicalism: An Independent Survey of the Two Latest Movements Affecting American Labor* (Cincinnati: Stewart & Kidd, 1913), pp. 14–15.
12. Irene Osgood Andrews, *Minimum Wage Legislation* (Albany, NY: J.B. Lyon, 1914), p. 9.
13. Harleigh Hartman, *Should the State Interfere in the Determination of Wage Rates?* (New York: National Industrial Conference Board, 1920), pp. 59–60.
14. "Position of the American Federation of Labor on the Legal Minimum Wage," Appendix III in Andrews, pp. 82–83.
15. Hartman, p. 65.
16. John O'Grady, *A Legal Minimum Wage* (Washington, DC: The Catholic University of America, 1915), p. 83.
17. See: Armstrong, pp. 69–79.
18. Hartman, p. 78; Felix Frankfurter, *District of Columbia Minimum Wage Cases: Brief for Appellees* (New York: Charles Young, [1921]), pp. 118, 120, 124, 134–35; and Felix Frankfurter, *Oregon Minimum Wage Cases: Brief for Defendants* (New York: National Consumers League, [1917]), pp. 114–37.
19. *Williams* v. *Evans* et al., 139 Minn. 321, 165 N.W. 495.
20. *Malette* v. *City of Spokane* (1914); quoted in Andrews, pp. 86–87.
21. *Adkins* v. *Children's Hospital* and *Adkins* v. *Willie A. Lyons*, Nos. 795 and 796, 261 U.S. 525 [October Term 1922].
22. Boris, pp. 749–51; Armstrong, pp. 146–48; Mary Anderson, *Women At Work: The Autobiography of Mary Anderson as told to Mary N. Winslow* (Minneapolis: University of Minnesota Press, 1951), p. 244; and Eileen Boris, *'Right to Work' as a 'Women's Right': The Debate Over the Vermont Knitters, 1980–85* (Madison, WI: Institute for Legal Studies, 1986), pp. 9, 33.
23. See: Burns, p. 362.
24. Shallcross, pp. 59–62.
25. See: Albert Syzmanski, "The Effect of Earnings Discrimination Against

Women on the Economic Position of Men," *Social Forces* 56 (Dec. 1977): 611–25; Jere R. Behrman, Robin C. Siddes, and Paul Taubman, "The Impact of Minimum Wages on the Distributions of Earnings for Major Race-Sex Groups: A Dynamic Analysis," *American Economic Review* 83 (Sept. 1983): 766–77.

26. Boris, "Regulating Industrial Homework," pp. 762–63.
27. Kathleen Christensen, "Women and Home-Based Work," *Social Policy* 15 (Winter 1985): 54–57; Joann Butler and Judith Getzels, *Home Occupation Ordinances* (Washington, DC: American Planning Association, 1985), pp. 1–3; and Tamara H. Wolfgram, "Working at Home: The Growth of Cottage Industry," *The Futurist* 18 (June 1984): 31–34.
28. From: Butler and Getzels, p. 4; Boris, '*Right to Work' as a 'Women's Right*,' pp. 2–3, 30–34; Christensen, pp. 56–57; and Bettina Berch, "The Resurrection of Out-Work," *Monthly Review: An Independent Socialist Magazine* 37 (Nov. 1985): 41.
29. From: Boris, '*Right to Work' as a 'Women's Right*,' pp. 14–18, 32.
30. See: *Minimum Wage Legislation* (Washington, DC: American Enterprise Institute for Public Policy Research, 1977), pp. 5–11; and Marian Wright Edelman, *Families in Peril: An Agenda for Social Change* (Cambridge, MA: Harvard University Press, 1987), p. 46.
31. This point is driven home persuasively in: Gerald Starr, *Minimum Wage Fixing* (Geneva: International Labour Office, 1981), p. 97.
32. For this compendium, see: Boris, '*Right to Work' as a 'Women's Right*' pp. 35–38.

Part V
THE COMMUNITY QUESTION

11

The Death of Peasant America

As the farm crisis reached its peak in 1985-86, the dwindling band of American farmers again dreamed radical dreams. The Washington apparatus was afflicted by that peculiar palsy that only "the farm question" seems able to induce. Republicans, in particular, were affected, for the modern agrarian crisis pits conservative against conservative. "It's almost a public utilitarian value to maintain the family farm," says Charles Grassley, senator from Iowa. "It's basic to the humanitarian responsibility of government." Yet the U.S. secretary of agriculture has reminded Americans "that the number of farms in this country has declined continuously for the last fifty years," that "we will lose more during the next four years," and the government cannot stop the change.

Indeed, the farmers have recently met an unusual level of hostility from some elements of the political right. Reflecting dominant assumptions in academia, University of California economist James Cothern scoffs at the old "agriculture fundamentalism," adding that the treatment of agriculture "as if it was a religious issue isn't going to work anymore."

Economist Robert Gillmore denies that farmers are more patriotic or virtuous than anyone else and concludes that Americans owe farmers nothing: "Government did not subsidize the income of blacksmiths when people started riding cars. Government expected blacksmiths to find other work. Farmers should be expected to do the same."

The conservative division on the farm issue is between those who give primacy to social results and those who give preference to economic results. The former view the family farm as the foundation of republican virtue and social order. Its preservation is mandatory, whatever the secondary economic consequences. The latter, in contrast, grant priority to the principles of limited government and the free market and willingly let the social consequences fall as they may.

The problem is that family farmers do embody a social character and an economic function which are indivisible and which do set them apart as a

157

unique socioeconomic class, one which the American political order has been loathe to recognize. Elsewhere in the world, the word "peasant" (stripped of its medieval connotations) is used to convey the linkage of family and farm; an inextricable mix of kinship, status, marriage, birth, death, occupation, property, profit, ancestors, and posterity. Even in contemporary Western Europe, according to one recent commentator, the "peasant economic system is built around the family and its perpetuation, the immobility of and lack of specialization of labor, a considerable interpenetration of economic and social roles."[1]

The "peasant" label, it is true, seems radically alien to America. We are more accustomed to thinking of the sturdy, independent yeoman farmer. Yet curiously, many Americans in this century have relied on the farming class to play the role of a peasantry, reinvigorating an otherwise failing urban system. Moreover, the shape of future rural policy depends on whether or not we consciously want to recreate a peasant class in America.

The ideological conflict behind the conservative split on the farm question needs to be clarified. The position held by economic conservatives is straightforward and consistent: food is the product of the agricultural sector and it must be produced efficiently through the mechanism of a free market. In his *Constitution of Liberty*, Austrian political economist Friedrich Hayek blasts "the irrationality and absurdity" of modern agrarian policy, "perhaps seen most easily in the United States." Restrictions on and subsidies to the "farmer or peasant," he admits, "may be the best way of preserving the kind of farming which we know and which many people (most of whom, one suspects, live in the city) wish to see preserved for sentimental reasons." Yet such an approach merely makes the agrarian class "more and more a sort of appendage to a national park, quaint folk to people the scenery." The farmer or peasant, Hayek explains, is prevented from making the mental and technological adjustments that would allow him to be self-supporting. Instead, he becomes a permanent ward of the state, a pensioner living off the rest of the population.

Hayek insists that the farmer or peasant, if he is to succeed, must progressively become a businessman. This would mean that many farmers and homesteads and the distinctly rural culture must vanish. Yet, Hayek concludes, we would be showing "more respect for the dignity of man if we allowed certain ways of life to disappear altogether instead of preserving them as specimens of a past age."[2]

The social conservative position on the agrarian question is a more complex amalgam of theoretical republicanism and the tradition of natural law. Its "bottom line" is very different: people, not grain or livestock, are the principal product of agriculture. Thomas Jefferson's well-known endorsement of a nation of yeoman farmers, each working his own piece of land, derived from this focus on human potential. "Cultivators of the earth," Jefferson wrote to John Jay, "are the most valuable citizens. They are the most vigorous, the most independent, the most virtuous, and they are tied to their country, and wedded to its liberty and interests, by the most lasting bonds."[3] When agrarian radicalism, or the Populist movement, first emerged in the United States during the 1890s, it stressed these same virtues of the producer and the family farm and gave emphasis to rural, grass-roots democracy.[4] As Theodore Roosevelt wrote in 1908: "No nation has ever achieved permanent greatness unless this greatness was based on the well-being of the great farming class, the men who live on the soil; for it is upon their welfare, material and moral, that the welfare of the nation ultimately rests."

Similar views were expressed by the so-called Southern Agrarians in the volumes *I'll Take My Stand* (1928) and *Who Owns America?* (1936). In the latter book, Andrew Lytle argued that farming, unlike any other occupation, should be considered as "a way of life," one deserving special attention from the state. Farmers, he reasoned, did not share "the spiritual sterilization, and often the physical, which comes from the modern technique of factory and city labor: the dissociation between work and the life of the senses." Small farms alone provided the widespread base for durable property ownership, which secured to citizens a stake in the commonwealth and so generated a concrete basis for patriotism. Lytle urged policies that would secure one-fourth or one-third of the American population on yeoman farms. He concluded: "Only when families are fixed in their habits, sure of their property, hopeful for the security of their children, jealous of liberties which they cherish, can the State keep the middle course between impotence and tyranny."[5]

Merging with this perception was the natural law doctrine, which viewed the rural family as the principal vehicle for social order and progress. One anchor for this tradition was Roman Catholicism, expressed in the United States through organizations such as the National Catholic Rural Life Conference. "Only that stability which is rooted in one's holding," Pope Pius XII explained in 1941, "makes of the family the vital and most perfect and fecund cell of society, joining up in a brilliant manner in progressive cohesion the present and future generations."[6] According to the Catholic perception, though, this function of rural life was threatened by the spread of urbanism and industrialism. "Today it can be said that the destiny of all mankind is at stake," Pius declared. "Will men be successful or not in balancing this influence [of industrial capitalism] in such a way as to preserve for the spiritual, social and economic life of the rural world its specific character?"[7]

The celebration and defense of rural peasant life became a significant political force in the Western world during the early decades of the twentieth century. The "Green International," composed of the new Peasant parties that had emerged in Europe after World War I, seemed to many observers in the 1920–30 period to represent the wave of the future. These parties, which briefly controlled governments in Bulgaria, Rumania, and Croatia, and which exerted strong influence in Poland, Sweden, Hungary, and Czechoslovakia, claimed that virtue sprang from the bond between man and the soil. Party theorists, such as the Bulgar Alexander Stamboliiski, stressed the atomization and alienation afflicting urban dwellers and contrasted this with the simplicity, humanity, natural community, democratic character, and regenerative power of the peasant population.[8]

In the United States, similar concern over the future of the farming class brought enhanced attention to the nature of the farm community. The discipline of rural sociology took shape during the same decade and rapidly accumulated evidence on the linkage between farm life and familism. Research showed, for example, that the presumed differential between urban and rural fertility was real. Even the mere presence of cities in a region had a negative impact on the fertility of rural population: the further a farm region was removed from a city, the higher the ratio of children to women.[9] Other studies proved that rural populations held "a considerable advantage over the urban with respect to reproductive efficiency by commencing effective fertility . . . a year to a year and a half earlier" and that the fertility differential between rural and urban populations had actually increased between 1910 and 1940.[10]

A report on the "human crop" born into a German Catholic parish in Kansas between 1891 and 1930 found a population characterized by "love of home and family life." Large families were common, those couples having completed their fertility cycle averaging 5.6 children. Divorces were few. Attachment to the land was also characteristic, half of those surveyed being farmers or farmers' wives. A similar study of fifty farm families in Illinois found them "happy and successful," their outstanding characteristics being "love of the land with its way of life, and the closeness with which they work, play, and plan together." Ninety percent of the wives gave as their goals the care and education of children, a happy home life, and owning the farm.[11] Studies of opinion polls between 1946 and 1950 also showed farmers to be more traditional and morally rigorous than city dwellers, with "strains of conservatism" showing up "most conspicuously in areas of personal and social concern."[12] In short, the mythologies of the American family farm—that it was child-centered, virtuous, and socially conservative—were all proving to be true.

Yet there were clear troubles in the countryside. The farming population, which still numbered 32.2 million in 1935 (25.3 percent of the total population), had fallen to 24.4 million ten years later, only 17.5 percent of all Americans. Some analysts suggested that "factory farms" would soon displace the remaining independent farmers. Those who looked to the family farm as the wellspring of American virtue and order recognized that such a deterioration in numbers could not long continue.

Among them was Harvard sociologist Carle Zimmerman. The family farm, he said, was a form of agriculture "in which home, community, business, land and domestic family are institutionalized into a living unit which seeks to perpetuate itself over many generations." As such, the family farm fed the larger culture with both people and virtue "as the uplands feed the streams and the streams in turn the broader rivers of life." He compared the decay of family farms in America and their replacement by "corporate, capitalistic and nonfamily forms of management in agriculture" to the rise of the latifundia of the late Roman empire. In both cases, such changes had created "a flight . . . of the independent and culturally stable people" from the countryside and heightened "individualistic and anti-social" attitudes.

The destruction of family farms, Zimmerman continued, was not a progressive development. Rather, it was "a menace" to national life. Americans, he explained, had not yet found a way to make urban family life "self-regenerating." The flow of good people from the country was essential, and Zimmerman urged creation of a farm policy that gave priority to family life.[13]

Others also emphasized the lateness of the hour, and saw massive governmental intervention as the only way to save the farming class. If present trends continued for another generation or two, sociologist Douglas Bowden said, "we won't have enough vitality left to generate any sort of solution." In order "to recreate and stabilize the all-important human values that can arise only out of an economically and socially stable farm life," he called for an end to "the evils of farm tenancy and absentee-landlordship." A National Agriculture Corporation should be created, one empowered to buy up agricultural land held by corporations and nonfarm owners and redistribute it to bonafide farmers, in exchange for long-term, low-interest, foreclosure-free notes.[14] At an international assembly on family farm policy convened in 1946 by the University of Chicago, analyst Horace Hamilton stressed the role of the family farm as a social institution. It produced "men of strong character and moral consciousness," the "kind of people and the kind of social values which make a society strong and secure," viable neighborhoods, good schools, and solid churches. By way of contrast, the farm-labor camps found on large-scale commercial farms spawned "poolrooms, honky-tonks, cheap picture shows . . . and flashy, back-slapping personalities." To save the family farm, he suggested taking the sale of farmland "entirely out of the free market," prohibitions on the breaking-up of family farms by inheritance into small, uneconomic units, and the vast expansion of public services in rural areas.[15]

One perceptive social scientist, though, saw a deeper dilemma rising from the conspicuous lack of class identity among American family farmers. Robert Rohwer argued that as a result farmers often opposed legislation specifically designed to promote family farming. The future of this mode of agriculture, he concluded, depended on the willingness of farmers to "value farming more than they prize competing values" such as free markets or urban living standards and to achieve a clearer understanding of "what family farming is and how it is tied up with other habits, practices, and values."[16]

One policy response to growing pressures to save the family farm was the Brannan Plan, presented to Congress in April 1949 by U.S. Secretary of Agriculture Charles Brannan. Among its provisions were a cap on price supports for basic commodities, designed to ensure that federal subsidies flowed primarily to family-sized farms, and the proposed introduction of direct payments to farmers raising livestock, fruit, and vegetables, amounting to the difference between the market and the "parity" price.[17] In tandem, these ideas would have delivered a guaranteed income to families on moderately sized farms.[18]

Yet for a complex set of reasons, including inconsistencies within the proposal, the Brannan Plan failed. With the election of Dwight Eisenhower in 1952, farm policy took a very different direction.

The central figure in this change was the new secretary of agriculture, Ezra Taft Benson. He shared common sentiments about the value of rural life. "The country is a good place to rear a family. It is a good place to teach the basic virtues that have helped to build the nation." Yet in the face of demographic change and economic pressures, he was also committed to the transformation of farming from a class-bound, peasant-like entity into a modern business enterprise. As he put it, "agriculture is not so much an important segment of our population as of our free enterprise system. It should be permitted to operate as such." Among those small businessmen who made a success of farming, the "family farm will endure and grow stronger." Yet there would also be a continued out-migration of marginal farmers who could make a better living outside agriculture. This was simply a part of the American system. As Benson concluded: "What right do we have in our generation to refuse to others any opportunity to earn what we proudly call an American standard of living?"[19]

One basic assumption behind this policy vision was embodied in Section 347a of the Smith-Lever Act (1955), which introduced the new concept of a "disadvantaged" farm, defined as "farm families on farms either too small or too unproductive or both." Federal policy was reshaped, often in subtle ways, to encourage the consolidation of these farms into larger units and the movement of the "surplus" agrarian population into other jobs. Benson is said to have put it bluntly: "Get big or get out." U.S. Department of Agriculture (USDA) officials confidently projected that the number of farmers could drop to only 500,000 and still meet the food and fiber needs for domestic and foreign markets. Programs were introduced to help small farmers find better jobs elsewhere and to assist the large numbers of farm youth "for whom there is simply no room in commercial agriculture" to prepare for nonfarm occupations.[20]

A second foundation to this policy vision was Benson's belief that the farm community was no longer needed as a wellspring of virtue. He pointed to accelerating dispersal of city people into suburban and rural areas. In Michigan, Benson explained, nonfarm people living outside towns and cities now actually outnumbered farmers. Many farmers, moreover, held part-time jobs in industry. These "diversified income" rural areas were rapidly replacing farm regions. Such trends suggested that the beloved rural values might survive even when divorced from the farm. What the United States needed, he concluded, was a comprehensive "rural policy," one independent of farm policy and designed to encourage and institutionalize this trend.[21]

Indeed, there was a growing body of sociological evidence that seemed to support such a belief and program. The hottest subjects in rural sociology circles by 1955 were the burgeoning suburbs, where all the "social laws" learned during the interwar years were apparently being broken. In 1953, researchers at the University of Texas enthusiastically described the emergence of "a new family form" in "the urban fringe," one which seemed "able to maintain sufficient fertility and integration to satisfy the [Carle] Zimmerman requisites and yet function adequately in the urban community." Young couples were pouring out of the cities [and, as was realized only later, off the farms] into the suburbs, where the birth and marriage rates were soaring, the decrease in the age of marriage accelerating, and the historic functions of the family seemingly strengthened. Another study found that 83 percent of the new suburbanites were intensely and intentionally "familistic," committed to a primary investment in family life, to marriage at a young age, to a short childless time-span after marriage, and to building communities composed of "people like ourselves." Following the relatively barren years of the Great Depression, the large-family system seemed to have returned to America.[22]

During the late 1940s, the marriage rate in "the urban fringe" was higher than in both central cities and farm areas. Then in 1949, in an unprecedented development, the number of children under five years of age per

1,000 women proved to be higher in the "rural nonfarm" [largely subur-
ban] area than in both urban and "rural farm" areas. Moreover, the percentage distribution of households with four or more persons present was
also highest in the suburbs. The farm was dethroned as the wellspring of
family virtue, solid marriages, and children. The middle-class ethos of the
postwar suburb had effected an extraordinary reconciliation between family values and the demands of modern urban life. As two demographers
noted, this totally unexpected reorientation of cultural values in America
toward the family had occurred "despite the concurrent presence of three
trends thought to be clearly inimical to fertility, namely, the rise in educational attainment, the large-scale entry of married women into the labor
force, and the increase in urbanization."[23]

Postwar America had successfully defied the laws of sociology. It was easy
to conclude that the farming class could now be relieved of its social and
moral burdens and quietly laid to rest.

By the early 1960s, in fact, rural sociologists began to exhibit a curious
new hostility toward their objects of study. Lee Burchinal, variously affiliated with the USDA and the U.S. Department of Health, Education and
Welfare, told a farm audience that the old rural family system was being
displaced. Giving a disturbing twist to the new urban family model, he
described an "emerging family system" which had its "modal representation among the college educated, professionally employed urban couples."
This system, he said, involved a new commitment to full equality between
men and women, a decline in the division of labor between the sexes
(particularly when dictated by the "dead hand" of rural culture), a more
democratic, "person-centered" view of children, increases in sexual experimentation and nonmarital sexual contacts, and more divorce based on a
new respect for "interpersonal relationships" rather than on the "functional economic interdependence and the social and legal sanctions" which
held traditional families together. Such views, he added, were also rapidly
spreading to rural and farm communities. Higher levels of education, a
rising standard of life in rural areas, and the specialization and professionalization of farm occupational roles were the forces accelerating this diffu-
sion process. The farm family, in consequence, increasingly took its cues
from urban culture, and evidenced a declining commitment to traditional
familism.

Burchinal saw this as generally positive. New sociological evidence, he
indicated, showed that farm living produced unhappy women and lower
levels of marital and personal satisfaction. The teenage boys choosing to
stay on the farm, moreover, were not model citizens, tending instead to be
"localistic" and brute-strength orientated with little interest in the "development of social relations." Those farm boys choosing not to farm,

moreover, had "greater emotional stability, greater independence and self-sufficiency, and a greater interest in people." Above all, Burchinal implied, the spread of new norms to the country offered traditional folk a chance to learn real love. He favorably quoted two other researchers:

> Love is an artistic creation which reaches its widest perfection in the sophisticated upper reaches of American society. It is a boon which a more leisurely, better-educated society has conferred upon its members. The progressive urbanization, acculturation, and education of the oncoming generation suggests there is likely to be correspondingly more expression of love in the future.[24]

Lauren Soth, editorial page editor of the *Des Moines Register*, joined in the debunking of rural America. The migration of farm people cityward, he said, was solid evidence "that the joys of the bucolic life will not offset much difference in hard cash." Farmers wanted to live more like their city cousins, "proof that they do not think life in the country is its own reward." Moreover, Soth said, farmers should no longer be viewed as the bulwark of democracy. Indeed, there was "some evidence" suggesting that farm people are "less concerned" than other groups about "the basic liberties of our constitutional system." As an example, he pointed to opinion polls during "the McCarthy spasm of infringements on individual freedom" which showed farmers to be "less opposed" to McCarthyism than other groups. Adding it all together, Soth reached the same conclusion as other agricultural professionals: "The great adjustment needed in agriculture still is to reduce the number of farmers."[25]

Reflecting these accumulating pressures, the 1950s proved to be the crucial decade in the transformation of American farming. Two-mule farms, still to be found in many areas of the South in 1950, were almost completely displaced ten years later by a highly capitalized form of operation. The number of farms declined from 5,648,000 at the start of the decade to 3,960,000 by 1960. The farm population itself had fallen from 23 million to 15.6 million, less than 8 percent of the nation's total. Remaining farm families also seemed to lose many of their distinctive qualities. As two rural sociologists put it in 1964: "Rural-urban differences in values are decreasing as America moves in the direction of a mass society."[26]

The last gasp of rural America as a viable culture-shaping entity came shortly after 1960. Speaking at Iowa State University, Roman Catholic Auxiliary Bishop George Speltz of Winona, Minnesota, still intoned the old verities, but they represented little more than a eulogy for a dying tradition. Through their distinctive character, he said, a rural people exercised "a profound influence on the biological and intellectual, spiritual and religious development of humanity." The progressive enlargement of farms and concentration of farm ownership, however, represented a profound danger to democratic land control and "to the rural family rooted in such ownership." It was incumbent on the state, Bishop Speltz said, to redress "the obvious imbalances between agriculture and the other sectors of the economy," for the values of reverence for the soil, love of God, love of country, and willing acceptance of honest toil could not be maintained for long on any basis other than agriculture. Yet he pointed to the great ambiguity in norms, goals, and values existing in modern America, and was not optimistic. In the process of change, Speltz said, "I think that important spiritual values will be lost to our nation."[27]

In the same period, the farming community vanished as a politically relevant defender of virtue. Pressure had been growing for a decade to end the disproportionate representation of the rural population in state legislatures, usually achieved by apportioning one or both legislative chambers by county or area rather than by number of people. As Senator John F. Kennedy had put it, cities could not get what they needed because "the urban majority is politically a minority, and the rural minority dominates the polls." In 1962, the U.S. Supreme Court held in *Baker* v. *Carr* that state legislative apportionment was subject to constitutional review. A year later, the Court struck down Georgia's county unit system that had given rural areas disproportionate influence in state elections. The Court delivered the coup de grace in 1964 with sweeping opinions ruling that congressional districts and both houses of the state legislatures must be apportioned according to population, not geographic area.

Farmers were struck dumb. Their advocates complained that the rulings had tossed into the ash can "one of the basic, time-honored cornerstones of our system of American representative government." Yet when a constitutional amendment proved to be a practical impossibility, there was nothing to be done. Freed from the rural yoke, state legislatures in the farm states and South began implementing a new set of values. They tossed out the Blue Laws, lifted restrictions on alcohol sales, loosened divorce and sodomy statutes, and purged other such "anachronisms." Rural America gasped, and died.

Gone, for better or worse, were the last political barriers raised against modernity and secularity by the forces of rural tradition. Gone too, in any instrumental sense, was a vision of the farm community as the reservoir of familism and virtue, the wellspring of children. Indeed, the farmer's status may have been precisely reversed. In a richly symbolic act, one response of the federal government to the farm problem of the 1982–87 period has been the provision of a grant to the state of Iowa for free vasectomies for troubled rural men. "Our argument [in seeking the grant]," said one state health official, "was that this was a particularly good idea in Iowa because of the high unemployment rate and the problems of farmers."[28] Admittedly, the welfare-state logic here is impeccable: Still too many farmers? Sterilize them!

As it turned out, though, this purposeful decomposition of rural America was based on a miscalculation. The style of familism born in the suburbs between 1945 and 1960, while real, turned out to be fragile. Under a new wave of ideological challenge, it crumbled. Those sociological laws once transcended by the suburbanites came howling back with a vengeance after 1965. Resurgent concern about "overpopulation," the large-scale entry of married women into the labor force, and the soaring divorce rate showed marriages predicated on interpersonal relations and sophisticated love to be prone to disruption. Pornography and abortion became common features on the national landscape.

Retrospectively, it also appears likely that "the new familism" of the suburbs was not entirely the result of a new family form created by indigenous urban dwellers, but rather the partial consequence of the migration of farm people to the suburbs and cities. This flow had begun in 1941, accelerated quickly, and lasted through the early 1960s. An estimated 15 million persons, a disproportionate number of them young adults, made the journey. It represented the last great contribution of human capital by America's farms to America's cities.

Even so, perhaps we can call on the farmers once again to serve as our peasant class, to be our reservoir of virtue, our source of good people, our easy salvation from our follies.

Surprisingly, despite recurrent troubles, the farming community continues to exhibit the traditional virtues of home and family. In 1983, for example, farm women ages 18 to 34 continued to be more fertile than nonfarm women, averaging 2.45 children per woman compared to 2.07 in the cities. While 13.3 percent of urban women ages 35 to 44 were currently divorced, only 2.1 percent of farm women were so situated. Ninety-three percent of farm children lived with two parents, compared to 73.7 percent of city children. Farm folks do remain—on average—morally better people.

Yet this time, they will not be able to bail us out, for the number of farm families, particularly younger families, is too low. The farm population now numbers 5,787,000 persons, only 2.5 percent of the population. Even those remaining are disproportionately old. Among the nonfarm population in 1983, 9 percent were ages 25 to 29; on the farm, only 5.6 percent were. Farm males, ages 55 to 64, represent 3.6 percent of the total U.S. male population in their age bracket; yet those between the ages 25 to 34 are a mere 1.58 percent of theirs. While farm families with children still do exhibit higher fertility, there are disproportionately fewer of them in the country than in the city: 42.5 percent compared to 48.9 percent.

In short, America's farms increasingly resemble old-age homes. We have exhausted their human capital. Significantly, farm numbers are so few that the dramatically lower divorce rate on the farm, when factored in with the urban rate, does not affect the overall national figure.[29]

The raw reality is that our nation's family farmers can no longer serve as our peasant class, reinvigorating an otherwise troubled social order and providing a stream of surplus youth for factories and offices. Put simply, the numbers are no longer there. A different policy course taken during the Truman or early Eisenhower years might have produced different results. Or, given the reluctance of American farmers to live up to "class" expectations, perhaps not. In any case, America's peasant "class" as a culture-shaping, family-sustained entity is now gone.

Notes

1. S.H. Franklin, *The European Peasantry: The Final Phase* (London: Methuen, 1969), pp. 5–6, 15.
2. Friedrich Hayek, *The Constitution of Liberty* (Chicago: University of Chicago Press, 1960), pp. 362–64.
3. Letter, Jefferson to Jay, August 23, 1785; in *The Best Letters of Thomas Jefferson*, ed. J.G. de Roulhac Hamilton (Boston and New York: Houghton Mifflin, 1926), p. 15.
4. Margaret Canovan, *Populism* (New York and London: Harcourt, Brace, Jovanovich, 1981), pp. 128–29.
5. Herbert Agar and Allen Tate, *Who Owns America?: A New Declaration of Independence* (New York: Houghton Mifflin, 1936), pp. 237–50. For a more recent expression of this tradition, see Hamilton Horton, Jr., "The Enduring Soil," in *Why The South Will Survive, By Fifteen Southerners* (Athens: The University of Georgia Press, 1981), pp. 57–67.
6. Pius XII, "La Solennita della Pentecoste, June 1, 1941," in *Principles for Peace*, ed. H.C. Koenig (Washington, DC: National Catholic Welfare Conference, 1943), n. 1692.
7. Pius XII, "Problems of Rural Life [Rome, 1951]," in *Christianity and the Land* (Des Moines, IA: National Catholic Rural Life Conference, 1951).
8. See: George D. Jackson, Jr., "Peasant Political Movements in Eastern Europe," in *Rural Protest: Peasant Movements and Social Change*, ed. Henry A. Landsberger (New York: Macmillan, 1974), pp. 259–315; and Canovan, pp. 112–26.
9. Edmund deS. Brunner and J.H. Kolb, *Rural Social Trends* (New York: McGraw-Hill, 1933), pp. 114–15.
10. Otis Dudley Duncan, "Rural-Urban Variations in the Age of Parents At the Birth of the First Child," *Rural Sociology* 8 (March 1943): 62–67; and T.J. Woofter, Jr., "Trends in Rural and Urban Fertility Rates," *Rural Sociology* 13 (March 1948): 3–9.
11. Gilbert Wolters, "The Human Crop of a Rural Catholic Parish," *Rural Sociology* 21 (Sept. 1956): 297–98; Cleo Fitzsimmons and Nellie L. Perkins, "Patterns of Family Relationships in Fifty Farm Families," *Rural Sociology* 12 (Sept. 1947): 300–03.
12. Howard W. Beers, "Rural-Urban Differences: Some Evidence from Public Opinion Polls," *Rural Sociology* 18 (March 1953): 11.

13. Carle C. Zimmerman, "The Family Farm," *Rural Sociology* 15 (Sept. 1950): 211–21.
14. Douglas Bowden, "The Good American Earth," *Rural Sociology* 4 (March 1939): 78–87.
15. Horace Hamilton, "Social Implications of the Family Farmer," in *Family Farm Policy: Proceedings of a Conference on Family Farm Policy*, ed. J. Ackerman and M. Harris (Chicago: University of Chicago Press, 1946): 110–13.
16. Robert A. Rohwer, "Family Farming as a Value," *Rural Sociology* 16 (December 1951): 330–39.
17. *Parity* is the farm income level derived from farm prices having the same purchasing power, per unit of product, as that enjoyed during the five relatively prosperous years immediately preceding the outbreak of World War I.
18. Reo M. Christenson, *The Brannan Plan: Farm Politics and Policy* (Ann Arbor: The University of Michigan Press, 1959).
19. Ezra Taft Benson, *Freedom to Farm* (Garden City, NY: Doubleday, 1960), pp. 109, 198–200.
20. See: Gilbert Fite, *American Farmers: The New Minority* (Bloomington: Indiana University Press, 1981), pp. 122–23, 136; Benson, p. 201.
21. Benson, pp. 200–201, 230–32.
22. E. Gartly Jaco and Ivan Belknap, "Is a New Family Form Emerging in the Urban Fringe?" *American Sociological Review* 18 (October 1953): 551–57; Wendell Bell, "Familism and Suburbanization: One Test of the Social Choice Hypothesis," *Rural Sociology* 21 (Sept.-Dec. 1956): 276–83.
23. Donald J. Bogue and Calvin L. Beale, "Recent Population Trends in the United States and Their Causes," in *Our Changing Rural Society: Perspectives and Trends*, ed. James H. Copp (Ames, IA: Iowa State University Press, 1964), p. 108.
24. Lee G. Burchinal, "The Rural Family of the Future," in Copp, pp. 160–62, 168–79, 184–89.
25. Lauren Soth, *Farm Trouble* (Princeton, NJ: Princeton University Press, 1957), pp. 22–28.
26. Olaf F. Larson and Everett M. Rogers, "Rural Society in Transition: The American Setting," in Copp, p. 53.
27. George H. Speltz, "Theology of Rural Life: A Catholic Perspective," in *Farm Goals in Conflict: Family Farm, Income, Freedom, Security* (Ames, IA: Iowa State University Press, 1963), pp. 35–49.
28. "Grant Gives Iowa Aid for Vasectomies," *Des Moines Register* (February 28, 1985): 1A.
29. U.S. Department of Commerce, Bureau of the Census, *Farm Population of the United States: 1983*, Series P-27, No. 57 (November 1984): 1–13; and *1980 Census of the Population. Volume 1, Chapter C: General Social and Economic Characteristics. Part 1 (United States) Summary* (PC 80-1-C1) (December 1983): Table 100, pp. 1–69.

12

The Curious Triumph of the Suburbs

The suburban revolution of the last forty years forms the physical context for the contemporary cultural struggle over the family. Its history bears examination.

In 1945–46, as 10 million servicemen returned home, the nation faced an unprecedented housing crisis. Home construction had virtually stopped during the Great Depression and was again postponed by World War II. The National Housing Agency estimated in late 1945 that the country needed 5 million new units immediately and another 7.5 million by 1955.

Fortunately, the federal government was able to act positively, offering one of the few examples of successful modern social policy. The Federal Housing Administration (FHA), created in 1934 but dormant during the war years, offered a program for insuring long-term mortgage loans at affordable interest rates. In 1939, the tax deduction for mortgage interest was introduced. The Veterans Administration mortgage-guarantee program, created in 1944, enabled veterans to borrow the entire value of a house without down payment. In 1947, Congress loosened the rent, wage, and price controls still stifling the real estate and construction industries. These measures were crowned by the Housing Act of 1949, which greatly increased opportunities for home ownership. With the family in mind, President Harry Truman explained the program's rationale: "Children and dogs are as necessary to the welfare of this country as is Wall Street and the railroads."[1] The result was a social revolution: the suburbanization of America. For the first time in world history the large majority of a nation's citizens were given the opportunity to own their own homes.

Suburbs, of course, were nothing new. The suburban ideal was actually born in late-eighteenth-century England, the product of market forces in union with middle-class commitments to religion, family, and tradition. The first suburb was probably the village of Clapham in Surrey, south of the Thames. In the years after 1790, a growing stream of pious and prosperous merchants removed their families from the moral and environmen-

171

tal pollutions of London. They looked to the village on the periphery (supplemented by the daily commute to The City) as the place where urban life could be reconciled with superior rural values. They called on the use of landscaping (spacious lawns, irregular street patterns, and carefully planted shrubs) and eclectic housing design to build their small Christian commonwealth. In Clapham, the evangelical leader and antislavery advocate William Wilberforce served as the spiritual force behind this new mode of urban living. Their village would represent a community of shared values, above all, the values of Christian duty, spontaneous family affection, and the love and nurturing of children. Family worship, "the united family kneeling in prayer," and the library, the prototype "family room," would be the suburban substitutes for the balls, theaters, and coffee houses of London.[2]

The women of Clapham turned with heightened enthusiasm to domestic tasks. Viewing their mission as the elevation of moral and religious life as the basis for renewal of civilization, the women of Clapham saw their distinct labors as decidedly superior to the mean tasks of their husbands. Typical was Marianne Thornton, wife of merchant Henry Thornton. A fervent evangelical before her marriage at the age of twenty-one, she turned her considerable energies to the construction of a Christian family. She bore nine children. Like other Clapham wives, she rejected the custom of aristocrats and the old London merchant elite of sending children to a wet nurse. She breast fed all of them herself, and devoted her life to raising and educating her offspring to the highest religious standards.[3]

Architect John Nash, in his 1820 design for the Park Village community in London, solved the final design problems confronting the suburban structure. With middle-class sentiments in mind, he sought a synthesis of a landscaped park and picturesque village. The design of each house, he believed, should establish an essential contrast between city and suburb, and incorporate within the structure itself the emotions of family life. Nash drew, in particular, on a mixture of Gothic, Romanesque, and "Old English Cottage" motifs that would reflect both an attachment to the historical landscape, and the virtues of stability, simplicity, and domesticity. Through his work, historian Robert Fishman has shown, suburbia became a commodity that could be endlessly reproduced and replanted in new locales.

This mode of living soon found its advocates in America. Foremost among them was Catharine Beecher, author of *Treatise on Domestic Economy*, published in 1841. With a vigor worthy of the women of Clapham, Beecher carved out a distinctive separate sphere for women, rooted in the home, that would salvage Christian virtue. Women called to build homes were "agents in accomplishing the greatest work that was ever committed to human responsibility. It is the building of a glorious temple, whose base shall be coextensive with the bounds of the earth." In each dwelling, the woman must become a self-sacrificing laborer, "necessarily the guardian of the nursery, the companion of childhood, and the constant model of imitation." As wives and mothers sank or rose in the scale of domestic virtue, so would husbands and sons, and, ultimately, the nation as a whole.[4]

Architect Andrew Jackson Downing served as the American counterpart to John Nash. The author of *Cottage Residences* (1842), Downing advanced the suburban synthesis of virtue and modernity born in evangelical England. He saw the ideal American house as an irregular cottage of the old English style, with heavy infusions of Gothic detail. The feelings inspired by architecture were what mattered, the ability to make "the place dearest to our hearts a sunny spot where social sympathies take shelter securely under the shadowy eaves, or glow and entwine trustfully with the tall trees or wreathed vines that cluster around, as if striving to shut out whatever bitterness or strife may be found in the open highways of the world."[5]

Suburbs of this sort began emerging in America after 1840. In Cambridge and other outlying areas of Boston, concern for the protection of the household grew in importance. John Ford, editor of the *Cambridge Chronicle*, lectured his readers on the importance of "sociability" in the home, and advocated standard plans for houses that were designed for the convenience of the homemaker. By 1857, Ford and other defenders of suburbia were extending the concept of domesticity beyond the house, and attaching it to whole neighborhoods: a domestic setting for the home was just as important as domesticity within the home. Developments that would undermine the residential middle-class nature of Cambridge or pull too many activities downtown must be avoided. The town's citizens, he wrote, already had business interests in Boston. If they also moved their "religious, educational, moral, and social interests" there, then "Cambridge cannot be a home, according to the New England idea of home."[6]

Architect Frederick Law Olmstead, designer of the new Chicago suburb of Riverside, Illinois in 1868, gave the most dramatic form to the suburban ideal. "I never lose an opportunity," he wrote to a colleague, to urge the "ruralizing of all our urban population and the urbanizing of our rustic population." "Savage conditions," he said, prevailed both "in the dense poor quarters of our great cities and manufacturing firms," as well as in the farm districts, "especially the sterile parts of the great West." In contrast, the suburbs combined the finest aspects of town and country and so marked "the best application of the arts of civilization to which mankind has yet obtained."[7]

By the 1920–30 period, transportation advances had made suburban living viable for significant and ever-growing numbers of Americans. Religious devotion surfaced less often as the motivating factor for architects and developers. Nonetheless, ideology of a sort remained fundamental to the suburban dream. Housing reformers such as Lawrence Veiller and John Nolan stressed the socially conservative values engendered by home ownership among blue-collar workers. Others urged an implicit American social contract between capital and labor, founded on the ideal of the family. As one business sloganeer from the 1920s put it: "After work, the happy home."

Yet the real "suburban revolution" began only after the Second World War. Lasting three decades, it fundamentally altered the American geographic and social landscapes. Between 1950 and 1970, the population of suburbia doubled from 36 to 72 million. Of the 13 million new homes built in the decade after 1948, 11 million were in the suburbs. Home ownership rose 50 percent during 1940–49, another 50 percent in the following decade, and still another 50 percent during 1960–69. By 1980, over 75 percent of American families—including blue-collar families—owned their own homes, and most of the latter were suburban homes. Such numbers were unprecedented and stand among the most extraordinary achievements of the modern American nation.

This post–1945 triumph of suburbia seemed, to observers, to represent a joint victory for "family" and "national" sentiments, reflected in the "intensity of sentiment about 'the American home.'" Talcott Parsons pointed to the extraordinary growth in the number of single-family dwellings and the climbing birthrate as signs of the "upgrading" of the American family.[8] Economic historian Walt Rostow looked to the suburbs, and saw embodied there a nation able and ready to carry the burdens of world responsibility and Cold War. He celebrated the fact that the "average American" was increasingly likely to live in a suburb and hold a white-collar job. There was, he continued, "a marked increase in the social homogeneity of the American population." While the pressures of the Cold War had imparted "a strand of garrison life to the society as a whole," they had also "converged with many of the trends built into our domestic dynamics," including suburbanization, bureaucratization, and the development and application of the social sciences. Under the strain of world leadership, Rostow insisted, suburbanizing Americans had "retained the old link between nationhood and ideal values."[9]

Stereotypical of the suburban housing boom were the enormous Levittown developments in New York, New Jersey, and elsewhere: 6,000-house projects built for the new market. Bill Levitt, president of Levitt & Sons, described himself as typical of the "new type" American businessman, who believed "they have a responsibility to their country as well as to their shareholders." The expanding suburbs, he added with Jeffersonian flair, formed the backbone of the nation: "No man who owns his own house and lot can be a communist. He has too much to do."[10]

And indeed, the social consequences of the suburban revolution were great. "Child centered" from their theoretical origin, the architecture of the new postwar communities gave special attention to family life and the needs of children: "family rooms," numerous bedrooms, and patios as "outdoor living rooms" became staples of the new style. Moreover, there were children in abundance. As one writer has put it: "The suburbs were conceived for the baby boom—and vice versa."[11] With housing opportunities opening up, marriages came earlier and fertility soared, particularly among the middle class. From 1940 until 1957, the fertility rate for women aged 20–24 almost doubled, while the fraction of women becoming mothers by age 25 climbed from one-half to three-quarters. Between 1948 and 1958, the number of families with two or more children at home rose 46 percent. In 1940, there were fewer than 11 million Americans under the age of five. Twenty years later, there were 20 million. The annual rate of U.S. population growth approached two percent, a figure previously considered by experts to be "impossible" in a modern nation.

Social commentators turned their attention to this altogether new development. Some liked what they saw. Editor Frederick Lewis Allen found the suburbs to be "wholly astonishing places," "gregarious communities" built for "an intensely domestic generation," the embodiment of a dream that "looks westward to California."[12] Max Lerner saw the suburbanites as symbols of America "resettling itself," heirs to the frontier tradition of founding new communities. They represented "a democracy of a kind," much more inclusive than the old "residential" and "restricted" neighborhoods of the cities and the earlier suburbs. Moreover, they were integrative, pulling together people of different classes, faiths, and ethnic backgrounds "to share . . . the experience of building a new community."[13]

In his classic work *The Levittowners*, sociologist Herbert Gans also celebrated the suburban environment. He found that "most new suburbanites are pleased with the community that develops." Levittown permitted its residents "to be what they want to be—to center their lives around the home and the family, to be among neighbors whom they can trust, to find friends, to share leisure hours and . . . to be of service to others." By any yardstick, he maintained, Levittowners treated their neighbors "more ethically and more democratically than did their parents and grandparents." Indeed, Gans concluded, the Levittowners differed little from the early-nineteenth-century Americans described by Alexis de Tocqueville, particularly in their devotion to religiously inspired morality, Franklinesque individualism, children, the equality of men and women, sexual modesty, and voluntary associations. The goal for the future, he insisted, must be to extend "the benefits of suburban life" to more people, particularly minorities and the less affluent.[14]

But the suburbs also generated powerful enemies. At first, they were confined to those upper-middle-class, Manhattan-based cosmopolitans who sneered at the antiurban values of the lower-middle and working classes. For *Harper's* editor Eric Larrabee, the uniformity of Levittown stirred "uneasy memories;" it was "potentially a monster."[15] Writing in *The New York Times Magazine*, Sidonie Gruenberg exclaimed: "Mass produced, standardized housing breeds standardized individuals, too—especially among youngsters."[16] John Keats' 1957 novel, *The Crack In The Picture Window*, ridiculed the suburban life of John and Mary Drone. In *The Split Level Trap*, psychologist Richard Gordon recognized the suburbs as the crucible of modern America, yet focused on the emotional problems found there, asking "where and why this disturbed modern community—this archetype of the modern world, this Disturbia—has gone wrong."[17]

But the true madness soon lay elsewhere. As part of the irrational wave of intellectual self-immolation that swept across America during the 1960s, the indictment against the suburbs grew. An extraordinary national achievement was recast as a nightmare.

First came the New Left. Writing in *The Nation*, Eve Merriam blamed the existence of "housewives" in their single-family homes on capitalism, a system that could not supply enough real jobs to go around and needed to fix women in the role of full-time consumers. She demanded an "examination and overhaul of our entire family structure" and of "the whole social structure and economic system it is hitched to."[18] Then came the environmentalists, who decried the "suburban sprawl" based on "energy profligacy" and the consumption of "non-renewable resources" brutally extracted from "often fragile ecosystems."

Finally, came the feminists. Betty Friedan showed the way in *The Feminine Mystique*, finding women's problems to be particularly endemic to suburbs, "those ugly and endless sprawls which are becoming a national problem."[19] Over the next two decades, the suburb as "enemy of woman" theme continued to gain momentum, as numerous books expanded this critique of American housing patterns and demanded radical change.[20] Representative is architect and university professor Delores Hayden's *Redesigning The American Dream*.

According to the author, the contemporary "housing crisis" facing Americans is really a crisis of gender. The 54 million single-family dwellings in the United States, she maintains, reflect social assumptions that "the most fanatical Victorian moralists only dreamed about," where maxims about "true womanhood and manly dominance" are reinforced by spatial design. Dream houses in suburbia, she continues, are places where "white male workers" act out "the fantasies of proprietorship, authority, and consumption" while "separating women," binding them to "the sacred rites of cooking and cleaning," and so "lowering an individual woman's status." She adds that today's suburbanites also "lack a sense of the world context of their housing problems," seen in their wasteful use of limited resources. Similarly, condominiums are blasted because they have too many cars and swimming pools and not enough daycare centers and "other services that are connected to the basic needs of life." Even in the face of the huge increase in the number of working women, she charges, neurotic Americans cling to their "sacred huts" fenced with white pickets because they remain city people trying to be farmers. Yet, Hayden adds, this nostalgic attachment to primeval housing types "is not a fully conscious, politically informed, aesthetic choice."[21]

Quite prepared to remedy that deficiency, Hayden advances "a complex social program and cultural agenda" designed to aid "new family forms" like single-parent families, working women's families, and gay families. Housing policy and architects must "repudiate the Victorian gender stereotypes" glorified in the post-1945 suburban boom, she argues, and instead seek to build the "non-sexist" city. She grows ecstatic over scattered experiments in woman-oriented housing: the Swedish high rise designed in 1935 by feminist Alva Myrdal and architect Sven Markelius, offering communal dining, a collective nursery, and in-house daycare; Vanport City, the "Kaiserville" built in Oregon in 1943 to accommodate husbandless women working in wartime construction; and Baldwin Hills Village in California, designed in the early 1940s with integrated daycare centers, community kitchens, and common laundries. These, Hayden argues, must be the models for the future.

Opposing "simplistic corporate solutions" to the housing crisis, Hayden calls for a "new coalition" of feminists, environmentalists, architects, and planners "to challenge the real estate lobby," to restructure the existing housing stock along more communal lines, to oppose most new construction of "sacred hut" housing, and to guide society into living patterns meeting the "real needs" of American "women and men." Racial integration is "not enough," nor is "a national daycare policy." Rather, the "quality" of the whole "white, male homeowner culture" found in the suburbs must be examined by activists who truly understand its full implications. A "general strike" by women, she implies, may even be necessary to pull down the wizened cultural edifice resting on the myth of the "sacred hut."[22]

Is there any truth in this analysis? Some, but not much. Of course, it is obviously true that more married women than ever before are working outside the home, that many use daycare centers, and that American housing patterns are based on certain deeply ingrained social assumptions about family life. But there is absolutely no evidence suggesting that significant numbers of Americans—women or men—are wearying of suburban life or demanding new forms of collectivized housing. Indeed, the evidence all points in the opposite direction. For example, during 1970–79—the decade that began with "counterculture" communes and ended with inner-city "gentrification"—the suburbs continued to grow far more rapidly than these exotic experiments. The suburbs accounted for a hefty 44.15 percent of the U.S. population in 1980, up from 40 percent a decade before. This fact can also be contrasted with Hayden's pathetically short list of women-oriented housing experiments. Even these, it appears, have no staying power, usually failing after several years. The "Myrdal-Markelius" house, for example, eventually shut down its collective dining area for underuse and inefficiency, and had to open its daycare center to outsiders to stay in business as residents aged or turned to "child free" lifestyles; the "Nina West" homes built in Great Britain for unwed mothers have succeeded only as temporary housing; Vanport City lies in the dust; California's Baldwin Hills Village degenerated into a haven for "problem families" and was eventually turned into condominiums, complete with a miniature golf course.

In short, Hayden might be dismissed as merely another example of an upper-middle-class "cosmopolitan," distraught over the values and free choices of most Americans, and seeking to coerce the unenlightened masses into accepting her vision for their lives.

Yet Hayden's work has deeper ideological importance. Indeed, it is symbolic of how the "isms" reborn during the 1960s—e.g., feminism and environmentalism—often veil a more radical cultural, economic, and political agenda.

One wag has suggested that much of what passes for "feminism" actually has very little to do with women and a great deal to do with socialism. Hayden's book is no exception. For example, she consciously draws her vision of social change from the Bolshevik-Soviet dream, positively quoting a 1926 revolutionary slogan: "a new life demands new forms." Materialistic assumptions, a la Marx, are found throughout her volume: the home should be seen essentially as "a domestic workplace"; rearing children is "the reproduction of labor power"; and so on. She labels "economic equity," collectivized services, and the close regulation of the building industry as necessary "to move beyond the conventions of gender imbedded in traditional housing design." Economic, social, and physical "planning" need also be "reunited," she adds. The reshaping of America's housing stock must be kept out of the hands of "profit-making . . . big corporations, national franchises, and their stockholders." Citizens must "end the owner-speculation in one-family houses, halt the flood of new commercial products and services that do little to help our current crisis about the nature of housing and family life, and create local [i.e., planned and socialized] economic development instead." She also wants to diminish private-property rights, eliminate tax benefits encouraging single-home ownership, and embrace new forms of collective housing control as the model for the future.[23]

Above all, Hayden wants to create the socialist paradise, the communal dream, where each person gives according to ability and takes according to her or his need. She waxes poetic about a community garden in Santa Monica where, in the words of one participant, "individuals simply take what they need. In some cases, people who may work at the greenhouse three or four days a week . . . may choose to take little or nothing, while an individual with less time to spend but more need might take whatever is ready to pick." Another of Hayden's dream housing arrangements is Woodruff House in Holland, a feminist collective. "Among the residents, two came from old age homes, several had been living alone, some left unhappy marriages, and one left an unhappy living arrangement with grown children. . . ." Members of this group, with brows undoubtedly furrowed, take care of each other when ill, study technical trades, attend women's rights demonstrations, and hold "regular feminist meetings."[24]

A second aspect of Hayden's deeper agenda lies in her effort to turn the once abnormal into the politically preferred. The implicit targets of her whole book are those norms of behavior that define and sustain the modern social order: commitment to family and children; adherence to religiously grounded values; sexual modesty; and personal responsibility. Subverting this culture at its most vulnerable spot, Hayden simply assumes that there are no longer categories of "normal" and "abnormal." Indeed, she labels once abnormal behavior such as illegitimacy, broken families, and homosexuality as "new" family forms, in some respects the inheritors of the future. "Gay" people, "single parent families," and other "pluralistic families" are, in her view, the victims of a benighted, suburbanized American culture. Carrying the argument full circle, she adds that over the next thirty years, most of the nation's single-family-housing stock need to be restructured to reflect these "basic demographic shifts." At the same time, the only new housing construction that can be justified is that programmed "to meet the special needs of the elderly, single parents, battered wives, and . . . single people." Families with children need not apply.[25]

At that point, then, social disintegration and moral breakdown have come full circle, and begin justifying themselves as "new," progressive, and deserving of preferential treatment. Such a change has real consequences.

The 1980 convention of the National Association of Home Builders, for example, offered a series of speakers who berated their audience for continuing to build for the "traditional" American family. "Builders will have to plan houses for living situations they might not approve of," one consultant said. A magazine editor called on builders to meet "the housing demands" of gays and divorced mothers.[26] To the degree that the housing and real estate industries follow such advice, so the social order that sustains a free, market-driven economy crumbles.

Tragically, such ideologically charged arguments obscure the true "housing crisis" in America. It is a crisis unrelated to the peculiar life-styles and glandular hedonism of the cosmopolitan class. Its effects fall rather on blue-collar and service-oriented workers and on minority groups struggling to achieve a better life. It is a crisis related in no way to gender. Instead, it results from a breakdown of the cultural and policy mechanisms that—until recently—enabled young families to purchase a home and also bear and raise children.

On the cultural side, as noted earlier, the concept of the "family wage" has all but vanished. Today, in contrast to thirty years ago, no significant political or cultural figure challenges the phrase, "equal work, equal pay." An indirect consequence of this change has been to leave the one-paycheck family with small children at a considerable relative disadvantage, particularly in the competitive search for affordable housing.

On the policy side, the mechanisms designed between 1937 and 1940 to deliver affordable housing to new families broke down about ten years ago under the impact of inflation, as evidenced in soaring home prices, high mortgage rates, climbing property taxes, and steep utility bills. Whereas half of American households could afford the median-priced new home in 1970, only 13 percent could in 1980, or in 1985. The child-centered world of the postwar housing boom, it seems, has been turned upside down.

Notes

1. "Housing Gets No. 1 Spot at Family Life Conference," *The Christian Science Monitor* (May 14, 1948).
2. Robert Fishman, *Bourgeois Utopias: The Rise and Fall of Suburbia* (New York: Basic Books, 1987), pp. 25–26, 36–38, 51–61.
3. See: E.M. Forster, *Marianne Thornton, 1797-1887: A Domestic Biography* (New York: Harcourt, Brace, 1956).
4. Catharine E. Beecher, *An Essay on the Education of Female Teachers* [1835]; excerpted in *The Educated Woman in America*, ed. Barbara M. Cross (New York: Columbia University Teachers College Press, 1965), pp. 67–83; and Kathryn Kish Sklar, *Catharine Beecher: A Study in American Domesticity* (New Haven: Yale University Press, 1973), p. 160.

5. Fishman, 123–124; Andrew Jackson Downing, *Victorian Cottage Residences* (New York: Dover Publications, 1981 [1842; 1873]), p. ix.
6. Henry C. Binford, *The First Suburbs: Residential Communities on the Boston Periphery, 1815-1860* (Chicago: The University of Chicago Press, 1985), pp. 171, 174.
7. Quoted in Fishman, pp. 128–29.
8. Talcott Parsons and Winston White, "The Link Between Character and Society," in *Culture and Social Character: The Work of David Riesman Reviewed*, ed. Seymour Martin Lipset and Leo Lowenthal (New York: The Free Press of Glencoe, 1961), pp. 116–17.
9. See: Walt W. Rostow, "The National Style," in *The American Style: Essays in Value and Performance*, ed. Elting E. Morrison (New York: Harper and Brothers, 1958), pp. 246–313.
10. Quoted in Eric Larrabee, "The Six Thousand Houses That Levitt Built," *Harper's* (Sept. 1948): 80, 84.
11. Landon Y. Jones, *Great Expectations: America And The Baby Boom Generation* (New York: Coward, McCann and Goeghegan, 1980), p. 38.
12. Frederick Lewis Allen, "The Big Change in Suburbia," *Harper's Magazine* (June 1954): 25–27.
13. Max Lerner, *America As A Civilization* (New York: Simon and Schuster, 1957), pp. 172–80.
14. Herbert J. Gans, *The Levittowners: Ways Of Life And Politics In A New Suburban Community* (New York: Pantheon Books, 1967), pp. 409–13, 419, 423.
15. Larrabee, p. 88.
16. Sidonie M. Gruenberg, "Homogenized Children of New Suburbia," *The New York Times Magazine* (Sept. 19, 1954): 14.
17. Richard E. Gordon, Katharine K. Gordon, and Max Gunther, *The Split-Level Trap* (New York: Bernard Geis Associates, 1961), p. 33.
18. Eve Merriam, "Are Housewives Necessary?" *The Nation* (Jan. 31, 1959): 96-99.
19. Betty Friedan, *The Feminine Mystique* (New York: W.W. Norton, 1963), p. 243.
20. See: Gwendolyn Wright, *Building The Dream: A Social History Of Housing In America* (New York: Pantheon Books, 1981); and Nancy Rubin, *The New Suburban Woman: Beyond Myth And Motherhood* (New York: Coward, McCann, & Goeghegan, 1982).
21. Delores Hayden, *Redesigning The American Dream* (New York: W.W. Norton, 1984), pp. 41, 43, 49–50, 102, 104–05, 141, 207.
22. Hayden, pp. 226-31.
23. Ibid., pp. 143, 146–47, 169–70, 176–78, 192.
24. Ibid., pp. 190, 203–04.
25. Ibid., pp. 12–14, 120, 181, 197.
26. Cited in Wright, p. 268.

13

Shopping Mall Morality

Broad elements of the American literati deeply despise the shopping mall. The intensity of their anger both shocks and baffles.

The latest public diatribe against the malls is William Kowinski's book, *The Malling of America: An Inside Look at the Great Consumer Paradise*. This author leaves no public charge against the shopping complexes untried. The word "mall," he emphasizes, comes from the same root as "maul." These huge shopping complexes are "the culmination of all the American dreams, both decent and demented." The mall is essentially fascist, as it "tries to control everything that goes on within its domain." Its environment "bathes you in sweet neutrality with soft light, candied music, and all the amenities that reassure and please without grabbing too much attention." Malls, Kowinski adds, create a zombie effect, where "victims" stay on for no good or apparent reason, lured by "its implicit promise of safety, sanctuary, and salvation. Of Nirvana?"

In later pages, the author really warms up. Shopping center managers instill their own corrupted values into young people, programming them to be "hard-core, lifelong shoppers." The mall is "a surrogate mother," "a protected fantasy environment," "a made-up Mickey Mouse kind of Main Street," an oppressive entity based on the psychological "repertoire of prostitutes [and] airline attendants." William Calley of Mai Lai fame, he adds with a knowing wink, left prison to work in a mall. Kowinski concludes that shopping centers actually may be an expression of the American nuclear nightmare. "The history of atomic terror," he notes grimly, "parallels the growth of malldom." Accordingly, Kowinski says it would be a fitting end for the nuclear bombs, when they finally come, to "find millions of Americans happily perambulating in the suspended animation of the mall."[1]

These are not isolated charges. *The Nation* magazine regularly takes swipes at suburban malls, one author labeling them the political equivalent of "Big Uncle." The more mainstream *Time* makes fun of these "gleaming oases of retail chic among the growing, monotonous tracks of ranches and split-levels," blasting their "voracious" appetite for electricity and labeling them "asphalt eyesores." All critics agree that the malls' primary sin has been the destruction of downtown shopping areas. Suburban malls, says one city planner, represent "every evil which goes along with a non-planned district" and bring "the destruction of our municipal wealth." As Yale architect Cesar Pelli explains, the appearance of a new mall has awesome consequences for its urban neighbors: "Towns disappear." Kowinski stresses the significance of that phase: "Move over, Godzilla and H.G. Wells. Who needs atomic breath or a Martian heat ray?" The mall destroys human community almost as quickly and with equal thoroughness.[2]

Where lies the truth? There is no doubt that the rapid spread of the shopping mall in the post-World War II era has had a profound influence on life in the United States and is symbolic of much deeper change. Yet the evidence is also clear that the new shopping centers did not "destroy" the business districts of the central cities. During the 1945–55 era, for example, the data show that a rising national birthrate tied to sustained growth in real personal income allowed downtown centers to show "considerable vitality despite the booming suburban trade." One study found the gain in dollar volume of retail sales between 1948 and 1954 to be 15.8 percent in the central cities and 44.1 percent in the suburbs. Simply put, a rising tide lifted all boats, albeit more quickly in the suburban fringe. Decline of retail trade in the cities actually set in parallel to the sharp fall in the U.S. birthrate, which began in 1958.[3]

Other studies have shown that retail "flight" from the central cities was a result, rather than a cause, of population changes. That is, people moved first, with the stores merely trailing behind. Looking at data for Detroit, John McDonald found that regional shopping centers did not independently cause the decline of the central business district; rather, the prior movement of people was the key. Looking at national data, sociologist Donald Steinnes discovered the same result: the suburbanization of people preceded the suburbanization of the stores.[4]

So, a mystery arises: why this irrational passion directed against the malls? Why do the intellectuals find collections of stores with names like Northland and Southdale, Eastridge and Westgate, Plaza Del Sol and Kings Plaza, Yazooville Shopping Center and Sherman Oaks so repulsive as to warrant an endless stream of diatribes and repeated political efforts to cut them off or shut them down?

A few clues might be found by tracing the reasons for the successful rise of the suburbs. Like all great migrations, the flow of Americans to new residences outside city limits was the result of both "push" and "pull" factors. Concerning the former, American cities were clearly in crisis by

1948. Urban crime rates were rising sharply; cities were growing more congested; racial tensions also grew. There was increasing potential for social violence and a progressive breakdown of any sense of community. In earlier decades, most workers and their families were limited in their choice of where to live: If they wanted to work, they had to live in the cities. The advent of the cheap automobile, though, revolutionized choices.

Politicians reacted crudely to the new situation. At the local level, their primary effort was to treat citizens and businesses as captives, fair game for ever higher tax rates and experiments in urban planning. At the national level, liberalism ran amok. In the federal courts and bureaucracy, activists used the rhetoric of freedom and mounted an attack on the moral foundations of the city. Prior to this new era of judicial and bureaucratic intervention, every American 'burg—large or small—basically enjoyed the power to enforce democratically determined moral standards as law. Vice and pornography were usually outlawed; the commonsense decency of average citizens could still—and usually did—animate those charged with creating and upholding legal standards. Vague abstractions about federally protected rights held little sway in neighborhoods, which enjoyed a considerable degree of informal autonomy in enforcing popular cultural choices and standards.

The new federal elites, though, could not stomach this democratic morality, and urban residents were soon taught lessons about the new order. Criminals had rights, the leaders determined; average citizens defending their families and neighborhoods did not. Government-funded "community activists" had rights; long-time inhabitants must accept their guidance or be silent. Anti-American protestors could spread their message wherever they chose; average people must listen. Pornographers were protected by the Constitution; families were not. Religion was divisive, a public eyesore, and must go; the Black Panthers, meanwhile, received federal funds. Schools must be vehicles for social engineering; local communities and standards be damned.

The modern liberal myth, promoted by Jane Jacobs and others, is that "real cities" are spontaneous, ad hoc creations thriving on unpredictable diversity and openness to change. By this reckoning, central cities are real; suburbs are false. In fact, the nation's major cities in this era were essentially transformed into so many prison camps, where an antidemocratic cabal of judges and bureaucrats forced their amoral, statist visions onto those unable to escape.

The "pull" behind the migration to the suburbs lay in the opportunity there to recover a form of moral community. The cities, characterized by crime, grime, unrest, and social experimentation, were increasingly poor places to marry, raise children, or praise God. In the wake of American demobilization after World War II, there were millions of men and women desperately and precisely looking for places to start a home, bear children, create a decent life, and find reasonable safety and peace. They were willing to sacrifice a great deal—time, career advancement, diversity, excitement, novelty—in order to have this minimum basis for social existence and a degree of security for their children.

The shopping center, as a national phenomenon, developed in response to this vast movement of Americans to the suburbs; it sought to meet the special commercial needs of a family-centered culture.

The architectural origins of the shopping centers lay in scattered experiments of the interwar period. Californians, living in the first completely automobile-centered culture, frequented Westwood Village and Farmer's Market in Los Angeles. Kansas City's Country Club Plaza, completed in 1925, confronted and solved many of the problems facing this new retail design form. By 1950, funding questions were resolved as life insurance companies found these huge commercial centers to be worthy places of investment. Massive federal programs for the construction of highways and interstates began shortly thereafter, and indirectly resolved the travel problems posed by the regional shopping center model.

The major theorist of the shopping center movement was Victor Gruen. Austrian-born and trained, Gruen fled the Nazi *Anschluss* of 1938 and came to the United States. A committed Social Democrat, he argued that capitalist industrialization had corroded the bonds of urban life, so that "life in the city soon became intolerable and those who could afford it led the march to the suburbs." Ironically, as a planner and urban sophisticate at heart, Gruen also held little love for the institutions of suburbia. The automobile had destroyed "the last vestige of community coherence." He saw the suburbs as "an arid land inhabited during the day almost entirely by women and children." Social planning, he insisted, was now needed "to bring order, stability, and meaning to chaotic suburbia" and to "provide crystallization points for suburbia's community life." The suburbs needed some equivalent of the Greek Agora, of the medieval cathedral with "the merchants' and craftsmen's stalls and stores surrounding it," of the town squares and Main Streets of small-town America. In a 1943 article for *Architectural Forum*, Gruen described what such a creation might look like:

> Shops could be grouped in one building surrounding a landscaped area. With the exception of the main entrance, the outside is modest in character. No advertising disturbs the appearance of the residential streets. On each end of the block there is parking space, and loading and unloading [of goods] are carried out behind screen walls. For shoppers there is a covered walkway connecting all the stores with the landscaped traffic; all necessities of day-to-

day living can be found: post offices, circulating library, doctors' and dentists' offices, rooms for social activities.

Gruen's vision took complete form in his design for Southdale, constructed near Minneapolis in 1956. His goal was to create a world where variety and motion would coexist with order and discipline. Southdale featured a totally enclosed, climate-controlled environment, constructed on two levels and anchored at either end by a major department store. Interior space featured sculpture, trees, and benches arranged to create an impression of downtown bustle and energy. From vantage points throughout the mall, shoppers could gaze across seemingly limitless vistas, emotionally stimulating when filled with people, forming a planned landscape of perpetual movement and change.[5]

Major department stores lay behind the development of the early regional shopping centers, such as Seattle's Northgate (Allied Stores) and Southdale (Dayton's). Yet a new breed of developers quickly arose, men such as A. Alfred ("Big Al") Taubman, the creator of the 1,700,000 square foot Woodfield Mall in Schaumburg, Illinois, and James W. Rouse, developer of Cherry Hill, Echelon Mall, and dozens of others, not to mention the "new town" of Columbia, Maryland.

Fueled by insurance company investments, the concept spread quickly. Shopping centers numbered in the few dozens in 1950. By 1960, there were 4,000 across the United States; in 1977, 18,000. In that latter year, the malls accounted for 45 percent of retail sales in the United States. Indeed, this staggering, exponential rate of growth represented a true economic upheaval, what economist Joseph Schumpeter once labeled a "big" disturbance, "disrupt[ing] the existing system and enforc[ing] a distinct process of adaptation." Shopping centers brought basic changes in the nation's whole distribution structure, compelling existing retailers to join them, adapt, or go out of business.[6]

The social and cultural consequences of the shopping center were even more decisive. The fairly rapid and unheralded growth of these new developments, according to geographer V.J. Bunce, represented a "revolution" in human action. *U.S. News & World Report* concluded in 1973 that the mall had displaced the city park and Main Street as "the core of community 'belonging' in America," the "center of American consciousness." *Management Review* saw large regional shopping centers as offering "a focus for communities and a sense of identity for the formless sprawl of suburbia." Writing in *The New Republic*, University of Chicago historian Neil Harris concluded that the malls were the most effective architectural servants of American dreams since the huge movie palaces of the 1920s. *Fortune* saw the malls "reshaping much of American life," seizing the social, as well as the retail, role once held by the central business districts. Harvard psychologist Robert Coles suggested that visits to shopping centers served as a basic community ritual, where normally isolated persons shared "common, albeit commonplace experiences." Indeed, researchers at the University of Kansas confirmed that shopping at malls had primarily a social, rather than a commercial, purpose. Most visitors to malls, they found, came in groups of two or more, and their primary attention was on their companions rather than on purchases or displays.[7]

Observers also noted the extraordinary mix of people rubbing shoulders within malls: the aged sitting on benches, engaged in observation and conversation; teenagers in game arcades, outside theaters, or simply in clusters in the commons; children with their parents or in supervised play areas; church women's groups who came in for the day by bus from nearby hamlets. The malls also served as cultural centers, featuring on their stages everything from oom-pah bands and grade-school choirs to the Chicago Symphony Orchestra (although few "heavy metal" groups). Even interfaith chapels and "churches on the mall" could be found.

In short, the malls had met, and even exceeded, the stated expectations of their creators. Shopping centers had become economic powerhouses, transforming the whole retail trade in the process. They had also emerged as the centers of social life for thousands of communities and tens-of-millions of Americans, becoming successful twentieth-century versions of the cathedral square.

Yet such explanations hardly seem adequate to account for the bitterness and anger of the malls' enemies, hostile to American success stories as they are. Nor do they reveal why the primary theoretician of the mall, Victor Gruen, turned with such disgust on his creation in the late 1970s. "I refuse to pay alimony for those bastard developments," Gruen wrote, referring to the huge new complexes going up around the country. These malls, constructed by "anonymous real-estate entrepreneurs . . . who just wanted to make a fast buck," were travesties, he said. They were delivering the "death blow" to already suffering city centers. They represented the rape of the environment, encouraging air pollution and the loss of farmland. They were "specialized ghettos," an "extreme" example of substituting "an artificial and therefore sterile order for naturally developed blends of urban forms." He called for their downfall.[8]

In truth, the malls in America had developed a life and purpose of their own. Escaping the grasp of both social democratic planners and profit-minded entrepreneurs, they took a unique shape. Representing neither the triumph of socialism nor of capitalism, the malls actually evolved into a new political-economic form, one bearing in structure an uncanny resemblance to the medieval manor. In wake of the collapse of democratic moral governance in the cities, the malls became privatized islands of simple decency, fortresses reared against the decaying American urban system. And that is what their critics cannot tolerate or forgive.

Fundamental changes often occur under our noses, their significance clear only in retrospect. Such a change occurred in American land law in the four decades after 1945. Prior to this time, estate tenures (meaning any contiguous arrangement of multiple tenants holding a lease from a common landlord) were rare in the modern Western world, and land management primarily a diversion for widows and speculators. All that changed after World War II, with the rise of an array of new forms of tenancy: industrial estates, mobile home parks, marinas, RV parks, medical clinics, professional centers, downtown complexes such as the Rockefeller Center, "new towns" like Reston, Virginia, and Columbia, Maryland, and, of course, shopping centers. Novel in the twentieth century, these multiple-occupancy, income-producing properties harken back to "the landed estates and manorial organizations of antiquity in which the internal, or domestic, public authority derived from the proprietary authority over the land."[9]

The medieval parallels extend to the legal and political realms. In these contexts, malls should be viewed as a community of landlord and tenants, as a process or an event rather than an entity, where space is divided between private and common areas and where mutual relationships are carefully defined in order to perpetuate the community. This necessitates a legal structure resting essentially on premodern bonds of obligation.

Its basic form rests in the written "mall law," the totality of leases in effect at any given time which defines the rights and duties of landlord and merchants. These leases serve as instruments of social policy, involving lateral extensions which create obligations for the lessee not only to the landlord but also to his neighbors in the center. Common clauses require tenants to participate in the merchants' council, to spend a minimum amount on advertising, and to coordinate store hours with other merchants. Furthermore, equality plays little role in defining such leaseholds. Some tenants enjoy disproportionate privileges—lower rent, veto power over new tenants, and so on. Indeed, each lease may contain a distinct set of reciprocal privileges and obligations, rough equivalents of the ancient royal charters jealously protected by medieval towns, villages, and guilds.

The second legal level encompasses the law of the shopping center's various subgroups: contracts between tenants and their employees; independent contractors; and suppliers. These latter categories, just as wives and children in earlier tenure systems, participate in the mall community "once removed." Another group drawn in are visitors to the community: the shoppers. They, too, are part of the mall's legal order, observing parking restrictions and posted dress codes as their obligations to the community.

A third legal level is represented by the informal, unwritten, customary understandings that arise within the merchants' community. This "common law" embraces principles such as "loyalty to the center," and encourages conformity for the protection and welfare of all.

Holding this legal-political system together is the mall manager, the modern equivalent of the lord of the manor. Unelected, the manager derives his power from control of the land or space. As head of the community, his job is to protect all of its participants. He must attract shoppers to the center, and secure their safety and good conduct while there. He must find solid tenants of the right sort, coordinate promotion, and sponsor civic and cultural activities that bind the center to the surrounding neighborhoods.

More importantly, the mall manager serves as a buffer between his tenants and other forms of political authority that impinge from outside: municipal, county, and higher governments with their array of permits and regulations and sometimes simmering hostility. In addition, tenants recognize that the manager is not partisan, but holds a unique interest in assuring the success of the center community as a whole. This puts the manager in the position to arbitrate disputes between leaseholders, to serve the peacemaking role, to become judge and enforcer.[10]

Economically, too, shopping malls harken back to a medieval style of organization. Like guild systems that enforced quality and price levels to assure a basic income for all, malls operate on the theory that the whole venture depends on the well-being of the little shops. Managements commonly exclude discount stores. Tenant mix is controlled to avoid excess competition: where one flower shop is wonderful; two may be disruptive. Individual merchants overly prone to pricecutting have on occasions been tossed out of the relevant merchants' associations.[11]

Most importantly, the malls serve as oases of moral preferences, "cathedrals" of commonsense decency. In these citadels of commerce, one commentator notes, "crime and squalor have been forever banned." When an outbreak of criminal activity occurs, mall officials respond by increasing private patrols, installing video monitors, and preferring charges against offenders. Maintenance and cleanliness standards are high, setting examples for all who enter the closed domain.

The mall is a private space, and its use is governed for basic moral ends. "We ask for simple decency," explains mall developer Jack Pearlstone, Jr., "that the kids not block our shoppers, use carpeted malls as picnic areas, or make insulting remarks to pretty young girls." Signs posted in a suburban Washington, DC, mall set out the principle: "Areas in Tysons Corner Center used by the public are not public ways, but are for the use of tenants and the public transacting business with them. Permission to use said areas may be revoked at any time." As a perceptive writer for *The Nation* has acknowledged, customers make demands on malls that they would not ask of Main Street merchants, "because they know that the center is a protected enclave controlling all the property it occupies." This allows mall authorities to expel troublemakers, keep out the deranged, and ban the partisans of unpopular or antisocial causes. "Why," asks one mall official, "should the maternity shop pay increased common area charges to [allow customers to] pick up leaflets distributed by a zero population growth group?"

Such environments are openly designed to create protected spaces for families. The amoral city of the post-World War II era was hostile to home life and children. Yet in the suburbs, both found affirmation, with the malls there to serve. As one British commentator symbolically noted in 1959, "stores in shopping centres display prominently the maternity garments and the children's clothes which their city cousins tuck away upstairs." The malls, moreover, transformed the very act of shopping from a specialized chore into a family outing, where women and children were protected from those human predators—pimps, drug dealers, pornographers, gang lords—that have been allowed the run of Main Street.[13]

In sum, the mall is designed to be neither purely efficient nor democratic. Like the lord of the medieval fortress, the mall manager aims at controlling competition, within certain limits, for the benefit of all members of his merchant community. Politically, the manager aims at resolving differences and preserving social relationships. Factionalism and voting are avoided; consensus shaped by the wise leader is sought. As the head of one mall's merchant council put it, "if [a proposal] comes to a vote, we don't want it." Communal unity must take precedence. Externally, the manager defends his community from hostile governments and barbaric intruders.[14]

In one of his most rueful passages, Kowinski complains that it may soon be possible for a single individual to be born, move from preschool through college, date, marry, advance through several careers, have children, receive medical care, be arrested, tried, and jailed, live a full life of culture and entertainment, and then die and be given funeral rites without ever leaving a single mall complex—"because every one of those possibilities exists now in some shopping center somewhere." The simple truth is that the malls are serving as havens for a normal, relatively decent life amidst the ruins of the postliberal, postdemocratic city.

Naturally, the enemies of the mall and the moral preferences it represents have been unrelenting in their efforts to prevent their construction, shut them down, or change their nature. Arguments against shopping centers have been clothed in "public interest," "free speech," and "environmental" garb. Yet the common goal has been to destroy the malls' legal-political autonomy and to subject them to the same forces which had earlier made the cities unlivable.

The original strategy was annexation. By the early 1950s, big-city administrators and planners looked with horror upon the growth of suburbs and the movement of retailers to the shopping centers. Some simply stuck their heads in the sand, hoping (in 1956) that the building of the centers had already passed its peak.[15] Other defenders of the old order grew more aggressive. Suburban shopping areas represented everything reprehensible in free choice and unplanned growth, they said. Accordingly, central cities must "annex the new areas in which suburban business development is taking place," and so bring them under the central regime.[16]

A more effective strategy involved turning to the federal courts and the familiar use of the First and Fourteenth Amendments to the U.S. Constitution to batter down the mall restrictions on disorder and antisocial conduct which private property rights had secured. The earliest relevant Supreme Court decision came in 1945 (*Marsh* v. *Alabama*), and actually involved a prohibition by a company-owned town on unauthorized preaching on a company street. The Court ruled that the firm could not prohibit free speech, reasoning that the more an owner "opens up his property for use by the public in general, the more do his rights become circumscribed by the statutory and constitutional rights of those who use it."

Over the next several decades, lower courts applied this precedent to a series of shopping center cases, ruling that barriers to entry by "unpopular" causes must be removed. The Supreme Court reaffirmed this line of argument, on a divided vote, in 1968 (*Amalgamated Food Employees Union* v. *Logan Valley Plaza*), ruling that a mall owner could not limit union picketing on his property. When private property was opened to the general public, argued Justice Thurgood Marshall, it lost its private character. "The shopping center here is clearly the 'functional equivalent' of the business district in *Marsh*," he concluded, and so subject to constitutional rights applied by the courts under the Fourteenth Amendment.

By 1971, though, four new Nixon appointees sat on the Court, setting the stage for a dramatic reversal of precedent. In *Lloyd Corporation* v. *Tanner*, the Court reaffirmed the integrity of property rights. The case involved the attempt by a mall manager to prohibit anti-Vietnam War leafleteers within the center. The lower courts, citing *Marsh* v. *Alabama* and *Amalgamated Food Employees Union* v. *Logan Valley*, had decided in favor of the war protesters. The Supreme Court, though, struck down the lower court decision. The First and Fourteenth Amendments, Justice William Powell reasoned for the majority, were limitations on state actions, not on the actions of owners of private property using that property for private ends. As he wrote: "The essentially private character of a store and its privately owned abutting property does not change by virtue of being large or clustered with other stores in a modern shopping center." In his dissenting opinion, Justice Marshall took particular umbrage that the American Legion and Disabled American Veterans had been allowed to hold a parade and sell poppies in the mall, while the war protesters had been turned away. Nonetheless, the private, protected status of the malls had been restored, and such expressions of popular preference once again had protection.

This precedent was strengthened in 1976 (*Hudgens* v. *NLRB*) when the Court ruled that the owner of an enclosed mall had the right to limit picketing on his property. Writing for the majority, Justice Potter Stewart concluded that private property became "public" only when it took on all the attributes of a town: i.e., it had become an independent municipality. For shopping malls, this meant that the "constitutional guarantee of free expression has no part to play."[17]

Stymied by the courts, the opponents of shopping centers quickly found another weapon: environmental regulation. Working through the U.S. Departments of Housing and Urban Development (HUD) and Transportation, the Jimmy Carter Administration sought "to discourage the proliferation of suburban malls that threaten the vitality of urban centers."[18] Federal agencies, for example, refused to provide funds for access roads and other improvements and blocked proposed malls in a number of cities.

Classical political battles over this question were fought in Minnesota and Vermont. In the former case, a proposed suburban mall near Duluth was challenged by authorities on the grounds that it would have an adverse impact on the central city. Using a new federal policy device, HUD prepared an Urban Impact Analysis (UIA) that suggested the city would lose jobs and taxes. Construction of the mall was stopped. In Vermont, the Pyramid Companies proposed building an 82-store complex between Williston and Burlington. Local politicians opposed the project, yet pro-mall forces in Williston eventually won a referendum forcing the local government to cease its opposition to the center. Nonetheless, a 1970 Vermont environmental law required that a regional commission prepare an "impact" statement. During the commission's fifty public hearings, worried politicians, the Sierra Club, and the Friends of the Earth came together to warn of "the threat to the Vermont way of life." In the end, they triumphed: The mall was killed and popular democracy again crushed by the backroom rulers of America.

With all this said, two questions remain: What of democracy? And what of the central cities?

As shown above, there is truth to the charge that malls are undemocratic. However, undemocratic does not necessarily mean unpopular or elitist. The flow of enthusiastic throngs—seven billion trips to shopping centers in 1984 alone—proves that they are wildly popular. Moreover, research shows that the malls are most used, as social institutions, by the less-well-off.[19]

Furthermore, the democratic failure did not begin with the malls. Rather, it began among the institutions of the left-liberal hegemony. Since World War II, as historian Christopher Lasch has recently noted, the left has relied on the courts, the federal bureaucracy, and the media to achieve its goals: "Once the voice of the common man, the left has come to regard common sense—the traditional wisdom and folkways of the community—as an obstacle to progress and enlightenment."[20] This destruction of democratic morality in the cities helped to produce the flight to the suburbs and the construction of the malls: given the abject failure of public institutions, moral standards could survive only in private spaces. The results were decidedly imperfect, not only in terms of politics and total moral vision but also commonly in terms of aesthetics. Nonetheless, it seems evident that true democracy will not be restored simply by crushing the malls and other privatized entities.

Which raises the second question: What of the central cities? What is to save them? The long-term answer is an end to the reign of activist judges, bureaucrats, and media pundits, and a restoration of commonsense morality on the streets. Short of that probably utopian dream, the answer lies in transferring the suburban solution to the cities: privatize urban institutions; let the basically decent moral sentiments of citizens take control in defined, limited areas. As the National Center for Neighborhood Enterprise has repeatedly emphasized, "privatized" public housing—where tenants have won back some control over their lives and, more significantly, over those of their immediate neighbors—can perform wonders in terms of restoring minimal order to the cities. More directly, retailers have moved back *en masse* to urban centers when the privatized suburban mall has been allowed to move downtown. Water Tower Place in Chicago, Galleria in Houston, and Fanueil Hall Marketplace in Boston are but a few of the dozens of examples of what one writer calls "suburbia's gift to the cities."

Of course, these downtown malls also have their critics. Architect Lawrence Halprin sees them as "merely walled enclaves with a suburban mentality." Psychologist Richard Evans complains that downtown mall patrons "begin to lose touch with the problems of the city, and the city as a sophisticated environment begins to lose its impact on the individual."

Of course, it is that very "sophisticated environment," complete with muggers and molesters, that ordinary citizens are trying to escape. A *Time* editor's casual summation is essentially correct: Shopping malls are "the modern equivalent of a fortress,"[21] attempts to preserve decent environments for normal family life in a troubled and disordered urban world.

Notes

1. William Severini Kowinski, *The Malling of America: An Inside Look at the Great American Paradise* (New York: William Morrow, 1985), pp. 25, 106, 316, 340–41, 346, 350–54, 357–59, 365.

2. Rose DeWolf, "Main Street Goes Private," *The Nation* 215 (Dec. 18, 1972): 628; "A Pall Over the Suburban Mall," *Time* (Nov. 13, 1978): 116; Ben Ehrlichman, "Cities Urged to Reach Out," *National Municipal Review* 41 (April 1952): 188-89; and Kowinski, p. 109.
3. Mabel Walker, "The Impact of Outlying Shopping Centers on Central Business Districts," *Public Management* 39 (Jan. 1957): 171; and James D. Tarver, "Suburbanization of Retail Trade in the Standard Metropolitan Areas of the United States, 1948–54," *American Sociological Review* 22 (Aug. 1957): 429.
4. John F. McDonald, "Some Causes of the Decline of Central Business District Retail Sales in Detroit," *Urban Studies* 12 (1975): 229–33; and Donald M. Steinnes, "Suburbanization and the 'Malling of America': A Time-Series Approach," *Urban Affairs Quarterly* 17 (June 1982): 401–18.
5. Victor Gruen and Larry Smith, *Shopping Towns USA: The Planning of Shopping Centers* (New York: Reinhold, 1961), pp. 11–24; the 1943 quotation from: Victor Gruen, "The Sad Story of Shopping Centres," *Town and Country Planning 46* (July/Aug. 1978): 350.
6. See: Perry Bliss, "Schumpeter, the 'Big' Disturbance and Retailing," *Social Forces* 39 (Oct. 1960): 72–76.
7. V.J. Bunce, "Revolution in the High Street? The Emergence of the Enclosed Shopping Centre," *Geography* 68 (Oct. 1983): 308; "How Shopping Malls are Changing Life in America," *U.S. News & World Report* (June 18, 1973): 43; Jack Morris, "Main Street Moves to the Mall," *Management Review 58* (May 1969): 48; Neil Harris, "Spaced-Out at the Shopping Center," *The New Republic* (Dec. 13, 1975): 26; Gurney Breckenfeld, "'Downtown' Has Fled to the Suburbs," *Fortune* 86 (Oct. 1972): 80; Edwin Warner, "Suburbia's Gift to the Cities," *Horizon* 20 (Sept. 1977): 16; and Tina Z. Adelberg and Maynard W. Shelly, "Notes on Satisfactions in Shopping Centers: I, II, III," *Psychological Reports* 21 (1967): 507–08, 536, 584.
8. Victor Gruen, "The Sad Story of Shopping Centers," pp. 350–52; also, quotation in "A Pall Over the Suburban Mall," p. 116.
9. Spencer N. MacCallum, "Jural Behavior in American Shopping Centers: Initial Views on the Proprietary Community," *Human Organization* 30 (Spring 1971): 4.
10. MacCallum, pp. 4–9.
11. See: Breckenfeld, p. 87; Bunce, p. 307; and "Baghdad in the Suburbs," *The Economist* (Feb. 14, 1959): 594.
12. See: Warner, p. 114; Breckenfeld, p. 88; DeWolf, p. 627.
13. See: "Baghdad in the Suburbs," p. 594; and R.L. Damer, "Shopping as a Family Expedition," *Geographical Magazine* 50 (Feb. 1978): 297–301.
14. From: MacCallum, p. 10.
15. Walker, p. 173.
16. Ehrlichman, p. 189.
17. See: Howard Ball, "Careless Justice: The United States Supreme Court's Shopping Center Opinions, 1946–76," *Polity* 11 (Winter 1978): 200–28; and Peter J. Kane, "Freedom of Expression in Shopping Centers," *Today's Speech* 22 (Summer 1974): 45–48.
18. "A Pall Over the Suburban Mall," p. 116.
19. See: Tina Z. Adelberg and Maynard W. Shelly, "Notes on Satisfactions in Shopping Centers: IV," *Psychological Reports* 21 (1967): 660.
20. Christopher Lasch, "What's Wrong with the Right?" *Tikkun* 1 (May/June 1986): 23–29.
21. See: Warner, p. 24.

Part VI
THE AGE QUESTION

14

The Ageism Scam

Modern American liberalism works to break up traditional forms of community and to transform the resulting pieces into victim classes beholden to government for their sustenance and security. A primary example of this process has been the treatment accorded the old.

The creation of the Social Security Act set loose new economic incentives that ate away, cancer-like, at existing family bonds between generations. Within each family, children were transformed from a blessing, a source of future security, into an increasingly questionable burden. The Act also gave strong impetus to the concept of mandatory retirement, which quickly displaced most other ways of dealing with the questions of age and work. Moreover, as social insurance evolved into a vehicle for massive income redistribution, the old assumed the role of a privileged political class, one increasingly living apart from children and grandchildren and one heavily dependent for its survival on the state.

Facing these circumstances, liberal social thinkers sought during the 1945–70 period to create a new understanding of aging, a new explanation of the place of the old in a modern welfare society. Two rival theories emerged. One sought to move the liberal tradition in an optimistic, seemingly rightward direction. Theorists gathering around Talcott Parsons described the instrumental restructuring of the family in America around the nuclear unit (husband-wife-children), and the "disengagement" process of the old that supported this change. A second theory, though, encouraged a leftward drift toward a radical condemnation of the American system. It cast the old as a minority group, the victims of prejudice or "ageism," a persecuted class needing state protection and succor. While the first theory had primary influence on liberal thought and action through the early postwar years, the latter triumphed after 1970 and remains dominant to this day.

In retrospect, it appears that this victory of the radical perspective was inevitable. Philosophical liberalism's difficulty in coping with the aged de-

199

rived from its very premises. In traditional societies, the old are revered as
leaders or priests of their religion, as defenders of inherited culture, as
interpreters of social order, as judges of the normal and deviant, as revered,
past-oriented guides to the future. Among modern American liberals,
though, such roles have been distrusted. Unbound by a consistent religious
metaphysics, suspicious of cultural expectations that violated the guiding
principles of efficiency and equality, contemptuous of the irrational aspects
of the past, and dedicated to freedom from inherited social restraints as an
end in itself, modern liberal theorists have worked to disenfranchise the old
from their traditional roles, to turn the aged into hollow shells. Unwilling,
then, to admit their own responsibility for transforming the old into a
marginal class, these same figures have turned the charge around and have
blamed this development on "society" or "capitalism."

The parallel here with the treatment of women is instructive. In both
cases, political theorists relabeled as "stereotypes" the forms of expected
behavior that had once conferred honor and dignity. Having so made war
on what it meant to be a woman or a grandparent, having stripped these
roles of any intrinsic value, liberal modernists confronted "empty" people
who needed to be given new status and identity.

Significantly, it was the theme-setting essay of the inaugural 1946 issue of
the *Journal of Gerontology* (the publication of the newly organized Geron-
tological Society) that fully acknowledged this imperative. "Now much of
the wisdom of the aged has become less valuable, if not misleading and
sometimes harmful," wrote author Lawrence Frank, "because of the rapid
march of events and of social and cultural changes." The necessary task, he
emphasized, was to replace "many of our cherished traditions and long-
standing social institutions and practices which have become obsolete." He
admitted that this effort was made "more difficult" by the steadily growing
number of older men and women, persons who tended to fear and to resist
change "at a time when it has become imperative to reduce the discrepancy
between the political, economic, and social practices of the nineteenth
century and the technological and other developments of recent years." Yet
he insisted that the effort must be made. Accordingly, the old need be given
a new social purpose so that they would not interfere with the process of
change.[1]

One attempt in this direction came from Parsons. He deviated from the
basic argument of the early-twentieth-century theorists who had said that
the American family was losing its functions. Productive activities, recreation, education, and even religious practice, these authors had suggested,
were no longer found in the home, but rather were being professionalized
and taken over by experts or the state. In contrast, Parsons argued that the
American family was actually undergoing an "instrumental" reorgan-

ization. True, some functions were eroding. In particular, kinship ties between generations had virtually disappeared. However, other functions were strengthening. Indeed, the nuclear family, focused on the tasks of rearing children, maintaining "highly personal relations," and providing psychological "tension management" for adults, was involved in "a quite definite upgrading process." This isolated family unit, he added, now served as the principal unit of kinship, community, and residence. Commonly headed by one major breadwinner, the nuclear family was the unit of social mobility and so proved to be surprisingly adaptable to "achievement values" and to the demands of economic efficiency. Accordingly, Parsons concluded that the restructured family and modernity had been successfully reconciled in the suburban middle-class family. In this modified family form, society had found its new equilibrium.[2]

Parsons, however, left a large gap in his vision of modern American social life. His early theory provided few specifics on the role to be played by the old and the retired. To his clear relief, this gap was finally filled by the work of sociologists Elaine Cumming and William Henry and the development of the theory of "disengagement." Cumming and Henry argued that disengagement was an inevitable part of the aging process, whereby many of the existing relationships between an individual and other members of society were severed, and those remaining altered in quality. Like the nuclear family itself, disengagement was geared to support a rational economic system focused on efficiency.

The authors said that disengagement began with an individual's new awareness of the shortness of life, a new expectation of death, and a decline in individual physical and mental abilities. As the number of personal contacts decreased, the individual experienced increased freedom from the control of norms governing daily behavior, which further accelerated the withdrawal process. An individual's life cycle was punctuated by ego changes, they noted. Specifically, a decline in knowledge and skills usually accompanied the aging process. Hence, the mechanism of "age-grading" was used to ensure that the young were sufficiently trained to assume authority while the old were retired before they lost their skill. Accordingly, society, rather than the individual, governed the disengagement process. Cumming and Henry added that the abandonment of life's central roles— work for men, marriage and family for women—resulted in a crisis of morale unless a transition to other roles appropriate to the disengaged state occurred. The primary change was from "vertical solidarities" (ties to children, for women; to bosses and subordinates, for men) to "horizontal" ones (retired friends). Over time, the well-disengaged individual became less assertive, more self-centered, less social, and reconciled to his or her new status.[3]

Putting his own optimistic gloss on the theory, Parsons argued that old age should increasingly be defined in consummatory terms. It was a period of "harvest," he said in 1963, when the fruits of previous instrumental commitments were gathered in, when the individual received rewards for a life well-lived and learned that "it is *good* to be old."[4] The emerging American world of compulsory retirement, sunny villages in Florida, leisure centers, and senior clubs was the institutional embodiment of the "disengagement" concept.

A countervision of the aged also emerged, one casting them as a persecuted minority. This alternative's subsequent success derived, in large part, from a critical weakness in the Parsons-Cumming theory: its reliance on mechanistic, normative explanations that proved susceptible to ideological attack. Such challenges soon arose from feminist and Malthusian theorists who saw the reorganized, strengthened suburban family as a menace to their goals of liberation, enhanced individualism, and zero population growth.

The alternative theory of aging, which first surfaced in 1953, was an early spin-off of the civil rights movement. Writing that year in the *Journal of Gerontology*, Milton Barron cautiously suggested that the old resembled American Negroes in many ways. He argued that a majority of Americans saw the aged as a menace, citing two published statements that had noted the danger of heavy pension taxes being imposed on the young and the existence of mandatory retirement. Barron said that employers maintained stereotypes of older workers—that they talked too much, tried too hard to please, were too set in their ways, lacked poise and grooming—which were belied by the facts. He added that the aged, particularly older workers, also manifested typical minority group reactions: sensitivity, self-consciousness, defensiveness, and self-hatred. Barron concluded that the aged "meet many of the criteria of a minority as defined in sociological theory" and encouraged researchers to use this focus in analyzing the problems of the elderly.[5]

Eight years later, sociologist Irving Rosow revived the theme, arguing that despite American affluence, "old people have become an underprivileged minority group of second-class citizens." He attributed this situation to "social change": the rapid growth in the economy, which had created jobs and opportunities for younger folk; the new inapplicability of one generation's experience to another; the decay of religion; and the transfer of responsibility for care of aged parents from family to the state. On the fact that political liberalism had encouraged or supported most of these changes, Rosow was silent. Rather, he focused on the consequences: young people now held "negative stereotypes about the old" and intentionally drove the latter into debilitating poverty. Americans exhibited "enthusiasms" for pastel refrigerators and mink washrags, he said, rather than showing concern about social justice. The young were alienated from the old, the old from the young, and man from man. The very "values and institutions" of America so undermined the position of the aged. Accordingly, Rosow argued that the old now needed to take away "a larger, more equitable share of what our society has to offer." They must, for example, be guaranteed health care. Social Security coverage must be made universal, with both taxes and benefits raised substantially, and the latter indexed so as to rise automatically with inflation.[6]

Revealingly, Rosow thought that such measures were so radical in scope that only a "catastrophic crisis" could bring them to fruition. Barely a decade had passed, though, before his agenda was fully achieved through Medicare and the Social Security Amendments of 1971. With semirevolution so won, with the aged having almost doubled their share of national income in a brief ten-year span, one might have expected the view of the elderly as a persecuted minority group to disappear. In fact, the rhetoric only grew in intensity as the concept of "ageism" was born. It soon entered the standard lexicon of American social crimes.

The term was coined in 1969 by gerontologist Robert Butler. Defined as "prejudice by one age group toward other age groups," ageism reflected "deep-seated uneasiness" on the part of the young and middle-aged toward the old as symbols of disease, disability, powerlessness, and death. Aging was "the great sleeper in American life," Butler concluded, an issue that would parallel racism as the great social question of the next twenty to thirty years.[7]

Central to the new focus on "ageism" were charges that "society" had denied the elderly their sexuality through the myth of sexlessness in the older years. This denial, according to sexologist Isadore Rubin, had made difficult, or impossible, the correct diagnoses of medical and psychological problems, had distorted family relationships, had perverted the administration of justice to older persons accused of sex offenses, and had weakened the self-image of the elderly. Among other corrective measures, Rubin urged marriage counselors to encourage masturbation among the old as a "valid outlet" and called for sex education classes in "golden age" clubs. While the old no longer deserved honor and dignity, they would be given guilt-free sex as compensation for their loss.[8]

Ageism gained a kind of theoretical support a few years later with publication of William Ryan's *Blaming the Victim*. This logically subversive volume purported to identify a "brilliant" new ideology which had been used by humanitarian liberals of the Parsons school to justify "a perverse form of social action designed to change, not society, as one might expect, but rather society's victim." This liberal ideology, he said, had gone beyond "conservative" ideas that simply dismissed victims as inferior, defective, or morally unfit. Instead, it had framed inadequacy as an acquired stigma of social, rather than genetic or moral, origin.[9]

What Ryan was actually objecting to was a normative social order of any kind, the attempt to give moral shape to society and to judge some persons as normal and others as deviant. As he readily admitted, *Blaming the Victim* was little more than a popularized version of the radical sociology of C. Wright Mills, which also disputed the use of moral and social codes to defend the normal. Ryan insisted, for example, that black poverty in urban areas was not due to the breakdown of family life, to soaring levels of divorce and illegitimacy, or to the malignant nature of the culture of poverty. Poverty, he said, was "primarily an absence of money." Defects were not to be found in individuals, but rather in the community, the environment, and the economic order. Racism, sexism, and ageism were the great cancers in the American system, he concluded. They could be cut out only through political action and revolutionary social change.

More theory, of a sort, came from the French intellectual Simone de Beauvoir. In her 1972 book, *The Coming of Age*, she sought to translate her earlier analysis of gender conflict to the situation of the old. As with her view of women, de Beauvoir's analysis rested on a bowdlerized Marxism. Society looked upon old age "as a kind of shameful secret," she said, around which had been built a "conspiracy of silence." The myths and cliches of bourgeois thought aimed "at holding up the elderly man as someone who is different, as *another being*." "The world" looked upon old people with disgust: "In them love and jealousy seem revolting or absurd, sexuality repulsive and violence ludicrous." With the entire civilization ruled by profit, the human working stock was of interest "only in so far as it is profitable. When it is no longer profitable it is tossed aside." Such treatment as "a piece of scrap," de Beauvoir declared, was the fate of the elderly under capitalism.

What was the alternative? De Beauvoir's answer was clear: "Those who condemn the maiming, crippling system in which we live should expose this scandal. It is by concentrating one's efforts upon the fate of the most unfortunate, the worst-used of all, that one can successfully shake a society to its foundations." Insisting on protection of the old "would imply a total upheaval of our society," she said; it would make clear "that everything has to be reconsidered, recast from the very beginning." As such, the fate of the elderly became the best argument for radical reconstruction on a socialist model.[10]

Backed by these theoretical schemes, the frantic charges began to mount. Writing in *Life*, Marcia Seligson argued that Americans wrenched the aged from society's mainstream, isolated them like lepers, stripped them of productivity, and dehumanized them in bleak institutions. American civilization, she added, mutilated the old and condemned them to live out their years "trapped in near poverty, numbing boredom, inactivity, indignity, dependence and the hopeless state of standing alone outside the swirl of humanity." Alex Comfort accused Americans of treating the old as "unintelligent, asexual, unemployable, and crazy." Philosopher Ronald Gross called ageism "the ultimate prejudice, the last discrimination, the cruelest rejection." California writer Irene Paull labeled the aged "an oppressed class." Anthropologist J. Scott Francher reviewed the content of television commercials and charged that the words "You've got a lot to live and Pepsi's got a lot to give," along with other aspects of America's youth culture, culturally disenfranchised the elderly. Such celebrations of youth, he continued, confronted the old with "many anxiety-inducing and tension-provoking situations," which led to their emotional breakdown and early death. Bill Oriol, staff director of the U.S. Senate Special Committee on Aging, hinted that a new holocaust was just around the corner: "There is ageism in this country, and it is real and growing. The truth is most people consider the elderly expendable."[11]

In her book *The Other Generation* (1977), Rochelle Jones carried these themes to their furthest lengths. Ageism in America grew out of our desire to end "aesthetic pollution," she said. Americans were offended by wrinkled skin, liver spots, and varicose veins. To exorcise our fear of death, we made those who were about to die redundant and irrelevant while they were still alive. Jones was particularly angry that society showed great anguish over the death of a child and such little sadness when the death of a very old person came. Indeed, she looked with envy on those societies where children were considered of so little value that they were not worth a funeral or a memory. The government, she also charged, blatantly cheated the elderly out of their fair share of national resources. Psychiatrists and other doctors discriminated against the aged because "the old are too depressing to work with." Newspapers treated the elderly "as if they were an alien race." In short, Jones concluded that ageism was "a serious and growing problem in the United States rapidly surpassing racism in prevalence," a problem clearly linked to industrial capitalism.[12]

These extraordinary charges generated demand for equally extraordinary countermeasures. In their volume *Ageism: Prejudice and Discrimination Against the Elderly*, Jack and William Levin swallowed whole Ryan's *Blaming the Victim* analysis and encouraged fundamental changes "in the very system that provides majority group members with a relatively comfortable style of life." Rochelle Jones described the emergence of a new political pressure group "composed of outraged older adults" who saw themselves as victims and who were fully aware that they got more only if the rest of society got less. Some groups, she noted with approval, were already resorting to terror tactics to force politicians to give them what they wanted. To secure justice for the persecuted, Jones insisted, the young and the middle-aged would have to pay higher taxes and reduce their own standard of living.

Maggie Kuhn, founder of the Gray Panthers, demanded an assault on the very foundation "of our competitive, wasteful, productivity-centered society." America was "sick," she said. The elimination of racism, sexism, and ageism required "sweeping changes in society as well as in personal attitudes and life-styles, social theories and policies, our national priorities and political processes." The remnant family should be dismantled, for example, in favor of "families of choice" based on mutual interests rather than kinship. With such an agenda, Kuhn argued, the old could become the revolutionary vanguard, working to topple capitalistic society and replace it with one truly humane and just. Paraphrasing Karl Marx, Kuhn wrote: "We who are old have nothing to lose! We have everything to gain by living dangerously! We can initiate change without jeopardizing jobs or family. We can be the risk-takers, daring to challenge and change systems, policies, life-styles, ourselves."[13]

Just as the campaign against "sexism" has been subtly translated into the forced proletarization of women, the resulting dismantling of the home, and the necessary collectivization of children, so the campaign against ageism has become but another variation of an old socialist/Marxist theme.

The most curious aspect of this effusion of books, articles, and rhetoric was that almost none of it was based on research. Prejudice, or ageism, was simply presumed to exist, and from that assumption the flights of theoretical and political fancy took off. Only well after the visions of the old as a minority group and a persecuted class had sunk deep roots did younger sociologists and gerontologists fan out to collect the hard data proving the argument.

The empirical results, though, were disturbing. Writing in 1965, for example, Gordon Streib found no support for the argument that the aged were a minority group. The aged, he found, had no collective history, no religion of their own, and no solidarity of work and interest. Despite the rise of retirement villages, most of the old still lived dispersed among the young. Their closest ties were to family rather than other old people. Survey data actually showed that most Americans believed that the old were *better* workers than younger persons. The old, Streib continued, also had no common identity, and were vastly overrepresented in state legislatures. Studies of local elite systems suggested further that those over age 65 exercised more influence in their communities than any other age category.

Many of the old, it was true, were economically underprivileged, yet these persons had been poor most of their lives. The old, moreover, did not prove to be "ghettoized," with fewer than 5 percent living in institutions.[14]

Taking another tack, Vivian Wood sought to show that the young held nasty, emotionally crippling behavioral expectations of the old. She found, however, "that young adults are considerably more aware of how older people think than are older people of how young people think." Moreover, it turned out that the old themselves were far more disapproving of unconventional behavior by the elderly than were the young. Persons in their twenties and thirties, for example, were *three times* more likely to approve of a retired couple wearing shorts when they went shopping downtown than were the old. Similarly, the young were far more likely than the old to approve of a retired couple frequenting nightclubs with a floor show. Simply put, the anticipated "ageist" stereotypes could not be found. (Indeed, in a curious manner, Wood had unwittingly stumbled onto an unsettling truth, discovering that the young actually dismissed the traditional functions of the old by giving little respect to patterns of behavior that reflected modesty, morality, or virtue and by expecting the old to live by a new code of life focused on personal and sexual fulfillment.)[15]

In the mid-1970s, a large team of social researchers headed by Eva Kahana noted that "we have almost no systematic information about the actual incidence of [ageism] or the extent to which older persons feel victimized," and resolved to fill the void. Using a large sample of elderly persons drawn from two Michigan communities, one middle-class and one blue-collar, the team devised complex measurements of social victimization. The results? "Or data indicate that, contrary to expectation of widespread reporting of problems, relatively few older people report discrimination or rejection by society or the family." In fact, the team found that the real concerns of the elderly were fear of crime, lax court systems, and undesirable neighbors. Once again, ageism could not be found.[16]

Rather, the social evidence that could be found tended to support the disengagement theory. Streib's research, for example, tended in this direction, as did the work of a team from Duke University's Center for the Study of Aging and Human Development, which used an "equality index" to measure the treatment of the elderly in 31 countries. They found that the status of the aged, relative to employment and education, was equal to that of the young only in underdeveloped lands such as Iran, Honduras, and Ghana. By way of contrast, status in developing lands was correlated with unequal treatment of age categories, followed by a differentiated form of equality in mature societies, reflecting the modern institution of retirement.[17]

Despite their repeated failures, though, the ageism theorists refused to concede the field. The Kahana team, for example, continued to insist that ageism was "a prevalent feature of modern USA society," something which "we all know exists," an "important" defining characteristic of American life.[18] Alex Comfort found sinister implications in the fact that 82 percent of young and middle-aged Americans thought that the old were "friendly," while only 25 percent of those over 65 thought their contemporaries were. This showed, he said, that the old had been imprinted with "negative attitudes" about their own age group because of the "fear of aging" shown by the young.[19]

What accounts for such deceptions? The simple reality is that ideology pays no attention to facts. It is impervious to research. Rather, it seeks to reshape interpretation of reality in line with its own presuppositions. In this case, modern liberalism assumed that American society was littered with discrimination: that racism, ageism, sexism, heterosexism, weightism, and species-ism (to name only a few of the identified prejudices) defined the modern American experience. This ideology demanded victims and victimizers, suffering classes and perverse exploiters. It envisioned a very small group of wealthy, middle-aged, heterosexual, slender, waspish, white males (the "majority") who collaborated to exploit women, Blacks, immigrants, young people, the poor, Hispanics, American Indians, Asians, children, the old, the overweight, the homosexual, and the nonhuman. If persons or creatures in these victimized groups were unaware of their victimization, this was simply because their "consciousness" had been insufficiently raised.

The great ageism scam, of course, had consequences. While never more than a small minority of the old took to the barricades to tear down the system, a new militancy fueled by a sense of victimization did begin to characterize more mainline political pressure groups, such as The National Council on Aging and the National Council of Senior Citizens. One positive change was a fresh campaign against mandatory retirement rules, leading to federal legislation that effectively scuttled such requirements. Such rules had always rested on dubious assumptions of a static economy and a limited number of available jobs and were being used by companies primarily to avoid difficult personnel decisions.[20]

Other consequences, though, were more disruptive. This same political militancy also led to passage of the Social Security Amendments of 1972, which vastly increased coverage and benefits with scant regard for the system's solvency or the burden to be borne by future generations. The ageism scam also had the effect of scuttling the civil rights campaign focused on the status and goals of black Americans. After 1960, civil rights leaders had struck alliance after alliance with newly aggrieved groups—e.g., women, the old, homosexuals—in a bid to build a grand coalition that would crush all discrimination. However, the result of this coalition-building with overwhelmingly white, overwhelmingly middle-class groups was simply to see the movement squander its historical and moral capital. The mistake of black leadership lay in buying into an absurd theory of victimization that cast a very small group of middle-aged WASP males as somehow persecuting the other 90 percent of the population. Where black Americans had legitimate moral grievances deeply rooted in American history, the complaints of feminists, Gray Panthers, and "gays" were of a different order: ideological, neo-Marxist, amoral attacks on the Western social and economic order. To cast their grievances as equal, to recite the lyric "racism, sexism, ageism, heterosexism," was to sacrifice that unique claim to redress and to link the black community to developments that have brought it ruin: the celebration of female-headed families; the embrace of sexual anarchy; the turn to state "solutions" for social problems.

Finally, growing numbers of the old were dragged down into the hedonistic pit, transformed from guardians of a heritage into hustlers pursuing easy sex and self-gratification. Television encouraged the change, as hip, sex-obsessed seniors became stock comic figures, seen, for example, among the residents of the Sunshine Home on *All in the Family*. Paralleling this change at the other end of the age spectrum was the emergence of the sex-wise, prepubescent child, another stock video character of the last fifteen years. This great leveling process has stripped the old of their dignity and the young of their innocence. The war against age "stereotypes" has actually proven to be part of the campaign against moral order of any kind; and the number of human casualties is mounting.

Through most of this debate, curiously, traditionalists or social conservatives sat on the sidelines. Except for occasional criticisms of the Social Security system (even then, usually for economic or fiscal reasons), conservative philosophers gave little attention to the proper place of the old in late-twentieth-century America, while politicians of a rightward bent offered little more to policy development than halfhearted attempts to delay the "cost-of-living adjustments" for state pensions.

This avoidance of the issue of aging has been unfortunate. Traditional voices, for example, might have explored the real "ageism" that exists in our society: the refusal of modern Americans to accept and honor the authentic values and traditions represented by the old, forcing the latter instead to live by the code of pleasure-seeking hedonism. Conservatives might have promoted ways of restoring the multigenerational family as a social and economic institution, noting that the survival of family life in any form will necessarily involve voluntary, but still compelling compromises with economic efficiency and personal freedom. Moreover, it is within tradition that alternative ways of viewing the old exist: not as "disengaged," state-dependent, or "persecuted" persons, but as interpreters of social order, as defenders of inherited culture, as leaders of religions, as past-oriented guides to a community's future.

Notes

1. Lawrence K. Frank, "Gerontology," *Journal of Gerontology* 1 (Jan. 1946): 8, 10.
2. Talcott Parsons and Winston White, "The Link Between Character and Society," in *Culture and Social Character*, ed. Seymour Martin Lipset and Leo Lowenthal (New York: The Free Press of Glencoe, 1961), pp. 116–19; and Talcott Parsons, *The Social System* (New York: The Free Press, 1951), pp. 186–88.
3. Elaine Cumming and William E. Henry, *Growing Old: The Process of Disengagement* (New York: Basic Books, 1961), pp. 168–71, 211–17.
4. Talcott Parsons, "Old Age as a Consummatory Phase," *The Gerontologist* 3 (June 1963): 53–54.
5. Milton L. Barron, "Minority Group Characteristics of the Aged in American Society," *Journal of Gerontology* 8 (Oct. 1953): 477–82.
6. Irving Rosow, "Old Age: One Moral Dilemma of an Affluent Society," *The Gerontologist* 1 (June 1961): 85–91.
7. Robert N. Butler, MD, "Age-ism: Another Form of Bigotry," *The Gerontologist* 9 (1969): 243–46.
8. See: Isadore Rubin, "The 'Sexless Older Years': A Socially Harmful Stereotype," *The Annals of the American Academy of Political and Social Science* 376 (Mar. 1968): 86–95.
9. William Ryan, *Blaming the Victim* (New York: Pantheon Books, 1971), pp. 3–12.
10. Simone de Beauvoir, *The Coming of Age*, trans. Patrick O'Brian (New York: G.P. Putnam's Sons, 1972), pp. 1–10, 543.
11. Marcia Seligson, "The Social Crime of Growing Old," *Life* (May 19, 1972): 22; Alex Comfort, "Aging: Real and Imaginary'; Introduction to Edith Stein, "What is Ageism"; and Irene Paull, "I Hate to Be Called a Senior Citizen"; in *The New Old: Struggling for Decent Aging*, ed. Ronald Gross, Beatrice Gross, and Sylvia Seidman (Garden City, NY: Anchor Books, 1978), pp. 7, 89, 122; and J. Scott Francher, "It's the Pepsi Generation: Accelerated Aging and the Television Commercial," *International Journal of Aging and Human Development* 4 (Mar. 1973): 245–55.
12. Rochelle Jones, *The Other Generation: The New Power of Older People* (Englewood Cliffs, NJ: Prentice-Hall, 1977), pp. 79–99.
13. Jack Levin and William C. Levin, *Ageism: Prejudice and Discrimination Against the Elderly* (Belmont, CA: Wadsworth Publishing Co., 1980), pp. 36–44; Jones, pp. 218–27; Maggie Kuhn, "Advocacy in This New Age," *Aging* Nos. 297-98 (July-Aug. 1979): 2–5; and Maggie Kuhn, "Foreword," in Levin and Levin, pp. vii–viii.
14. Gordon F. Streib, "Are the Aged a Minority Group?" in *Middle Age and Aging: A Reader in Social Psychology*, ed. Bernice L. Neugarten (Chicago and London: The University of Chicago Press, 1968), pp. 35–46.
15. Vivian Wood, "Age Appropriate Behavior for Older People," *The Gerontologist* 11 (Winter 1971): 74–78.

16. Eva Kahana, Jersey Liang, Barbara Felton, Thomas Fairchild, Zev Harel, "Perspectives of Aged on Victimization, 'Ageism,' and Their Problems in Urban Society," *The Gerontologist* 17 (1977): 121–29.
17. Gordon F. Streib, p. 45; and Erdman P. Palmore and Kenneth Manton, "Modernization and Status of the Aged: International Correlations," *Journal of Gerontology* 29 (Feb. 1974): 205–10.
18. Kahana, pp. 127–28.
19. Comfort, p. 80.
20. The key congressional act was passage of the 1978 Amendments to the Age Discrimination in Employment Act of 1967, which extended the measure's coverage through age 70. For a detailed description of their impact, see: "Age Discrimination in Employment Act," *Prentice-Hall Labor Relations Guide* 349 (Englewood Cliffs, NJ: Prentice-Hall, 1982), pp. 1601-24.

15

The Dilemma of Social Security

Americans live in an incomplete welfare state. Our system of Social Security, the legend tells us, has been built pragmatically through the push, pull, and compromise of rival interest groups. This has been in contrast to Western Europe, where welfare policies resting on broad, abstract theories of social democracy have predominated.

Many see this as the great virtue of the American system. By sticking to interest group politics, they say, we have bypassed many of the problems associated with the more comprehensive welfare states. It is certainly true that the costs of those theoretically integrated systems absorb much larger shares of their respective Gross National Products. Sweden's state expenditure on income maintenance, for example, was 30.7 percent of its GNP in 1977, compared to only 14 percent of GNP for the United States.

Yet the American avoidance of comprehensive welfare state theory has had one negative consequence. It is now apparent that our system of old-age security was constructed on a fundamental social contradiction. Indeed, it is a contradiction that now threatens the very survival of that system. More disturbingly, it also promises, before it is done, to consume the family unit in America.

It seems appropriate to begin by returning to the theorists and learning where we went wrong. Warnings over the disastrous course in which the United States was heading were published as long ago as 1941. The Cassandras in question were not sour conservatives, seeking to block humane legislation. Rather, the warnings came from the pens of Swedish Social Democrats Alva and Gunnar Myrdal, two primary architects of their nation's welfare system.

The Myrdals argued that the root contradiction in America's new Social Security system lay in the shift from family-centered to state-centered old-age support. In the long era before the creation of socially funded pensions, they noted, economic incentives bound the generations within a family tightly together. Persons in their most productive years, roughly ages 18 to

65, supported their parents in the latter's old age as a culturally and legally enforced duty. These young and middle-aged adults also had a strong incentive to bear and successfully rear children themselves, in order to provide for their own security when they could no longer work. Those who avoided the responsibility of having children so left themselves at risk.

This family-centered form of security is common to most traditional societies. Significantly, though, it was still operative in the United States as late as 1929. Indeed, during the 1920–29 period alone, five states joined the majority of other jurisdictions in enacting statutes to enforce the moral duty of children to support their parents. Eleven other states passed new laws making failure to care for one's destitute parents a criminal offense. In his definitive history of the treatment of the aged in America, W. Andrew Achenbaum concludes that, in the absence of the Great Depression, this orientation would probably have continued indefinitely into the future. The pressure for change simply was not strong enough to overcome American traditions of family integrity and personal responsibility. Most workers, he suggests, would have stayed in the labor force as long as possible, funded their own retirements through savings and private insurance annuities, and relied on their children and other family members as their back-up source of security.[1]

The Myrdals explained that a socially funded pension system drastically loosened these family bonds. In the welfare state, government provided pensions to the elderly as a right. These pensions were paid by transferring income, through payroll or other taxes, from current workers to current retirees. Through this one stroke, then, the bonds of economic security between the three generations in a single family were cut. One's own children were no longer needed as an investment towards security in later life. In fact, the "value" of children was precisely reversed. In the welfare state, where income and payroll taxes were mandatory, one could *improve* one's immediate standard-of-living, and suffer no long-term consequences, by having only one child, or—even better—none at all. As Gunnar Myrdal described the situation: "While practically all married people try to limit the number of their children to some extent in order to defend the family standard of living, and while an increasing number carry out this limitation to the extreme, practically no one [now] breeds children as an investment . . . to secure support in old age." From the individual's perspective, nothing would be sacrificed. "Let others bear the children who will support me in my old age," became the logical response to the welfare state's new incentives.

Myrdal said that it was this clash over the economic effects of bearing children—society's need for generations of children sufficiently large to pay for promised future pensions and other welfare benefits in conflict with the incentives found in each family unit which made childbearing econom-ically foolish—that formed the "burning" core of the modern population question.[2] Wife Alva Myrdal argued that, in both Sweden and (implicitly) the United States, the generations in the productive age categories between 1920 and 1940 would "go down in history as the most ravenous of all." On the one hand, they had increased their immediate consumption by bearing, on average, fewer than two children per family and spending on themselves what should have gone toward the needed additional children. On the other hand, these same generations had created Social Security pensions, giving themselves tax-free, labor-free income in their old age. Such "consumption at both ends," she said, spelled ruin for a nation in the long run.[3]

Other sober voices offered the same warning. Great Britain's Royal Com-mission on Population, created in 1944 to investigate the consequences of that land's low birthrate, concluded that the game was running out. Be-tween 1890 and 1947, the commission noted, Britons had relied on the decline in their birthrate and the resulting shrinkage of the "dependency ratio" (as defined in its report, children under age fifteen + retired persons ÷ adults aged 15–64) to help increase the average standard of living in the land. Among the benefits which adults had granted themselves was retire-ment income. The Old Age Pension Act of 1908 made financial security for the aged a government responsibility. In the short run, fewer infant mouths to feed had made more available to divide up among those already alive. Britain now faced, however, the prospect of rapid growth in the number of the old, which would drive the dependency ratio back up. The dilemma was compounded by the fact that even a contemporary increase in the birthrate would only further raise the dependency ratio for at least two decades, or until the new children would become working adults. These developments, the commission concluded, "must aggravate the budgetary difficulties of the next generation, which in any case are likely to be for-midable."[4]

Such warnings fell on deaf ears. The American Social Security system was locked into a very different set of demographic, sociological, and eco-nomic theories which dominated the decade of the Great Depression. Sig-nificantly, their overall thrust was against children, families, and growth.

The old-age insurance portions of the Social Security Act were drafted by the Committee on Economic Security (CES), appointed by President Franklin Roosevelt in 1934. Its principal members were: Barbara Armstrong, professor of law at the University of California-Berkeley; Mur-ray Latimer, a member of the Railroad Retirement Board; J. Douglas Brown, a young Princeton economist; and Otto Richter, an actuary. In giving shape to this measure, they fell under the sway of certain academic theorists,[5] and operated from three basic assumptions:

1) *The American birthrate, already at a historic low, would probably fall still further.* Writing in 1930, demographer P.K. Whelpton predicted that the decline in the U.S. birthrate—already to the zero-growth level—would continue, with "no stopping place . . . indicated on the surface." This downward trend, he said, emphasized "the rapidity with which the age composition of the population is going to change," and the need to "overhaul" American social and economic institutions to care for the rapidly growing number of elderly. Robert R. Updegraff, in a 1932 article for *Advertising and Selling,* warned the business community that the American population, after centuries of rapid growth, was quickly approaching stagnation. "What is it going to mean to American business when its market stops growing? When sales quotas strike the reality of there being no more people this year than there were last?"

In the massive study *Recent Social Trends in the United States,* commissioned by President Herbert Hoover in 1929 and published four years later, demographer Warren S. Thompson joined Professor Whelpton in suggesting that the new stagnation in America's population size had played a role in worsening the current depression. In the past, they noted, the United States had had an implicit growth-oriented population policy, which encouraged large families and immigration in order to fill new communities, settle the land, work in growing factories, and people the nation. Over the last several decades, though, the rapid spread of birth control and growing Malthusian propaganda about alleged overpopulation seemed to have fundamentally changed attitudes. Indeed, they said, "if a continued decline in the birthrate is a desired end, it seems that the present mode of life can be little improved upon." The penalization of parenthood through the lack of distinction in wages between those who did and did not bring up children, the financial premium placed upon exclusive devotion to one's career, the exclusion of families with children from many desirable apartments and houses, "the pity lavished by their more 'emancipated sisters' upon women who rear families rather than devote themselves to business, lectures, travel, and bridge," the desperate struggle of white-collar workers to maintain consumption patterns equal to their neighbors, and "many other factors which discriminate against the man and woman who devote any considerable time and energy to their children"—such developments clearly discouraged the founding of families and birth of children.[6]

2) *The American family system was collapsing.* The theory emerged in the early decades of this century that the family system found in the United States was weakening and, as a consequence, voluntarily transferring most of its functions to the state. In his statistically bogus, but nonetheless influential, three-volume *Social History of the American Family* (1917), Arthur Calhoun argued that "American history consummates the disappearance of the wider familism and the substitution of the parentalism of

society." Since many natural parents were totally unfit for parenthood, society was now coming "to accept as a duty" the upbringing of the young. Ever more children passed "into the custody of community experts who are qualified to perform the complexer functions of parenthood . . . which the parents have neither the time nor knowledge to perform."

Giving the same argument a more scientific gloss, sociologists William F. Ogburn and Ernest R. Groves emphasized the "considerable and increasing disorganization of the family." In his contribution to Hoover's *Recent Social Trends*, Ogburn described "the decline of the institutional functions of the family." The modern family, he noted, produced less of its own food, furniture, and clothing than before. "Religious observances within the home are said to be declining." Recreation now focused on theaters, dance halls, and ball parks. Home baking and canning disappeared. Married women entered the workplace. The schoolteacher could be viewed "as a substitute parent in regard to the function of training the child." The "personality function" of the family, elsewhere described as the only task remaining within the home circle, was also failing as education and social change widened the gap between generations. Finally, even the protection of the very old members of the family by their offspring was disappearing, due to smaller families and greater mobility of the population. The implication was clear that the state needed to absorb this function, too.[7]

3) *Economic stagnation had become a permanent fixture, and only a finite number of jobs were available.* The economic consequences of a declining population were a popular theme during the early 1930s. Such a demographic shift, it was noted, involved a decrease in the number of consumers in the population relative to producers, which tended to reduce demand and so resulted in a kind of structural unemployment. Moreover, as the total number of consumers in a society approached a stationary level, innovations in production and other improved efficiencies created additional, "organic" unemployment as industrial capacity raced past consumer demand. The cessation of population growth, the economists added, also increased the risks of capital investment and imperiled the expansionist psychology on which capitalism rested. In combination, these changes produced permanent economic depression. As remedy, some theorists argued that more and better state economic planning was needed. John Maynard Keynes, in his 1937 Galton Lecture, stated that a stationary population could still enjoy a rising standard of living if government undertook a more positive state investment policy. Other economists were less sanguine. In a population without growth, they concluded, there were but a limited number of jobs to be had. Unemployment could be reduced only by artificially increasing the dependency ratio: namely, by moving some workers out of the labor pool through forced retirement.[8]

In an article widely read in progressive American circles, Swiss economist L. Hersch drew together all three assumptions. Assuming that the fall in the birthrate in the Western World was a *fait accompli*, noting the diminished capacity of the Western family to serve as a source of old-age security, and emphasizing stagnating populations as "a powerful factor" in producing permanent unemployment "in our time,' Hersch proposed a series of corrective remedies. Significantly, all of them found their way into New Deal programs.[9] They were: (1) a reduction in the average hours of work per person; (2) a progressive limitation of the age for wage-earning work, both by setting a minimum age below which no adolescent might be employed and a maximum for mandatory retirement; (3) an improvement in the purchasing power of the masses through an increase in real wages; (4) the granting of free or reduced-cost services by state authorities; and (5) a state fiscal policy resting on the progressive taxation of large fortunes and high incomes, used primarily to soak up the "excess capital" in the system and transfer it to the less-well-off, so as to increase their immediate purchasing power.

Even within this scheme, though, Hersch admitted to an implicit contradiction: in a stagnant population, the proportion of insured workers paying "contributions" to the old-age insurance programs would naturally diminish, over time, as the population aged; meanwhile, the need to redistribute available work by the forced retirement of some laborers would further reduce the number being taxed and increase the number drawing benefits. In short, the system would slowly self-destruct. Hersch had no answer to this dilemma, other than to encourage more immigration. The old-age pension system, and Western living standards generally, could be maintained only by leeching off the biological vitality of other peoples.

There were serious flaws in the research and reasoning behind all these assumptions. As the post-World War II era would show, demographic trends were far more malleable than thought possible. In addition, we now know that the family was not so much "losing functions" as it was seeing them stripped away by aggressive new coteries of "experts" in the "helping professions." The belief that only a finite number of jobs existed in the American economy had a certain logic in the peculiar circumstances of the Great Depression; the two decades after 1945, though, witnessed more normal economic conditions. Moreover, the contradiction openly described by Hersch (and later intuited by the Myrdals) revealed the basic scheme to be unworkable.

Nonetheless, the CES and other New Deal architects swallowed these assumptions whole. The basic trade-off in the new Social Security system was not the "compact between generations" now so enshrined in congressional speeches. Rather, it was a deal cut to meet the specific conditions of the Great Depression: the young would pay for the support of the old through social insurance and so be relieved of the care of their own parents; the old would retire at 65 in order to give their jobs to the young. As Senator Robert Wagner, chief sponsor of the Social Security bill, explained to the Senate on the opening day of debate: "The incentive to the retirement of superannuated workers will improve efficiency standards, will make new places for the strong and eager, and will increase the productivity of the young by removing from their shoulders the uneven burden of caring for the old."[10] According to Barbara Armstrong, chief theoretician behind the old-age measure, the primary motivation behind the bill was a redistribution of work through forced retirement. "That's why that little ridiculous amount of $15 (the limit on monthly earned income for those on Social Security) was put in. Let [the retiree] earn some pin money, but it had to be on *retirement*. And retirement means that you've stopped working for pay."[11]

The birthrate was declining, and there was nothing the state could or should do about it; the family was losing its functions and should be replaced by the state; the number of jobs in a stagnant population was limited, and government should redistribute them: the new Social Security Act rested on these articles of faith. The Amendments of 1939 further expanded the social insurance aspects of the scheme, granting the first cohort of recipients benefits far exceeding contribution levels. The contradictions in the scheme were left for future generations to sort out.

For the next quarter century, though, the Social Security system was relatively problem-free. Social Security, or FICA taxes, to begin with, remained almost insignificant for several decades. In 1947, the maximum "contribution" was only $30 per year; as late as 1965, the top figure was still a modest $174 annually. At such levels, the demographic incentives within the system had little, if any, impact. In addition, events conspired to reverse, for two amazing decades, all three of the assumptions on which Social Security had been reared. This put off, for a time, the need to face the systemic time bomb.

To begin with, the birthrate started climbing again. From a low of 18.4 births per 1,000 persons in 1936, it climbed to 26.6 in 1947 and stayed at a relatively high level through 1962. This promised a vast new cohort of young employees for the workplaces of the 1960–80 period, and so removed the immediate danger of a crippling dependency ratio of retirees to workers. Second, the years between 1945 and 1960 witnessed the new flowering of family sentiments, with large families back in vogue. Even relative to the support of elderly parents, American families seemed solid, and the impact of Social Security relatively weak. In 1957, over half of the elderly still reported receiving some income support from their children, compared to only 41.6 percent receiving some support from Social Security. As late as 1960, a large majority of widowed women 75 years and older still lived with relatives. Third, the dramatic economic boom during this period fueled a huge increase in the number of American jobs.

Shortly after 1960, though, the old trend lines began to return. Concern about overpopulation fueled the massive propaganda campaign, described earlier, to sharply reduce the American birthrate. The new critics of the American family began heaping abuse on the "pathologies" of the suburban home, and alternative life-styles, usually "child free" and "flexible" (meaning no long-term responsibilities), became the vogue. The late 1960s also witnessed the first tremors in the international economy, which resulted in the stagflation and general recession of 1973–83.

Over the same years, the U.S. Congress made major changes in the coverage and benefit levels of Social Security. These alterations were part of a massive flood of legislation which started in 1965 with Lyndon Johnson's Great Society and ended in 1977 with the collapse of liberal self-confidence under Jimmy Carter. The most bizarre aspect of this legislative binge was the blatant contradiction lying at its heart. On the one hand, the rapid creation of new federal agencies and nearly geometric increases in funding levels for social programs were justified by published assumptions of rapid economic and revenue growth, both of which were premised on a continuation of growth-oriented demographic trends from the Baby Boom era. At the same time, Congress was passing legislation designed to end population growth (e.g., Title X funding for family planning services; programs of "population education"; Medicaid abortions; and the net transfer of the income-tax burden onto parents with children) and to slow down, even halt, economic growth (e.g., creation of the Environmental Protection Agency; the original Clean Air and Clean Water Acts).

This combination of growth and antigrowth assumptions could also be seen in the legislative maneuverings behind the Social Security Amendments of 1972. Between 1965 and 1970, Congress had regularly increased Social Security benefits and taxes, largely in line with the rise in the cost of living. Yet publicity surrounding the 1971 White House Conference on Aging and a newly militant "Gray Lobby" shouting "ageism" generated a proposal to increase benefits immediately by 20 percent and to index all future benefit levels to inflation. At the time, Robert J. Myers, former chief actuary of the Social Security system, warned the nation that Congress had based its plan on demographic assumptions keyed to the relatively growth-oriented days of the 1960–63 period. Even the most pessimistic projection from that time period, he noted, showed a significantly higher birthrate for 1971 than had actually occurred. Thus, while the United States had nearly reached the zero-population-growth (ZPG) level, it was still passing legislation assuming steady population expansion for decades to come.[12] During debate, Senator Carl Curtis of Nebraska informed his colleagues that the new taxes necessary to pay for this increase would fall most heavily on those low- and moderate-income families already burdened by trying to establish a home, buy a car, and carry the income and sales tax burdens. Senator Fannin of Arizona vehemently attacked his colleagues who justified "extravagant spending schemes" on assumptions of rapid growth and yet were also "the ones who most often are the advocates of zero population growth and even zero economic growth in the name of ecology."[13] Nonetheless, the measure won almost unanimous approval.

As a result, old-age benefits and FICA taxes rose steadily after 1971 to no longer insignificant levels. The tax on employee's income is now 7.51 percent, up to an annual maximum of $3,380 (the employer pays another 7.51 percent). For the self-employed, the maximum tax (computed at 15.02 percent) reaches $6,759, a portion of which is offset by an income tax credit. These increases were bonded to loosened eligibility requirements and increased benefits far exceeding contributory requirements. Indeed, Social Security became a vehicle for massive income redistribution, which did lift the large majority of the aged-poor above the poverty line. A clearer picture of the aged's financial status also emerged. In 1980, two-thirds of all elderly owned a house fully paid for. This compared to only one-eighth of those under 55. Social Security, moreover, had almost totally displaced family-based support, the percentage of the aged receiving aid from their children falling from 52.5 percent in 1957 to a mere 4 percent. Indeed, the elderly were now *twice as likely* to report providing financial help to children as to report receiving it. After in-kind aid was added in, the elderly actually enjoyed a higher average per capita income than the non-elderly.[14]

Such massive changes based on state-mandated income redistribution, of course, have their costs. Some have been visible, such as the further deterioration of intergenerational living patterns (seen in the decline in the number of widows over age 75 living with relatives, from 60 percent in 1960 to 33 percent in 1980). Less noticed has been the disproportionate burden of the FICA tax which falls on young families. Take, for example, a married couple with five children, father's age between 25 and 34 (while in some respects an exceptional case, there are approximately 200,000 families in the United States with this structure). The average income of such a family in 1983, according to the U.S. Census Bureau, was $19,712. After deducting federal and state taxes and FICA contribution,[15] net per capita income is $2,413. Compare this to the average income of a two-person household in which the householder is 65 years or older, of $20,143. Since a significant share of this is tax-free Social Security payments, the per capita net income in this household probably is near $9,500. Add to this the likelihood that the family of seven is renting a house or paying a mortgage while the elderly couple owns its home outright,[16] and one discovers that the elderly couple enjoys a living standard advantage roughly five times greater than that of the young family.[17]

Let us assume that such a distribution of income is fair, a reward earned for a life of labor. It nonetheless remains clear that a young, newly married American couple, contemplating this situation and their "life-style" and consumption plans, can do nothing to improve their current or future standard of living by cutting back on support of the aged. That is mandated by law, automatically taken from their paycheck(s), and can be expected to increase steadily in the years ahead. Yet they *can* improve their financial situation by delaying childbearing, or even better, by not having children at all. Certainly, economics will not be the only factor in their childbearing decision, nor is it likely to be even a major factor when the first child is considered. But the state-imposed disincentive is certainly there. Relative to old-age social insurance, moreover, they can rely on *others* to carry the burden of bringing the needed children into the world. Social insurance imposes no penalties—indeed it gives rewards—for remaining "child-free." This, of course, was exactly the situation that the Myrdals said would occur in an incomplete welfare state, and it has been associated with a decline in the American total fertility rate well below the zero-growth level.[18]

Cross-national research strongly affirms this connection between expansion of the welfare state and a ruinous fertility decline. In a series of articles, sociologist Charles F. Hohm has consistently found that "after controlling for relevant developmental effects, the level and scope of a country's social security program is casually and inversely related to fertility levels." This has proved true for both less developed and developed countries: indeed, even "the reverse-causation hypothesis" has been confirmed: lower fertility levels result in subsequent increases in Social Security expenditures, with no apparent stopping point. In every land, larger social security benefits mean fewer babies, and fewer babies mean larger benefits.[19]

Curiously, though, few seem to notice, even fewer to care. In 1980–81, there were great expressions of concern over the viability of the Social Security Trust Fund as the demographic dishonesties lying behind the 1972 Amendments began crashing home. Jimmy Carter's Commission on Pension Policy, in its May 1980 report, warned of a doubling in the dependency ratio of the retired relative to workers by 2035. Stephen Crystal labeled the problem so acute as to mark "the beginning of a new era in social policy." Nathan Keyfitz, writing in *The Public Interest*, described looming fiscal disaster. Both Crystal and Keyfitz pointed to worker/retiree ratios of only 2 to 1 by the early twenty-first century. The former calculated that 65 percent of the federal budget would be consumed by old-age benefits in 2025.[20] Yet when the administration and Congress finally acted in 1983, they merely raised payroll taxes again, pulled more categories of employees into the system, briefly delayed a single year's cost-of-living adjustment, and raised the retirement age to 67 in 2025. No attention was paid to the deeper symptoms of disorder.

Indeed, in a perverse closing of the New Deal circle, most contemporary academic defenders of the existing system are slinking back intellectually to the 1930s, quite prepared to sacrifice family life *and* children to the voracious jaws of the welfare state. John Myles dismisses any "crisis" in Social Security. He notes, correctly, that the elderly already constitute 16 percent of the populations of West Germany, Austria, and Sweden, a figure not far from the 18 percent to be seen in America by 2025. Moreover, West Germany already has a ratio of Social Security contributors to beneficiaries of less than 2:1 and has not suffered from intergenerational backlash or hostility. What Myles does not directly report is that the fertility rate in all three lands is at only 60–70 percent of the zero-population-growth level. In West Germany, the total fertility rate has been described as being in a "free-fall." If continued over more than two generations, such a figure represents effective national extinction. Putting on a smile, though, Myles actually *welcomes* the progressive disappearance of newborns, noting that this will allow total public expenditures on behalf of the elderly to increase without placing any net new burdens on those of working age. The system can live, for a time, by consuming its ghost children.[21]

Similarly, Eugene Friedman and Donald Adamchak mock the scare stories, arguing (again correctly) that the projections of "dependency burden" used have looked only at the burden of the retired. Using different data, they calculate a progressive *decline* in the *total* dependency ratio (all dependents ÷ all workers) from 127.0 in 1980 to 85.5 by 2050. Hidden behind their comforting figures, though, are these two assumptions: (1) *all* women, ages 18 to 65, will work outside the home (there will be no full-time mothers); and (2) the nation will enjoy pure zero population growth (2.1 children born to each woman).[22] The two, though, are mutually contradictory. Even today, when there are still a not-insignificant number of young American women trying to create a family on traditional lines, the "implicit reproduction rate" is already negative. Data from Canada and the United States suggest that the full-time working mother commonly bears only one child.

Honesty on this issue, it seems, is hard to find. That is why Norman Ryder's essay "Two Cheers for ZPG" is so refreshing.[23] After praising the contemporary political campaign for zero population growth, after urging enhanced government initiatives to reduce the birthrate even further, after labeling the family "unsuccessful as an agency for the maintenance of aged dependents," and after welcoming a slowdown in economic growth, Ryder gets to the heart of the matter. The real issue, he says, is whether biological survival is all that important. "A collective commitment to population replacement," he notes, "is a defensible posture only if we assume that whatever it is that we are proud of must be transmitted biologically." Americans, he suggests, might see themselves instead from "a sociocultural standpoint," and so satisfy their "thrust toward immortality . . . by efforts to ensure that future generations share our values, whether or not they share our genes."

In the end, we learn that the final consequence of the existing welfare state is biological extinction. The grim humor lies in Ryder's belief that he could find self-respecting immigrants who would want to "share values" with a decadent intelligentsia presiding over collective suicide.

The Myrdals identified only two ways out of the contradiction posed by old-age pensions in the welfare state: either scrap state-funded pensions altogether, and return the problems of security in old-age to private and family resources; or complete the welfare state—making it whole—by also socializing the costs of bearing and raising children, and so removing "the living standard penalty" imposed by children.

Being good socialists, the Myrdals naturally concluded that "only the second alternative needs . . . to be given practical discussion in modern democratic countries."[24] They went on to develop a comprehensive plan for completing the welfare state, including free health care for families, free state daycare, maternity and child clothing allowances, and a host of other state family services. In the ideal welfare state, they implied, bearing and rearing a child would not cost its parents a single dollar.

Unfortunately, forty years of experience with Social Democratic family policy in Sweden shows that the second option has failed. To begin with, despite the expenditure of impressive sums for family welfare programs—including the creation of universal children's allowances—the state was never able to provide enough to eliminate fully the living standard penalty. Between 1965 and 1983, in fact, the real value of family benefits steadily declined, losing out both to inflation and to the competition for shares of the state's increasingly strained budgetary pie. Second, an aggressive state family policy opens the family unit up to manipulation for other ends. While sincerely created as a means of helping families and of sustaining the population level, government intrusion into the Swedish family today is motivated primarily by the goals of securing gender and class equality and free access to "choice" of life-style. Finally, it appears that parents relieved of financial, social, and moral responsibility for their children soon lose interest in offspring altogether. According to a growing chorus of observers, Sweden has become a society oriented away from children. Even school-teachers—Social Democrats all—claim that the number of insecure, emotionally neglected children has skyrocketed in recent decades. Sweden already resembles the nightmarish land described by one of its demographers in 1978: "a country with an increasingly declining population, populated mainly by old people and only a small number of children; a country where the former day nurseries are used as pensioners' dwellings and where industry is kept going by an increasingly aging workforce."[25]

All of which drives the argument back to the first option. It is political dogma in America today that Social Security is untouchable. Nonetheless, it may be time to re-examine the principles upon which the American welfare state is built. The nation might begin by thorough debate of four questions recently posed by policy analyst William Gribbin: How do Social Security rules affect family structure? How does the system encourage or discourage patterns of caring and sharing between generations within a family? How does its future relate to levels of childbearing and to the policy incentives and cultural attitudes that affect those rates? How should the elderly be treated in the society of the third millennium?[26] Answers to these questions, it is clear, lead in radically new directions.

Notes

1. W. Andrew Achenbaum, *Old Age in the New Land: The American Experience Since 1790* (Baltimore and London: The Johns Hopkins University Press, 1978), pp. 127–128.
2. Gunnar Myrdal, *Population: A Problem for Democracy* (Cambridge, MA: Harvard University Press, 1940), pp. 197–200.
3. Alva Myrdal, *Nation and Family: The Swedish Experiment in Democratic Family and Population Policy* (London: Kegan Paul, Trench, Trubner & Co., 1942), pp. 87–88.
4. Royal Commission on Population, *Report* (London: His Majesty's Stationery Office, 1949), pp. 111–12; and *Report of the Economics Committee* (London: His Majesty's Stationery Office, 1950), p. 31.
5. This intellectual connection is shown in: William Graebner, *A History of Retirement: The Meaning and Function of an American Institution, 1875–1978* (New Haven and London: Yale University Press, 1980), pp. 186–200.
6. P.K. Whelpton, "Population: Trends in Differentials of True Increase and Age Composition," in *Social Changes in 1929*, ed. William F. Ogburn (Chicago: The University of Chicago Press, 1930), pp. 873, 876–77; Robert R. Updegraff, "The American Market Faces Middle Age," *Advertising and Selling* 19 (Aug. 18, 1932): 13–14; and The President's Research Committee on Social Trends, *Recent Social Trends in the United States, Volume I* (New York and London: McGraw-Hill, 1983), pp. 51, 53–55.
7. Arthur W. Calhoun, *A Social History of the American Family: From Colonial Times to the Present* Vol. III (New York: Barnes and Noble, 1945, [1917]), pp. 165–75; William Fielding Ogburn, *American Marriage and Family Relationships* (New York: Henry Holt, 1928), p. 106; and William F. Ogburn "The Family and Its Functions," in *Recent Social Trends in the United States*, pp. 661–63, 666, 672–76, 687, 699, 708.

8. See: Alva and Gunnar Myrdal, *Kris i Befolkningsfragan* (Stockholm: Bonniers, 1934), pp. 101–04; "Political and Economic Planning," *Population Policy in Great Britain* (London: P.E.P., 1948), pp. 83–84; Warren S. Thompson and P.K. Whelpton, "A Nation of Elders in the Making," *The American Mercury* 19 (April 1930): 385–97; and W.B. Reddaway, *The Economics of a Declining Population* (London: George Allen & Unwin, 1939), particularly pp. 229–45.

9. L. Hersch, "The Fall in the Birth Rate and its Effects on Social Policy," *International Labour Review* 28 (Aug. 1933): 159–62. The influence of this article is noted in Graebner, p. 190.

10. *Congressional Record*, 74th Congress, 1st Session (June 14, 1935), p. S9286.

11. From the Barbara Armstrong Memoir, Columbia University Oral History Collection; quoted in Graebner, p. 186.

12. Robert J. Myers, "Social Security's Hidden Hazards," *Wall Street Journal* (July 28, 1972).

13. *Congressional Record*, 94th Congress, 2nd Session (June 29, 1972), p. S23320; and (July 31, 1972), p. S26029.

14. Hugh Heclo, "The Political Foundations of Anti-Poverty Policy." Paper presented at the conference, "Poverty and Policy: Retrospect and Prospects," sponsored by the U.S. Department of Health and Human Services (Dec. 6–8, 1984), p. 27; and Stephen Crystal, *America's Old Age Crisis* (New York: Basic Books, 1982), pp. 16, 18, 32, 57.

15. The former two estimated at a total of $1,500, the latter calculated at the 1983 rate of 6.7 percent.

16. Calculated as a $3,000 annual differential.

17. Figures from: U.S. Department of Commerce, Bureau of the Census, *Money Income of Households, Families, and Persons in the United States: 1983*, series P–60, No. 146 (April 1985), Table 9.

18. U.S. Department of Commerce, Bureau of the Census, *Statistical Abstract of the United States, 1985* (Washington, DC: U.S. Government Printing Office, 1985), p. 57, Table 81.

19. Charles F. Hohm, et al., "A Reappraisal of the Social Security-Fertility Hypothesis: A Bidirectional Approach," *The Social Science Journal* 23 (Dec. 1986): 149–68.

20. Crystal, pp. 4–5; Nathan Keyfitz, "Why Social Security is in Trouble," *The Public Interest* 62 (Winter 1980): 102–19.

21. John Myles, *Old Age and the Welfare State: The Political Economy of Public Pensions* (Boston and Toronto: Little, Brown, 1984), pp. 103–10.

22. Eugene A. Friedman and Donald J. Adamchak, "Societal Aging and Intergenerational Support Systems," in *Old Age in the Welfare State*, ed. Anne-Marie Guillemard (London: Sage Publications, 1983), pp. 53–72.

23. Norman Ryder, "Two Cheers for ZPG," *Daedalus: Journal of the American Academy of Arts and Sciences* 102 (Fall 1974): 45–62.

24. G. Myrdal, p. 201.

25. Ingvar Holmberg, "Births Down, Aging Up: What's the Impact?" *Social Change in Sweden* No. 4 (New York: Swedish Information Service, 1978), p. 5.

26. From: William J. Gribbin, "The Family in the Formulation of Public Policy," *The Journal of Family and Culture* 1 (Spring 1985): 32.

Part VII
A QUESTION OF STATE?

16

From Patriarchal Family
to Matriarchal State

"Privatization" is a relatively new political word. It describes the process whereby modern welfare states divest themselves of the ownership of goods and resources or of the detailed regulation of private activities. Usually, state economic activity is the focus.

There may be merit, though, in transferring the concept to the social policy realm and raising a call to "privatize" the family. It is certainly true that the private/public distinction lies at the heart of America's current family problem. Recent historians of the family, including Philippe Aries and Tamara Hareven, have made the argument that the traditional American view of family life as "private" is historically peculiar, bound only to the modern system of bourgeois capitalism. They argue that extensive public intrusion into family life is the normal pattern of human existence, and they would like to see much more of it in our time.[1]

It would be foolish, of course, to misuse the privatization paradigm and to force an analysis of the family into an inappropriate economic framework. For many Americans, family life is primarily a question of metaphysics with no apparent connection to demand curves and measures of marginal utility. Nonetheless, a focus on the public intrusion into private family life is a first, central task in setting a modern family policy agenda.

It seems appropriate to begin by exploring the true history of philosophical thought on the family and the state. An honest look at the development of the Western Christian philosophical tradition reveals that, for most of this civilization's history, the autonomy of the family relative to government was virtually unchallenged. This understanding was born with Aristotle, who, in rejecting Plato's utopian vision of a shared community of wives and children, argued that all human society began through "a union of those who cannot exist without each other; namely, of male and female, that the race may continue." This marital bond, expanding into the household, served as "the first" social institution. When several of these house-holds united, Aristotle said, the village was born, and as several villages came together, the state sprang into existence. While in a metaphysical sense the state was prior to the household, since the whole must precede its parts, the foundation of social order clearly lay in the natural society of the home.[2]

The Christian theological tradition carried forward this understanding. Augustine, the fifth-century Bishop of Hippo, saw the union of man, woman, and their children as the sole "natural bond of human society," the place where humans learned the power of love and friendship. In contrast, his opinion of the state was low. "What are kingdoms but great robberies?" he wrote. "For what are robberies themselves, but little kingdoms? The band itself is made up of men; it is ruled by the authority of a prince; it is knit together by the pact of confederacy; the booty is divided by the law agreed on." It is true that medieval theologian Thomas Aquinas saw the human as "a social animal" and understood the state to be an institution complementing familial bonds. Newborns depended on the family group for their birth and early nurture, while the state also "provided public services beyond the means of one household, and for moral advantage." Aquinas was clear, though, that the state's role was one of service to and support of the family. The sixteenth-century reformer Martin Luther stressed that marriage was the first and primary social bond, a natural community instituted by God for the bearing and raising of children and for the renewal of society. As he wrote: "There is no higher office, estate, condition, or work than the estate of marriage." Luther saw government as an imperfect human device instituted by God to maintain order by preventing vice and by punishing those who offended society, so protecting the natural community of the family.[3]

This traditional vision carried into modern times. In his 1891 encyclical *Rerum Novarum*, Pope Leo XIII declared: "Behold, therefore, the family, a very small society indeed, but a true one, and older than any polity! . . . For that reason it must have certain rights and duties of its own entirely independent of the state." Leo denounced the temptations of the state to displace the family, to weaken marriage, or to undermine parental authority, and called on governments to permit maximum freedom of action for families.[4]

American theologians and writers of the nineteenth century shared, and often elevated, these sentiments. Writing in 1852, theologian Benjamin Mosby Smith of Union Theological Seminary blessed the "family constitution" founded "in the marriage union of one man and one woman" as "still, essentially, an organization for government, and secular and religious instruction." In the design of God's universe, he said, the family was instituted for "the multiplication of mankind," the protection of children, the promotion of piety and the strengthening of church, neighborhood, and state.[5] In a series of popular books for women, Catharine Beecher raised what she called "the family state" into the institution which "Jesus Christ came into this world to secure." She saw "the family state" as "the aptest earthly illustration of the heavenly kingdom, and in it woman is its chief minister." Man and woman were called to daily self-denial and self-sacrifice on behalf of children, an activity commanded by God and pleasing in His sight.[6]

Recent centuries, though, have witnessed the eclipse of this religiously grounded defense of family autonomy. Instead, the family has increasingly found itself under siege, an attack that one commentator has labeled "sweeping and unremitting."[7] In light of the privatization concept, it is instructive to note that this intervention of the state into family life and the progressive restriction of family autonomy has often occurred for reasons identical to those long used to justify state intervention into the economy and state ownership of resources and industry. These include:

(1) *The spread of statist philosophy.* Beginning with the seventeenth-century philosopher Thomas Hobbes, a major strain of secular liberal thought emphasized the negative tension between the individual and the family unit, and the need to use the power of the state to "free" persons from their families.

In a famous passage penned in 1642, Hobbes declared as "certainly false" the Aristotelian argument "that man is a creature born fit for society." Rather, he said, it was perfectly clear that "all society . . . is either for gain, or for glory; not so much for love of our fellowes, as for love of our selves." This universal quest for and exercise of power even extended into the family, where "dominion over the infant" was claimed by selfish mothers and the honor shown parents by children was "nothing else but the estimation of another's power."[8]

Philosopher John Locke attempted to put a more human face on the emerging society of free, competitive men, and was able to carve out "a sort of rule and jurisdiction" by parents over children when the latter were small. Translated into modern jargon, Locke saw parents as responsible for the "socialization" of children as free individuals. However, Locke could identify no role in his system for the institution of marriage beyond the reproductive function. Indeed, once children were able to care for themselves, the marital bond "dissolves itself" and the sexual partners were "at liberty till Hymen . . . summons them again to choose new mates."[9]

Subsequent liberal theorists have professed similar ambivalent or hostile attitudes toward the family. In the nineteenth century, for example, John Stuart Mill attacked the family structure of early Victorian England as the equivalent of slavery for women, the seedbed of despotism, and the source of human misery which "swells to something appalling." Writing for this tradition in 1971, John Rawls concluded that the central liberal principle of fair opportunity could never be achieved in a family-based society. "Is the family to be abolished then?" he asked. "Taken by itself and given a certain primacy, the idea of equal opportunity inclines us in this direction."[10]

This antifamily aspect of secular liberal theory left a wide opening for the more extreme statists, with the eighteenth-century French philosopher Jean Jacques Rousseau as their common progenitor. While Rousseau did offer a highly romanticized portrait of the family in his early novel *Emile*, his fully developed political views left no role for this natural community. Rather, he said, man necessarily entered a social compact in which "each of us puts his person and all his power in common under the supreme direction of the general will." It was essential "that there should be no partial society within the State." Indeed, Rousseau argued, "the newly born infant, upon first opening his eyes, must gaze upon the fatherland, and until his dying day should behold nothing else." Accordingly, he charged, the traditional prerogatives of parents should be superseded by the state.[11]

A century and a half later, this same secular liberal vision found support among Progressive American theorists. "The new view," wrote historian Arthur Calhoun in 1918, "is that the higher and more obligatory relation is to society rather than to the family; the family goes back to the age of savagery while the state belongs to the age of civilization. The modern individual is a world citizen, served by the world, and home interests can no longer be supreme."[12]

Marriage and family life, in the Progressive view, were tied to the "relentless workings of the profit system." More contemporary children of Rousseau, such as political economists Samuel Bowles and Herbert Gintis, continue to stress that a capitalist economy and the autonomous family are merely two aspects of a common oppression. Hiding behind the "privacy" label, they say, these institutions are the true sources of imperialism, violence, racism, religious intolerance, and the oppression of homosexuals. They charge that only the "post-liberal" state—loosely defined as hyper-individualism linked to an extraordinarily long and mutually contradictory list of state-protected rights—can defeat these repressive institutions, implement true democracy, and serve as an authentic "repository of loyalty, learning, identity, and solace."[13]

(2) *The abuse of freedom by some becomes a justification for restricting the freedom of all.* The modern state's earliest restrictions on family government, and the origins of the concept of children belonging to the state, lay in reactions by governments to abuses of parental authority. Prior to the mid-eighteenth century, family government in England, France, and the

American colonies rested with the father. It was to him that the policing of children belonged. The state merely served as an adjunct to this authority, even putting its prisons at the disposal of fathers for the punishment of rebellious children.

In France, the first limitations of this right of paternal correction followed a conscious decision by the Royal High Courts to bring more rigorous state control over social life. Investigations by the attorney general of the High Court of Paris discovered several scandalous cases, in which children who were imprisoned at their fathers' direction were found unable to speak or walk. Accordingly, while "young people of good family" who ran afoul of the law were left for a time to the discretion of their parents, a decree of 1763 specified that "children of the working classes" who misbehaved "may be incarcerated" and henceforward would belong to the State. The French Revolution accentuated this trend toward imposing controls on the exercise of parental authority, now requiring that even fathers of "good families" secure court permission and show "grave reasons for discontent" before exercising their right of punishment.

In the mid-nineteenth century, state officials came to recognize that this law actually offered the government a valuable means of regulating families. In order to determine the veracity of these "reasons for discontent" and the degree of their gravity, the civil courts established a system of investigation resting on a new device, "the social enquiry." In this subtle shift of bureaucratic procedure, the parent was transformed from the focus of rights and responsibilities into an object of suspicion. Following standard bureaucratic procedures, the state now sought to eradicate "savagery" and diversity from the social fabric. The child, authorities recognized, could serve as their lever of control. In the actuality or threat of the child's temporary or permanent removal, the state and its allied philanthropic societies found a powerful weapon to impose their morality. The new goal was to restructure families of the laboring classes into stereotypical units, uniform and universal, and susceptible to discipline and regulation to achieve efficiency of production.

Following the law of 1889, any father claiming the ancient right of paternal punishment might, by the end of the social investigation of his family, find this right turned against him and see his children seized by the state. A Marseilles lawyer described the process by which The Organization of Visiting Nurses would conduct its social enquiry:

> Through the intermediary of highly dedicated and experienced assistants this organization drew up a detailed and exhaustive record of particulars on the father, child, and whole family. This record was returned, in duplicate, to the public prosecutor's office. One copy was sent to a specialist doctor. .... A medical card was prepared, to which any other useful particulars, especially

of a psychological nature, were appended. The second copy was sent to the office of vocational guidance, which was also in possession of a complete curriculum vitae of the minor, to be examined if necessary. . . . The public prosecutor finally put the whole dossier together and . . . drew up his own proposals.

The twentieth century witnessed the culmination of this change. Parental powers were now considered delegated by the state, while the role of parents was to learn and observe the rules of public hygiene and to direct their children into molds devised by government. A 1958 decree finally and quietly abolished the right of paternal punishment, giving sole discretion to juvenile judges. The new order received clarification in the law of 4 June 1970, which redefined "parental authority" as "a set of rights and duties *conferred upon* parents [by the state] in the interest of the child, to ensure its protection and development." All children were now, in essence, wards of the state; parents merely the designated and carefully watched agents of government, charged with state responsibilities for state ends. As political economist Philippe Meyer has put it: "This then is the reign of the social enquiry, of medico-psychological expertise, of powers of guardianship over a family's economic behavior wielded by the authorities of social welfare until such time as the family be subdued or dislocated."[14]

In Great Britain and the United States, state intervention into the family proceeded on a parallel track, with cases of an abuse of liberty used to justify displacement of the patriarchal family by the matriarchal state. The first target was the ancient legal control of a father over his children, to the exclusion of the mother. As the legal scholar Blackstone explained in the late eighteenth century, "A mother, as such, is entitled to no power, but only to reverence and respect."[15] American law rested on the same principle. James Kent of Columbia University noted half a century later that "the father (and on his death, the mother) is generally entitled to the custody of the infant children, in as much as they are their natural protectors."[16]

Isolated abuses of paternal authority again gave the state justification for intervention and for restrictions on ancient prerogatives, to the ultimate benefit not of mothers, but of government. In an emotional oratory before the British House of Commons in 1837, Sargeant Talfourd described examples of abuse of this power by certain husbands and pleaded for "some mitigation of the mother's lot . . . some slight control over the operation of that tyranny which one sex has exerted over the helplessness of the other." The resulting Act of 1839 effectively transferred some authority from fathers to the courts. In the United States, the 1859 Constitution for the State of Kansas set a model, rapidly adopted elsewhere, mandating that government provide "for the protection of the rights of women . . . [including] their equal rights in the possession of their children." By the early twentieth century, the courts and state welfare authorities commonly decided on the disposition of children, increasingly to the benefit of the mother.

In the same era, outcry over child labor practices in both England and the United States led to state restrictions on the parental control of off-spring. Exposés of specific abuses led to a series of English laws designed to discourage (1833) and end (1873, 1936) child labor through the implementation of compulsory education. In the United States, the Fair Labor Standards Act of 1937 had the same effect.

This drive to protect children from the decisions of their parents also served in America to justify state restrictions on family choice in education. The shift did not occur unchallenged. At the 1890 meeting of the National Education Association, for example, Texas state school superintendent Oscar Cooper labeled compulsory education laws an affront to ancient Anglo-Saxon traditions and "a radical reconstruction" of basic American institutions. He declared: "If there are not limits to the interference of government with the rights of the family; if the will of the majority has a right to do whatever it may please with the minority, even though that minority be but one, we shall have substituted for our free institutions . . . socialistic despotism."[17]

Yet the drive for social conformity and the perceived need to secure rights for children independent of their parents proved stronger than parental rights. The Indiana Supreme Court, in a 1901 ruling validating that state's compulsory education law, exemplified the victorious spirit. As the court succinctly explained: "The natural rights of a parent to the custody and control of his children are subordinate to the power of the state."[18] The same reasoning was used to justify the new juvenile justice system, where court officials and social workers joined together to supplant parents. As the Illinois Supreme Court ruled in 1913, the relevant statute simply extended "a protecting hand to unfortunate boys and girls, who by reason of their own conduct, evil tendencies or improper environment, have proven that the best interests of society, *the welfare of the state*, and their own good demand that the guardianship of the State be substituted for that of natural parents."[19]

(3) *The periodic "public crisis."* Just as bad economic theory linked to a downturn in the economic cycle produced the Great Depression and the institutions of the New Deal, so has poor social science tied to media outcries over some "peril" to the nation resulted frequently in new government intrusions into the family. Recent decades have been witness to the "child abuse" crisis, the "teenage pregnancy" crisis, the "child care" crisis, the "working mother" crisis, the "population" crisis, and "the youth suicide" crisis, all seen as justifications for new federal programs that would necessarily restrict or supplant the failing family.

An earlier episode involved the linkage of psychology, sociology, and eugenics. In the 1907–20 period, fear of "the menace of the feeble minded" actually became a major force in American social thought, with extraordinary legal and policy consequences. In the most famous study, widely reported in the press, psychologist Henry Goddard of New Jersey's Vineland Training School for the Feebleminded described the results of his application of the new Binet intelligence test to juvenile delinquents. He discovered that among 56 wayward girls between the ages of 14 and 20, 52 were "clearly mental defectives." In a similar study of 100 juveniles at the detention home in Newark, he found 66 percent to be "distinctly feebleminded." Goddard concluded that a large portion of crime resulted from feeblemindedness.[20]

Other investigators followed his lead and discovered equally shocking results. A psychologist attached to the juvenile court in Denver, Colorado, found that the majority of delinquents were feebleminded. "We know further," he said, "that two-thirds of these cases of feeblemindedness are due to heredity, and that feebleminded people reproduce at twice the normal rate of the general population. But instead of sterilizing or segregating these people, we are buying them Bibles." The Massachusetts Commission for the Investigation of the White Slave Traffic gave Binet tests to 300 prostitutes and discovered that over half were feebleminded. Moreover, "[t]he general moral insensibility, the boldness, egotism and vanity, the love of notoriety, the lack of shame or remorse, the absence of even a pretense of affection or sympathy for their own children . . . the desire for immediate pleasure . . . the lack of forethought or anxiety about the future—all cardinal symptoms of feeblemindedness—were strikingly evident in every one of the 154 women." Other researchers discovered widespread feeblemindedness among drunks, orphans, tramps, and paupers.

The linkage of feeblemindedness to heredity was dramatically portrayed in a lurid 1912 book by Goddard and Elizabeth Kite, *The Kallikak Family*. Investigating the background of "a little moron girl" institutionalized at Vineland in 1897, they discovered that she was but one of 480 descendants of Martin Kallikak ("Old Horror"), the illegitimate son of a Revolutionary War soldier who bequeathed the Kallikak name to an unnamed "feebleminded girl" he had met in a tavern. Of these descendants, 46 proved to be of normal intelligence, while 143 were feebleminded, and the rest doubtful or unknown. The family had produced 26 illegitimate children, 33 prostitutes, 24 alcoholics, three epileptics, and three criminals. The legitimate Kallikak line, meanwhile, had produced a distinguished series of doctors, lawyers, judges, and educators. The hereditary nature of feeblemindedness seemed proved, and newspapers drove home the implicit message: the sterilization or institutionalization of that nameless colonial girl would have spared New Jersey a great deal of misery.

Other "family studies" quickly appeared: on the Pineys, a group of inter-related degenerate families in the Pine Barrens of New Jersey; on the Happy Hickory family, a five-generation family of the feebleminded in Ohio; and on the Dack family, the shiftless descendants of an Irish immi-grant couple in Pennsylvania. Feebleminded families breeding crime, pros-titution, and poverty seemed to be everywhere. State studies from the period, using dubious statistical techniques, also suggested that large num-bers of criminally oriented morons ran loose among the general popula-tion. The press had a field day.[21]

In 1911, the Eugenics Selection Committee of the American Breeders' Association created the ponderously named Committee to Study and to Report on the Best Practical Means of Cutting Off the Defective Germ-Plasm in the American Population. Its subsequent report concluded "that society must, at all hazards, protect its breeding stock" and that lifetime segregation, supplemented when necessary by forced sterilization, offered the greatest prospects for success. Leaders within the Progressive move-ment, believing that humankind could shape its own destiny, enthusi-astically embraced the eugenics campaign.

At the urging of a reformatory physician, Indiana passed the first state law governing the sterilization of the feebleminded in 1907. By 1917, 14 other states had followed its lead, including: New Jersey, the law signed by Governor Woodrow Wilson in 1911; California, in a 1913 statute signed by Progressive Governor Hiram Johnson; and Wisconsin, in a law endorsed by the Progressives on the University of Wisconsin faculty and signed by the Progressive party governor. The decade also witnessed dramatic growth in the number and size of institutions for the feebleminded. In New York alone, the number of persons so institutionalized doubled.

It was not until the 1920s that flaws in the original Binet tests were uncovered, particularly the nearly obvious tendency to inflate the number of feebleminded. Advances in genetic science also suggested that the link-age between heredity and intelligence was more complex than previously assumed. Nonetheless, over 50,000 Americans were forcibly sterilized in the interwar years before the enthusiasm had passed.[22]

The champion "public crisis," recurring at frequent intervals, has been juvenile delinquency. The 1890s, the 1920s, and the 1950s each witnessed an upsurge in concern over juvenile crime, and each panic spawned new state intrusions into the family. The root problem, it is now clear, lay in the transition of American society from its rural and small-town origins to an urban entity. The "delinquency" label has served for nearly a century as a convenient device of social control, labeling poor children in terms of their deviant or "potentially deviant" behavior, fixing the blame for the traumas of urbanization on parents, and justifying the new institutions of the matriarchal state.

The "delinquency crisis" of the 1950–65 period is representative. In their 1961 book *The Twenty Billion Dollar Challenge*, Kenyon Scudder and Kenneth Bean described the situation as "a national emergency." It was no longer a question of *whether* national action would occur; the question only was *when*. Juvenile delinquency was a social problem "just as deadly" as an opposing army or killer virus. Moreover, the perceived problem was merely the tip of the iceberg, "for probably less than one-third of those who commit delinquent acts are known to the authorities." These "hidden delinquents," who had yet to officially commit a crime, posed the real challenge for creative policy intervention.[23]

Scholars weighing in at a more sophisticated level laid blame squarely on the failure of the family. According to sociologist Harry Shulman, ongoing social change meant that the family was rapidly diminishing in importance as the basic social group in American society. Parents were losing control over their children, and there was great wear and tear on traditional standards of right and wrong. He concluded that this "weakening of parental decision in a hundred small issues taken together has led to a social revolution in manners and morals." Government must fill the void.[24]

Some commentators of the era laid blame on lurid comic books, some on working mothers, and some on broken homes.[25] Others denied that broken homes, "as such," played any role in causing delinquency: parental malfunction, on an individual basis, was the culprit.[26] Yet all commentators, expert or popular, could agree that the family in some way was at fault. As Benjamin Fine of the *New York Times* summarized: "Whether the family was broken, with one or both parents absent due to separation, divorce, desertion, or death, or the family was disorganized as a result of frustrations and instability, the end result was the same: maladjusted children who become involved in delinquency."[27]

Scholars of the situation also agreed on another point: attempts to reinstate "old values" of family and religion would never work. "Social change" demanded creative "social construction" and aggressive state intervention into the family. During the "youth crime" crisis of the 1840s, the forced institutionalization of the poor children in reform schools had been the chosen method. In the 1950s, commentators placed their faith in psychiatric therapy. "Problem families," Harrison Salisbury concluded, must accept psychiatry or lose their children. Some psychiatric social workers advocated "aggressive casework," where they would "reach out" to those families not willing or yet required to seek treatment and bring them into the comforting arms of the therapeutic state. Two prominent psychiatrists called for the creation of "family hospitals," state-funded institutions where teams of psychotherapists could work on whole families "at risk" of producing delinquents. They advocated a model used in the Netherlands, involving "a system of family diagnosis" based on "a four-way rating of families." The "treatment of the full family," they said, would require large teams of experts, including psychoanalysts, psychiatrists, pediatricians, psychologists, social workers, sociologists, anthropologists, and lawyers, "among others." These "staff structured" communities of targeted families would be expensive, they admitted. Yet family-wide treatment represented the only promising solution to the juvenile delinquency crisis.[28]

Under these accumulated pressures, the family has faded in legal and cultural significance. Meanwhile, both the state and the individual have staked claims to heightened importance. This growth in personal autonomy, though, is more apparent than real. "Freed" from the burdens and restrictions once imposed by the inherited communities of family, village, and religion, the radical individual actually finds himself naked and alone, unsure of the casual and easily discarded bonds offered by other free personalities, and beholden to the awful embrace of the therapeutic state.

Notes

1. See: Philippe Aries, *Centuries of Childhood: A Social History of Family Life*, trans. Robert Baldick (London: Cape, 1962); and Tamara K. Hareven, "Family Time and Historical Time," *Daedalus* 106 (Spring 1977): 69–70.
2. Aristotle, *Politics*, I: 1252a–1253b; II: 1261a–1263b.
3. St. Augustine, *The City of God*, Book IV, Ch. 4; St. Thomas Aquinas, *Philosophical Texts*, trans. Thomas Gilby (London: Oxford University Press, 1951), pp. 371–74; and *Luther's Works* (Philadelphia: Muhlenberg Press, 1962), Vol. 28, pp. 17–20; Vol. 45, pp. 18, 154.
4. In *Two Basic Social Encyclicals* (Washington, DC: The Catholic University of America Press, 1943), pp. 15–17, 47–49, 59–61.
5. Benjamin Mosby Smith, *Family Religion: or the Domestic Relations as Regulated by Christian Principles* (Philadelphia: Presbyterian Board of Education, 1852), pp. 7–18, 30–35, 155–59.
6. See: Catharine E. Beecher and Harriet Beecher Stowe, *The American Woman's Home* (New York: J.B. Ford and Co., 1869), Ch. 1.
7. Philip Abbott, *The Family on Trial: Special Relationships in Modern Political Thought* (University Park, PA: The Pennsylvania State University Press, 1981), p. 4.
8. Thomas Hobbes, *De Cive: The English Version* (Oxford: Clarendon Press, 1983), pp. 42–48, 122–24.
9. John Locke, *Of Civil Government (Second Essay)* (Ann Arbor, MI: Edwards Brothers, 1947), pp. 35–37, 41–44, 51–54.
10. John Stuart Mill, *The Subjection of Women* (Cambridge, MA: The M.I.T. Press, 1970), pp. 22, 28–29, 36–37, 48; and John Rawls, *A Theory of Justice*

(Cambridge, MA: The Belknap Press of Harvard University, 1971), pp. 74, 301, 462–63, 511.

11. Jean Jacques Rousseau, *The Social Contract* (New York: E.P. Dutton, 1950), pp. 4–5, 15, 27; and quotation from Rousseau's *The Government of Poland*, found in Abbott, pp. 55–56.

12. Arthur W. Calhoun, *A Social History of the American Family* (New York: Barnes & Noble, 1945 [1918]), pp. 171–72.

13. Samuel Bowles and Herbert Gintis, *Democracy and Capitalism: Property, Community and the Contradictions of Modern Social Thought* (New York: Basic Books, 1986), pp. 4–20, 178–79, 193–95.

14. Philippe Meyer, *The Child and the State: The Intervention of the State in Family Life*, trans. Judith Ennew and Janet Lloyd (Cambridge, England: Cambridge University Press, 1983), pp. 28–39.

15. Sir William Blackstone, *Commentaries on the Laws of England in Four Books, Book I*, 12th ed. (London, 1793), p. 453.

16. James Kent, *Commentaries on American Law*, Vol. II, 11th ed. (Boston: Little, Brown, and Co., 1867), p. 205.

17. *Journal of Proceedings and Addresses of the National Education Association* (Washington, DC: NEA, 1891), p. 187.

18. *State of Indiana v. Bailey*, 157 Indiana 324 (1901).

19. *Lindsay v. Lindsay*, 257 Illinois 328 (1913). Emphasis added.

20. Henry H. Goddard, *The Kallikak Family: A Study in the Heredity of Feeble-mindedness* (New York: Macmillan, 1912).

21. See: Mark H. Hallen, *Eugenics: Hereditarian Attitudes in American Thought* (New Brunswick, NJ: Rutgers University Press, 1963), pp. 93–110.

22. John Chynometh Burnham, "Psychiatry, Psychology, and the Progressive Movement," *American Quarterly* 12 (Winter 1960): 458–61.

23. Kenyon J. Scudder and Kenneth S. Baum, *The Twenty Billion Dollar Challenge: A National Program for Delinquency Prevention* (New York: G.P. Putnam's Sons, 1961), pp. 27, 233–34.

24. Harry Manuel Shulman, *Juvenile Delinquency in American Society* (New York: Harper & Brothers, 1961), pp. 380–85.

25. Robert C. Hendrickson and Fred J. Cook, *Youth in Danger* (New York: Harcourt, Brace, 1956), pp. 80–82, 195–96; and Harrison E. Salisbury, *The Shook-Up Generation* (New York: Harper & Brothers, 1958), pp. 121–25.

26. Richard S. Sterne, *Delinquent Conduct and Broken Homes* (New Haven, CT: College and University Press, 1964), pp. 93–96.

27. Benjamin Fine, *1,000,000 Delinquents* (Cleveland and New York: The World Publishing Co., 1955), p. 81.

28. Salisbury, pp. 214–15; and C. Downing Tait Jr. and Emory F. Hodges Jr., *Delinquents, Their Families, and the Community* (Springfield, IL: Charles C. Thomas, 1962), pp. 79–80, 117–20.

17

Child Savers and the Therapeutic State

The contemporary panic over child abuse, trumpeted in the pages of *Time* and *Newsweek* and encouraged by a spate of television productions featuring parents beating or molesting their natural children, is nothing new. "Child-saving" has a long and troubled history in America. It represents a peculiar combination of genuine concern, hysteria, the misuse of authority, and the systematic denial of constitutional rights to both children and parents.

One 1984 case, while perhaps extreme given the numbers and publicity involved, is symptomatic. James Rud, a trash collector and baby-sitter, was arrested by police in Jordan, Minnesota (population 1,836) for sexually molesting two children. Once in custody, he plea-bargained with the prosecutor and, in exchange for a reduced sentence, described his involvement in a large child-sex ring composed of Jordan parents. With no further investigation, police arrested the parents and seized the children, placing the latter in the care of social workers. Once in custody, the children were grilled for hours by a battery of experts. Therapists stripped the children down and performed physical exams. Doctors stuck their fingers in the little girls' vaginas, asking, "Is this what they did to you, and do you think it went in that far, and did it bleed?" Anatomically correct dolls were given to the children so they could "role play." Many of the children were told that if they revealed the truth about their abusing parents, the families might be reunited. The children started to confess. More experts came. Citizens who complained about police tactics were arrested, and their children also seized. In all, 24 adults eventually faced charges. Yet as the months passed, the prosecutor failed to come up with any hard evidence. The hymens of the little girls were all intact. None of the children showed any signs of physical harm. In desperation, the prosecutor turned to some of the accused and began plea-bargaining. One of them, a police officer, was offered a new identity, relocation, no jail time, even money in exchange for testimony against the other adults. He refused the offer, demanding a trial. In

September, the first couple brought before a jury was acquitted. The prosecutor began hinting about the parents' involvement in ritual murders. In November, Rud admitted in a radio interview that he had lied: there was no sex ring; he had made it all up. The children also recanted. Yet the prosecutor was unmoved, and the children remained in custody until the state attorney general intervened.[1]

The parallel here with the Salem witch trials is sobering enough. A more disturbing element of the story is the bonding of a blatant antifamily ideology to the historic child-saving philosophy and mission. The consequence of this change is an America turned upside down, with the law becoming a weapon held at the throats of families throughout the land.

The legal tradition involving state intervention into the parent-child relationship ought first to be clarified. Under the English common law, the father was entitled to the custody of his children by legal right. (A mother's right to custody was not established until the late nineteenth century.) In the American colonies, this custody relationship or "sacred trust" was seen as related to the parents' duties to maintain and educate their children. Recognizing that an orderly society required that parents have discretion in disciplining within the home, the common law held a presumption in favor of the reasonableness of parental action. In cases of severe abuse, the criminal law took hold. The courts also developed a general rule that a parent could not be held liable in a civil suit for the excessive punishment of a child.

Yet alongside this affirmation of parental rights, the law also recognized the power of the courts to intervene into families and take away children in order to protect the interests of the larger community. The Elizabethan poor laws (1601), for example, established the principle that the children of those receiving public relief should be taken away and bound as apprentices. Concern for social conformity and the training of good work habits led the Virginia Burgesses in 1646 to pass a statute which noted that "parents, either through fond indulgence or perverse obstinacy, are most averse and unwilling to part with their children" and so directed county commissioners to select and take away two children each year, age 7 or 8, to be sent to James City for employment in the public flax houses. In colonial Massachusetts, "tithingmen" were appointed in every neighborhood to "diligently inspect" the families under their supervision, concentrating particularly on "all single persons that live from under family government, stubborn and disorderly children and servants, nightwalkers, tipplers, Sabbath breakers . . . or whatever else course . . . tending to debauchery, irreligion, profaneness, and atheism amongst us." Violators faced fines, imprisonment, or the loss of children.

When the U.S. Constitution was written, one of the powers specifically not delegated by the states to the federal government was control of family law and governance. In contrast to most European constitutions, our foundational document makes no direct mention of children, families, parenthood, marriage, or the family's relationship to the state. This omission reflected the keen interest in the family held by local communities and an unwillingness to subject such sensitive questions to uniform, national answers. But when the federal government began expanding its sway over national life, this omission generated troubling consequences. As one legal scholar has noted, federal judicial cases do mention family privacy and family integrity, "but in reality the family as a unit is less protected than corporations."[2]

The relatively weak constitutional protections afforded families became apparent during the 1820s with the emergence of the "child-saving" movement. The New York House of Refuge, the first juvenile reformatory in the United States, opened its doors in 1825. Setting the pattern for the next one hundred years, this institution blurred over the distinctions among abused, neglected, poor, and delinquent children. By institutionalizing through court order those children who fell into any or several of these categories, the House of Refuge sought to separate real or potential youthful offenders from adults and so prevent children from entering a life of crime. While adult criminals, particularly recidivists, were considered at the time to be subhuman, children were said to have moral possibilities if only they could be rescued from their corrupted parents and brutish living conditions. As the famed penologist Enoch Wines wrote in 1880: "They are born to [crime], brought up for it. They must be saved."

The reform school movement which swept the nation during the nineteenth century represented a bonding of traditional values to coercive social engineering. The new penology emphasized the corruptions of the city, "its saloons, low dives, and gangs of bad boys." It defended and sought to instill in its charges the values of sobriety, thrift, industry, prudence, and realistic ambition. Whenever possible, reform schools were set in the countryside. Agricultural training formed the core curriculum. Institutions were organized on "the family system," where a couple of "sound Christian character" would govern the children organized in "cottages." Even the mistreatment or abuse of children, leading to their separation from the family, was understood in decidedly moral terms. The model 1889 Michigan statute, for example, defined an "ill-treated child" as one "whose father, mother or guardian is a habitual drunkard or a person of notorious or scandalous conduct or a reputed thief or prostitute, or one who . . . by any other act or example or by vicious training, depraves the morals of such child."

Under the new laws, the courts were empowered to seize children of "unworthy parents" and to place them in the care of private or public institutions. The famed "Mary Ellen" case of 1875 involved the physical abuse of a child mistakenly placed as an apprentice in the home of her illegitimate father. In response, Societies for the Prevention of Cruelty to Children sprang up in many large cities. Through legislation, they soon acquired extraordinary police powers of investigation and arrest.

However affiliated, though, the new child-savers represented a well-funded and highly educated elite, enjoying the economic backing of private philanthropists. As with the seventeenth-century Puritans, their fundamental goal was to defend the safety and mores of the social order. Predictably, the objects of their attention were almost exclusively the poor, the non-Anglo-Saxon, and the immigrant, those lacking enculturation into mainstream society. These were the categories of parents who saw their children "saved."[3]

More troubling than this crude approach to assimilation was the use of summary justice to seize and institutionalize children without any substantive legal protections. Robert Turner, superintendent of the Chicago Reform School, described the process in 1871: "If on the judge's examination of him and his parents . . . it was considered best for the welfare of the boy that he should come to the Institution, an order . . . was made out to that effect, charging him with no crime, recording no criminal proceedings against him, blotting out all previous charges, and consigning him . . . to a Boarding School." True, as the child savers hoped, the youth had been spared incarceration with hardened adult criminals. Yet in exchange for this special treatment, the "delinquent" child had no jury trial subject to the rules of evidence, enjoyed no privilege against self-incrimination, had no access to legal counsel, and faced an indeterminate sentence, remaining in the reformatory until released by the committing judge. Parents also saw their rights of custody stripped away, without the niceties of due process, through an inquisitorial hearing into their character.[4]

The constitutionality of neglect laws empowering the state to seize children was repeatedly challenged during the nineteenth century. But, with only a few exceptions, they were sustained. The key decision came in 1839, after a father secured a writ of *habeas corpus* to secure the release of his daughter from the Philadelphia House of Refuge. The managers of the institution fought the writ, arguing that the Bill of Rights did not apply to children. The Pennsylvania Supreme Court decided for the managers, not only on the Bill of Rights argument but also on the doctrine of *parens patriae* ("the parenthood of the state"). This ancient concept was drawn from English chancery laws justifying the English Crown's assumption of the parental role in order to protect the estates of orphaned minors. The Pennsylvania court, looking for a legal device to get around due process, now extended the doctrine to the termination of parental rights: "May not the natural parents, when unequal to the task of education or unworthy of it, be supplanted by the *parens patriae*, or common guardianship of the community?"[5] The court also ruled that reformatories were "residential schools," not prisons; thus, commitment to them was not governed by due process.

This doctrine of *parens patriae* would underlie "child-saving" work in America until the present. Predictably, its emphasis on the "parenthood" of the state led to ever broader claims of authority by the child savers and courts. As the Illinois Supreme Court, in a sweeping judgment, ruled in 1882:

> It is the unquestioned right and imperative duty of every enlightened government, in its character of *parens patriae*, to protect and provide for the comfort and well-being of such of its citizens as, by reason of infancy, defective understanding, or other misfortune or infirmity, are unable to take care of themselves. The performance of this duty is justly regarded as one of the most important of governmental functions, and all constitutional limitations must be so understood and construed so as not to interfere with its proper and legitimate exercise.[6]

With the constitutional floodgates down and the family legally disarmed, the welfare-state mentality began seeping in.

Alongside the general adoption of *parens patriae* as a guiding legal principle, there was a distinct line of dissent, rooted in a defense of family rights and natural liberty. The most dramatic decision in this regard came in a case involving Daniel O'Connell, age 14, who was committed to the Chicago Reform School in 1870. His father subsequently demanded Daniel's release on the grounds that his son had committed no crime. The Illinois Supreme Court so ordered, arguing that the boy's constitutional rights had been violated. The *parens patriae* doctrine, the court opined, was subject to the restraints of divine law. "The parent has the right to the care, custody and assistance of his child," the court reasoned. "The duty to maintain and protect it is a principle of natural law. . . . Before any abridgement of the right, gross misconduct or almost total unfitness on the part of the parent, should be clearly proved." The court also cut through the window dressing, acknowledging that reform schools were, in fact, prisons. In a flourish of indignation, the court declared:

> The State, as *parens patriae*, has determined the imprisonment beyond recall. Such a restraint upon natural liberty is tyranny and oppression. If, without crime, without the conviction of any offense, the children of the State are to be thus confined for the 'good of society,' then society had better

be reduced to its original elements, and free government acknowledged a failure.[7]

This line of argument found relatively few echoes. As already noted, within a dozen years the very same Illinois court embraced *parens patriae* as "one of the most important of governmental functions." Only a handful of decisions such as the 1885 ruling by the New Hampshire Supreme Court, which compared the forced institutionalization of children without charge or formal hearing to the activities of the notorious English Star Chamber, supported the alternate constitutional vision of the relationship between family and state found in *O'Connell*.

The juvenile justice movement emerging after 1890, the first overt linkage of social science and social work to the law, has been enshrined in liberal mythology as a radical break with the past and a progressive, humane advance in public policy. It was, in fact, none of these. In the procedural sense, the informality of the new juvenile courts—no formal charges, no trial, no rules-of-evidence, no right of counsel, no right to confront one's accusers, indeterminate sentencing—merely represented new codifications of constitution-straddling systems existing since mid-century. Similarly, "coercive prediction," involving the identification of probable delinquents and their removal from their families, simply continued a process already well-embedded in penological theory. Sociologically, the objects of attention—the children saved and their unfit parents—continued to be drawn almost exclusively from immigrant, poor, and minority families. Institutionally, the reformers' claims of revolutionizing the kinds of places where children were kept were only partly correct. The principal beneficiaries of this movement were usually the private "industrial schools," which came away with more business than ever.[8]

The true origins of the movement lay in a peculiar ideological mix of social-gospel Protestantism, feminism, and socialism. The new generation of child savers emerging in the late nineteenth century were overwhelmingly female. Reared in the wealthy class, these women faced the problems posed by a superabundance of leisure. Few of them had more than one or two children. All of them had a great deal of time on their hands, and all fretted about charges of "parasitism." Some such as Charlotte Perkins Gilman succumbed to the radical feminist temptation. The patriarchal family and the housewife were doomed, she said, by the advance of science and industrial production and the decay of capitalism. The private home was a "primitive" entity, a "clumsy tangle" of rudimentary industries "that violated all of the modern rules." Others such as Louise Bowen, Ellen Henrotin, Julia Lathrop, and Jane Addams sought only a modified female role. Child saving, they argued, was a reputable task for women seeking to extend their traditional housekeeping functions into the community. As Mrs. Bowen told the Friday Club of Chicago: "If a woman is a good housekeeper in her own home, she will be able to do well that larger housekeeping." Yet even this moderate variety of feminism involved a special commitment to social engineering. "Whenever and wherever we find [woman]," D. D. Randall told a national conference on charity in 1884, "she is always the fearless and uncompromising apostle and the inspired prophet of a higher and better humanity." It was through this new surge in child saving that the social work profession—partly maternal, partly feminist—was born.[9]

The Illinois Juvenile Court Act of 1899 appeared to shouts of acclamation, atop the first crest of the Progressive reform movement and buoyed by "a massive propaganda campaign."[10] Within twenty years, most states had established juvenile courts on the Illinois model. America had learned that "all was not well with that ancient institution, the family," concluded one advocate. Like "Christianity on the eve of destruction of Grecian art and philosophy," the juvenile court movement had miraculously risen up to avert the consequences of a great doom.[11]

Animated by the ideals of social work, the juvenile courts, in theory, transcended legal functions to merge with social service. Juvenile crime would be decriminalized. All minors at risk of becoming delinquents would be made wards of the state and would be treated as children needing protection. The juvenile court was symbolic of the state's parenthood, it was said, with the judge assuming the role toward the child of a "wise and kind" father. "Seated at a desk, with the child at his side, where he can on occasion put his arm around his shoulder and draw the lad to him, the judge, while losing none of his judicial dignity, will gain immensely in the effectiveness of his work."[12] Natural parents, whether "weak, ignorant, greedy, or degraded," were also to be treated as clients and given therapeutic services, with "the best interests of the child" at heart.

On the official level, the system still seemed cast in the middle-class mode, defending the bourgeois social order. The creators of the new system carried with them a dedication to home and family life. In contrast to the old poor law tradition, which advocated separating children from poverty-stricken parents, the opinion grew that home life should be preserved whenever possible and therapeutic and financial aid given to intact families. According to Miriam Van Waters, perhaps the most widely read defender of the juvenile court system, social workers held a clear view of the healthy family, where "the father is dominant but not cruel or mean," where the mother "is comfortable" and "not restlessly seeking her life gratification apart from mate and children" (although, "like Jane Addams," she may "do something for the community" by "spreading the cloak of her mothering a little wider"), and where both parents "genuinely love and enjoy children." She concluded: "No child has a good home if these fundamentals are lacking."[13]

Yet a more disturbing theme entered into the defense of the juvenile courts, suggesting that they were still less concerned with justice than with social control and a form of coercive assimilation. Judge Julian Mack readily acknowledged that most of the children who came before the court were "naturally the children of the poor . . . foreigners, frequently unable to speak English." Their parents, Mack said, "do not understand American methods and views, the amount of education demanded by law or what the modern requirements for childhood are." The state, he concluded, stood ready to use the powers of the juvenile court to reshape their lives in accordance with these views and requirements. Cultural differences, in short, would not be tolerated.[14]

At a still deeper level, the therapeutic state and the juvenile justice system implicitly threatened even the middle class. Van Waters, in her book *Parents on Probation* (1927), argued that "hardly a family in America is not engaging in the same practices, falling into the same attitudes, committing the same blunders which . . . bring the court families to catastrophe." Parents could no longer "shield themselves behind *natural* rights," she said. It was "only a question of time before the parent's psychological handling of his child" would be subjected to the scrutiny of the state. Indeed, she looked forward to the day when the court's current interest in defending the middle-class status quo would be scrapped, and when the juvenile justice system redirected its efforts toward "a different goal, happiness and well-being of individuals." In this *humanistic* environment, Van Waters exclaimed, children would no longer be "separated from parents who violated traditional moralities: they would be severed from parents who violated the right of the child to sanity and integrity of mind and body." On that great day, the parent would throw himself into the therapeutic arms of social work, "willingly cooperate in a plan for his own welfare," and then face "the superparent, which is mankind," with a "face stained with tears," saying: "Sure, I'll make good."[15]

This "humanistic socialism" rarely surfaced so explicitly. For most of its history, the juvenile justice system remained loosely governed by middle-class values. Even the rising tide of juvenile delinquency during the early 1950s, which so worried contemporaries, was apparently a statistical artifact produced by a short-term strengthening of these values. According to one analyst, the supposedly rising level of delinquency was actually produced by an enhanced "middle class sense of normalcy and uniformity," rooted in the new suburbs, which made Americans more sensitive to youthful disorders than in the past.[16]

Ten years later, though, this sustaining moral consensus was losing its grip. For instance, parental immoralities that had until recently been seen as warnings of possible criminality in children—e.g., the presence of alcohol or the failure to provide a Christian education—were losing their negative cast. Agreement on what constituted "neglect" also faded. A joint legislative committee reviewing New York's Family Court Act in 1962 finally concluded that the term had acquired so many different meanings that a common definition was not possible. "[T]his diversity was not a proper matter of governmental regulation," the committee concluded, "so long as basic standards [food, shelter, and clothing] were not violated."[17]

Morally adrift, the system soon became known for its procedural nightmares, arbitrariness, and cruelty. Cases were poorly prepared and inadequately presented. The whims of the judge, rather than case history, sealed the fate of countless children and parents. Finding sufficient foster homes for juvenile delinquents, particularly those from minority groups, proved impossible. Moreover, many juvenile reformatories of the era had undergone changes in terminology, but little else. Cell blocks were known as "adjustment cottages." Guards were "supervisors." Isolation cells were "meditation rooms." Whips, paddles, blackjacks, and straps were "tools of control." The call for "family relations" within such institutions, one legal scholar concluded, had proven to be no more than wishful thinking: "Without ready access to family life for the children coming before it, the juvenile court lost much of its *raison d'etre*."[18]

Despite this vacuum at its core, the system had taken on a life of its own, and it churned ahead. Only in 1966 did the U.S. Supreme Court acknowledge that the juvenile courts delivered the worst of both worlds: the child received neither the legal protections accorded adults nor the promised care and regenerative treatment.[19] The following year, in its *Gault* decision, the Court declared that juveniles had the same constitutional rights to due process as adults: rights to a notice of charges, to a public hearing, to counsel, and to a confrontation of hostile witnesses; the privilege against self-incrimination; and so on. "Under our Constitution the condition of being a boy does not justify a kangaroo court," wrote Justice Abe Fortas in the majority opinion. He directly attacked the doctrine of *parens patriae*, noting that "its meaning is murky and its historic credentials are of dubious relevance. . . . [T]here is no trace of the doctrine in the history of criminal jurisprudence." Fortas concluded: "Juvenile court history has again demonstrated that unbridled discretion, however benevolently motivated, is frequently a poor substitute for principle and procedure."[20]

Yet over the same years that the juvenile court system was crumbling, the *parens patriae* doctrine found new life in a fresh crusade against child abuse. The 1960–69 period marked the first time in nearly a century that great public attention focused on the complex problem of protecting children from abuse by their own parents. This interest derived from two sources. On the medical front, advances in pediatric radiology during the 1950s led to journal articles describing long bone fractures in children that were linked to the "indifference, immaturity and irresponsibility of parents." In 1962, several physicians coined the phrase, "battered child syndrome." Major media outlets such as *Life*, *The Saturday Evening Post*, and *Good Housekeeping* were soon featuring such articles as "Parents Who Beat Children" and "Cry Rises From Beaten Babies."[21]

Also fueling a rising sense of indignation was a general attack on the American middle-class family model launched after 1960. The impact of these attitudes was most pronounced among sociologists and social workers, whose professional journals were soon full of articles on the "wretchedness" of marriage, the brutality of parents, the joy of homosexuality, and the deep moral commitment behind the "child-free life-style." Such ideas also seeped into the popular media, suggesting that there was something basically wrong with most American families.

In combination, these developments proved to be a powerful stimulus to action. Between 1963 and 1967, all fifty states approved "reporting laws," commonly requiring physicians, teachers, and social workers to report suspected cases of child abuse to child welfare agencies or police authorities. Significantly, most of these laws involved the circumvention of long-standing legal protections, including: a denial of the physician-patient privilege and the husband-wife privilege under the rules of evidence; immunity from civil or criminal liability for those identifying suspected abusers; and a general presumption of guilt (commonly involving seizure of the children) until the parents could establish their innocence. With no organized opposition—indeed, with the support of organizations ranging from the National Association of Social Workers to the Daughters of the American Revolution—the "reporting law" movement enjoyed rapid and complete success.

After 1970, Title XX of the Social Security Act also began funneling large sums of money to state and community welfare agencies in order, among other purposes, to provide social services to neglected and abused children. This change both "federalized" the abuse and neglect issues and secured for social workers "the foremost position" in conducting programs of "child-mistreatment management."[22]

Despite these moves, the frantic concern over child abuse has seemed only to grow in intensity. Wildly divergent statistics aggravate the situation.

The number of reported cases of physically abused children, nationwide, was 6,617 in 1968, a figure that rose slowly in the years that followed. Such real numbers are indeed tragic. But they pale beside the "estimates" of abuse that have flooded the media. A 1971 article in the *New York Times*, for example, calculated 500,000 children in America abused annually, whether "physically, sexually, or emotionally."[23] More recent media estimates of abused children have risen to 6 million. As two scholars of the question have concluded, "the definitional chaos that has surrounded the problems of child abuse and neglect has precluded . . . rationality."[24]

Indeed, emotion has taken hold. Seeking to root out the "epidemic" of child abuse in America, many states have abolished the statutes setting an age below which children are presumed to be incompetent as witnesses, have abandoned the requirement for corroborative evidence, and have changed hearsay rules to allow videotapes and out-of-court statements as evidence. The U.S. Department of Health and Human Services, working through the states, has funded creation of School-Based Multi-Disciplinary Teams (SBMDT's) trained to enter schools and ferret out "abusing families." These cadres of social workers and psychologists are authorized to examine a family's sources of income, history, living conditions, resources, history and frequency of problems, "attitudes," self-image, parenting skills, spousal relationship, impulse control, and degree of community involvement. Those failing to measure up to SBMDT standards face therapy, loss of children, and/or formal charges.

Hysteria soon claims victims, and that is indeed occurring. The number of reported cases of child sexual abuse, for example, has *tripled* since 1981, to 250,000. Yet even the child savers admit that nearly 80 percent of these reports are unfounded, up from 40 percent only five years before. Some estimates of annual false abuse charges exceed one million.[25] In his recent report on the Jordan "sex ring" scandal, Minnesota's attorney general found "many instances" of parents being charged with abuse at a time when their children "had either denied the abuse or had not even been interviewed" and of parents being arrested and charged with abusing their own children "even though these children denied the abuse through several weeks of interrogation and separation from their parents." The growing list of parents and teachers falsely accused of child abuse and suffering from permanently damaged reputations has finally drawn the attention of the mainstream media. Cries of alarm are even heard on the left, with the magazine *Mother Jones* protesting that men are rapidly leaving the daycare and elementary-teaching professions, fearful of the consequences of touching a child.[26]

Now it is true that hysteria eventually wanes, that people lose emotional interest in a given subject and return to more mundane pursuits. Unfortunately, there are indications that this round of child saving will not settle into some workable balance. To begin with, the social work profession has, with only scattered exceptions, institutionalized the anti-middle class, anti-family values embraced during the 1960s. A review of the professional journals of the child savers, such as *Family Relations*, reveals the "new values" at work. In an altogether characteristic article, Eleanor Macklin advocates a new "family life curriculum" for high school students that would abandon the traditional family (adults marry someone of the opposite sex, have children, remain faithful, and live together until death). Instead, she proposes "education for choice," including the affirmation of childlessness, the presentation of a "single-parent-family" as "a viable lifestyle," the training of high schoolers in androgyny and skills for handling adultery, and support for gay rights. Each child should learn to write his or her own "lifestyle script." She suggests, for example, that a specific child might, all at once, "choose to stay single, have children, co-parent, make a permanent commitment, be sexually nonexclusive, have a same-sex partner, and live communally."[27] This inversion of values by the child savers has had direct consequences, as seen in the foster placement of two Massachusetts boys, aged two and three, with a male homosexual couple. "We can't discriminate based on anything," explained one social service executive.[28]

The "new" values of the child savers even link up with the assault on the free-market system. According to David Gil: "Violence against children in rearing them may . . . be a functional aspect of socialization into a highly competitive and often violent society, one that puts a premium on the uninhibited pursuit of self-interest and that does not put into practice the philosophy of human cooperativeness." As a result, he calls for "a revolutionary change not only in the child-rearing philosophy and practices of American society but also in its underlying value system."[29]

It appears that the bourgeoisie spawned the child savers, only to see them turn on their creators. The "terror" once confined to the immigrant poor and urban minorities is now spreading to the small towns and suburbs.

A second reason for pessimism is that child saving has become quite a lucrative business. In Sweden, always a decade ahead of America in the evolution of social policy, an investigative magazine has discovered there are *ten times* as many children in foster care, on a per capita basis, as in neighboring Norway and Denmark. The reason? Foster parents, commonly trained in social work, could earn 7,000 *kronor* (roughly $1,200) per month, or more, for every child they took in. Moreover, half of this income, called a support allowance, was tax-free, the hardest kind of income to find in tax-happy Sweden. In one case, a couple annually earned

$50,000 for caring for three foster children. Crudely put, legalized child-snatching in Sweden pays well.[30]

In the United States, financial considerations also appear to be fueling the child-abuse boom. Psychiatrists, testifying for the prosecution on vague concepts such as "the child sexual abuse accommodation syndrome," have pulled down $1,000 a day for their efforts.[31] In the Jordan, Minnesota case, therapists grilling the children for weeks on end earned $100 an hour for their efforts. As one renegade psychologist, W. R. Coulson, admits: "Therapists love child abuse because it makes more work for them. There hasn't been a lot done on the fact that the growth in statistics on child abuse comes from people to whose advantage it is to discover it."[32] The economic law appears to hold: supply (in this case, of therapists) creates its own demand.

Most tragically, the current level of hysteria and the ideology of child saving cover up the raw truths about child abuse. The constant media focus on abusive parents from intact, suburban families belies the fact that a greatly disproportionate number of the serious physical abuse cases are found in the otherwise celebrated "female-headed families," commonly involving the illegitimate father or mother's current boyfriend. Researchers at the University of Pennsylvania have also confirmed that stepparents and their stepchildren are much more likely to be involved in abuse than are natural parents and children. Indeed, an intact nuclear family is a child's surest *defense* against abuse.[33] The attack on the middle-class and traditional values actually cloaks the growing problems of real neglect caused by a spiraling divorce rate and working mothers with "latch key" children. As Coulson suggests, the concentration on child abuse allows these categories of child abandoners "to steer attention away from their own sin by pointing at this awful thing which others do."[34]

There is mounting evidence, moreover, showing that the intervention of state officials into families may actually *increase* the incidence of child battering. In one study, the incidence of "rebattering" among families supervised by state authorities was 60 percent; among families in a control group without supervision, the "rebattering" rate was only 30 percent.[35] It is also striking how little attention is given to the children who are abused or die in state institutions, "shelters," or foster care, perhaps the most widespread of officially covered-up crimes. As three eminent scholars have concluded, "[t]he law does not have the capacity to supervise the fragile, complex interpersonal bonds between child and parent. As *parens patriae* the state is too crude an instrument to become an adequate substitute for flesh and blood parents."[36]

The storm and fury over the allegedly abusive middle-class family blurs another disturbing fact: the linkage of child abuse to legalized abortion. During the 1960s, the advocates of abortion-on-demand argued that this policy change would reduce the number of unwanted pregnancies and so reduce child abuse. In fact, the exact opposite may have occurred. In a 1979 article for the *Canadian Journal of Psychiatry*, Philip Ney showed that those Canadian provinces (British Columbia and Ontario) with the highest rates of legal abortion were also the provinces with the highest and most rapidly rising rates of child abuse. In contrast, provinces with low abortion rates (New Brunswick, Newfoundland, Prince Edward's Island) also enjoyed low, even declining, levels of child abuse. Ney postulated that women's choice of abortion had led to diminished restraints on rage, a devaluation of children, an increase in guilt, heightened tension between the sexes, and ineffective bonding between the mothers and subsequent children. All of these factors, he noted, are closely correlated in the medical literature with abusive behavior toward children.[37]

Looking at the decaying juvenile justice system in 1969, Anthony Platt concluded that the programs of the child savers had both diminished the constitutional liberties of youth and parents and aggravated the very problems that were supposed to be solved.[38] The new round of child saving focused on abuse seems destined for the same historical judgment.

Notes

1. For an excellent survey of this case, see: E. Michael Jones, "Abuse Abuse: The Therapeutic State Terrorizes Parents in Jordan, Minnesota," *Fidelity* 4 (Feb. 1985): 28–33.
2. This discussion from: Jeanne M. Giovannoni and Rosina M. Becerra, *Defining Child Abuse* (New York: The Free Press, 1979), pp. 36–42; and Mason P. Thomas Jr., "Child Abuse and Neglect; Part I: Historical Overview, Legal Matrix, and Social Perspectives," *North Carolina Law Review* 50 (1972): 299–300, 304–05.
3. See: Anthony M. Platt, *The Child Savers: The Invention of Delinquency* (Chicago: University of Chicago Press, 1969), pp. 45, 51–58, 62–66, 74; Giovannoni and Becerra, pp. 44–49; and Sanford J. Fox, "Juvenile Justice Reform: An Historical Perspective," *Stanford Law Review* 22 (June 1970): 1206–09.
4. Fox, pp. 1213–15.
5. *Ex parte Crouse*, 4 Wharton Pa. 9 (1838).
6. *County of McLean* v. *Humphreys*, 104 Ill. 383 (1882).
7. *People ex. rel. O'Connell* v. *Turner*, 55 Ill. 280–87 (1870).
8. See: Fox, pp. 1221–28; Thomas, pp. 323–25.
9. Charlotte Perkins Gilman, *Women and Economics: A Study of the Relation Between Men and Women as a Factor of Social Evolution*, ed. Carl Degler (New York: Harper and Row, 1966 [1898]); Pratt, pp. 42, 75–82; and Christopher Lasch, *The New Radicalism in America, 1889-1963: The Intellectual as a Social Type* (New York: Alfred A. Knopf, 1965), pp. 46–56.

10. Fox, p. 1230.
11. Miriam Van Waters, "The Juvenile Court from the Child's Viewpoint," in *The Child, the Clinic and the Court*, ed. Jane Addams (New York: New Republic, 1925), pp. 218–19.
12. Julian Mack, "The Juvenile Court," *Harvard Law Review* 23 (1909): 104.
13. Miriam Van Waters, *Youth in Conflict* (New York: New Republic, 1932), pp. 65–66.
14. Julian W. Mack, "Legal Problems Involved in the Establishment of a Juvenile Court," in *Social Work and the Courts*, ed. Soponisba P. Breckenridge (Chicago: The University of Chicago Press, 1934), p. 200.
15. Miriam Van Waters, *Parents on Probation* (New York: New Republic, 1927), pp. 3–6, 35, 167.
16. Herbert A. Bloch, "Juvenile Delinquency: Myth or Threat[?]" *The Journal of Criminal Law, Criminology, and Police Science* 49 (1958): 303–09.
17. Quoted in Thomas, pp. 343–44.
18. Fox, p. 1233.
19. *Kent v. United States*, 383 U.S. 541 (1966).
20. *In re Gault*, 387 U.S. 16–18, 27–29. Also: B James George Jr., *Gault and the Juvenile Court Revolution* (Ann Arbor: University of Michigan Institute of Continuing Legal Education, 1968), pp. 29ff.
21. See: Stephen J. Pfohl, "The 'Discovery' of Child Abuse," *Social Problems* 24 (Feb. 1977): 310–23.
22. Giovannoni and Becerra, pp. 69–70.
23. *New York Times*, Aug. 16, 1981, p. 16.
24. Giovannoni and Becerra, p. 255.
25. Scott Kraft, "False Sex Abuse Charges Pose Growing Problem," *Kansas City Star*, Feb. 11, 1985, pp. A–1, 6; Douglas J. Besharov, "Unfounded Allegations: A New Child Abuse Problem," *The Public Interest* 83 (Spring 1986): 23–24; and Mary Pride, *The Child Abuse Industry* (Westchester, IL: Crossway Books, 1986), p. 13.
26. Derk Richardson, "Day Care: Men Need Not Apply," *Mother Jones* 10 (July 1985): 60. Also: David L. Kirp, "Hug Your Kids, Go To Jail," *The American Spectator* 18 (June 1985): 33–35.
27. Eleanor D. Macklin, "Education for Choice: Implications of Alternatives in Lifestyles for Family Life Education," *Family Relations* 30 (Oct. 1981): 567–77.
28. See: Randall Keith, "Hayes Questions DSS Moves Involving Children, Gay Couple," *The [Quincy, MA] Patriot Ledger*, May 10, 1985.
29. David G. Gil, *Violence Against Children: Physical Child Abuse in the United States* (Cambridge, MA: Harvard University Press, 1970), pp. 141–42.
30. "De tar vara barn!" ["They Take Away Our Children!"], *Contra* 8, No. 3 (1982): 3–5.
31. Kirp, p. 33.
32. Quoted in E. Michael Jones, p. 32.
33. Joy J. Lightcap, Jeffrey A. Kurland, and Robert L. Burgess, "Child Abuse: A Test of Some Predictions from Evolutionary Theory," *Ethology and Sociobiology* 3 (1982): 61–67.
34. E. Michael Jones, p. 33.
35. From: Michael Freeman, "Child-Rearing: Parental Autonomy and State Intervention," in *Family Matters: Perspectives on the Family and Social Policy*, ed.

Alfred White Franklin (Oxford and New York: Pergamon Press, 1983), pp. 146–51.

36. Joseph Goldstein, Anna Freud, and Albert J. Solnet, *Beyond the Best Interests of the Child* (New York: Free Press, 1979), pp. 11–12.

37. Philip Ney, "Relationship Between Abortion and Child Abuse," *Canadian Journal of Psychiatry* 24 (Nov. 1979): 610–20.

38. Platt, p. 5.

18

Youth Suicide and the Fate of a Nation

There are few human tragedies greater than a youth taking his own life. In America, a social and political system intended to offer unprecedented opportunities and freedom to all citizens has clearly and utterly failed the suicidal adolescent.

Between 1955 and 1977, the number of such suicides in the United States rose by 300 percent. Every year now, about 5,000 Americans between the ages of 15 and 24 kill themselves. A smaller, albeit disturbing number of children under age 15 also choose to end their lives.

Strong, almost obsessive, media attention to the phenomenon has been primarily a product of the years since 1980. *People, Newsweek, Time, Forbes, McCall's, U.S. News and World Report, Good Housekeeping,* and *Harper's Bazaar* represent only a partial list of the magazines that have recently given feature attention to the self-destruction of the young. Several made-for-TV movies, including CBS's *Silence of the Heart,* have also played on the adolescent suicide theme.

Inevitably, perhaps, governments have begun to turn the youth suicide crisis into an occasion for expanding their sway. On the state level, a 1983 California law is considered the model. The measure establishes a Youth Suicide Prevention School Program Fund, which supports demonstration projects in the public school systems of selected counties. On the federal level, the U.S. Department of Health and Human Services has formed a Task Force on Youth Suicide. In addition to representatives from the National Institute on Mental Health, the Administration for Children, Youth, and Families, and other agencies, the Task Force includes the leadership of the American Association of Suicidology, the American Psychological Association, and the American Psychiatric Association. It has focused on identifying risk factors and "prevention and intervention strategies." Within Congress, Representatives Tom Lantos (D-CA) and Gary Ackerman (D-NY) have proposed measures that would provide federal funding for teen hotlines, suicide prevention programs, training courses for adults, and public service announcements.

Before rushing into the creation of a national suicide prevention program, though, it seems appropriate to step back for a moment and assess what is already known about youth suicide. Is there actually a crisis? Who stands behind this call for expansion of the welfare state? What are the causes of the rise in the suicide rate? Do governments hold the solution? In a curious way, too, the answers to these questions about the self-destruction of our young open up far broader issues relating to the health and fate of the American republic.

Contrary to popular belief, the facts behind youth suicide suggest that we do not now face a crisis, in the sense of a rapidly growing or radically changing problem. It is true that between 1960 and 1977 there was a dramatic increase in the number of youth suicides. Yet even in 1975, near the peak year, their actual number was quite small. Within a nation of 220 million people, the total number of suicides among 5–9 year–olds was zero; among 10–14 year–olds, 170; among 15–19 year–olds, 1,594; and among 20–24 year–olds, 3,142. More importantly, the suicide rate (suicides per 100,000 persons in specified age categories) for American children, ages 5–14, and youth, ages 15–24, has held fairly steady since then. Among black males in the latter age category, the rate declined from 12.7 in 1975 to 11.1 in 1981, partially balancing a small increase among white males from 19.3 to 21.1. Among females, the rate for Whites, ages 15–24, was unchanged at 4.9 percent between 1975 and 1981; among Blacks, there was actually a 25 percent decline (from 3.2 to 2.4). When viewed globally, moreover, adolescent suicide in the United States is not a notably serious problem. Among young males, the U.S. suicide rate of 19.7 is below the rates found in Switzerland (33.5), Austria (33.6), Germany (21.2), and Norway (20.2). For young women, the American rate (4.6) also falls below that found in Denmark (5.0), France (5.0), and Japan (6.4).[1] In short, the overall trend of the last ten years suggests that the United States is not experiencing a growing incidence of youth suicide. If anything, the problem is receding.

Nonetheless, the cries for government action are rising in intensity. Why? Answers become apparent as we examine the rhetoric of the new youth suicide campaign. A common technique, for example, is to argue that the problem is far bigger than it appears. Writing in *Child Welfare*, Donald McGuire and Margot Ely state that "experts in the field" agree "that the statistics severely mask the reality": many suicides, they say, are incorrectly labeled accidents; parents conceal suicide attempts; and so on. There is, the authors add, a continuum of self-destructive impulses, leaving virtually all young persons at risk to some degree. Psychiatrist Cynthia Pfeffer plays the same game, arguing that while the suicide rate for children, ages 6–12, is low (it is well under .1 per 100,000), "suicide threats and attempts are not rare . . . and may be increasing." She points to one study at an outpatient psychiatric clinic which found 33 percent of children to have "contemplated, threatened, and/or attempted suicide." Through conjectural statistics, an almost insignificant number is elevated to a third of the population.[2]

Other advocates of state intervention craft arguments that are surprisingly similar to those that have been used in the push for sex education. According to Charlotte Ross, director of the pacesetting San Mateo (CA) County Suicide Prevention and Crisis Center and defacto theoretician for the movement, youngsters "desperately want to know about suicide." Educators need to strip away the religious taboos surrounding youth suicide, and "replace the cloak of mystery . . . with information that offers ways for adolescents to help both themselves and each other." Michael Peck blasts adults who avoid frank discussions about suicide around youth. Such denial is reminiscent "of the earlier need to deny teenage sexuality" and equally crippling in its implications. It is time to cut out the shame that surrounds suicidal thoughts, and confront them in an honest, therapeutic manner.[3]

Youth suicide intervenors cast parents in an odd, seemingly contradictory light. On some occasions, inadequate parents are blamed for the tragedy. According to Ross, today's teenagers must go through the normal agonies of adolescence while their world is being shaken by "social tremors" such as divorce, remarriage, and "reconstituted families." In a 1984 article, *Good Housekeeping* stresses how "statistics show" that teen suicides "frequently come from intact homes, where deep-seated problems may be more difficult to detect." The CBS movie, *Silence of the Heart*, portrays the suicide of 17–year–old Skip Lewis, "an affable preppie" whose "adoring parents . . . are so convinced of their son's mental stability that they consistently ignore the warning signals." McGuire and Ely blame a "crippling emotional home environment" and bumbling parents for creating youth suicide.

McCall's emphasizes that suicidal teens come from families "where anger and grief are not seen as normal human responses," families without psychological sensitivity. In her state-funded action program, Charlotte Ross pursues a strategy where psychologists seek to create for teens in the schools "a supplemental *or substitute family* designed to facilitate growth.[4]

On other occasions, though, action advocates go out of their way to deny that divorce, working mothers, or family problems are to blame. In her *People* magazine lament about her son Justin's suicide while she was at work, mother Anne Spoonhour emphasizes that neither she nor her husband feel any guilt about the death: "We both accept that this was his decision and not ours." In the same issue, Pamela Cantor, president-elect of the American Association of Suicidology, directly denies that divorce and working mothers are to blame: "What is important is that both parents be involved with their children, whether they are divorced or together." *McCall's* stresses that the variables surrounding a teenager's suicide are not a cause: "A parental divorce, for instance, will not make a teenager kill himself. Having a complex network of step-parents and siblings is not a cause of teen suicide, and neither are working mothers [nor] single-parent families." In a *Forbes* article, the ubiquitous Charlotte Ross denies that families with suicidal children have any structural flaws. The parents she works with, in fact, have been "some of the loveliest people you would want to meet." Alongside this no-fault personal morality, advocates do cast blame on violent American society and television (*Good Housekeeping*), racial bigotry (*U.S. News and World Report*), loaded guns around the house, and brutal parents (*People*).[5]

Lurking behind such disjointed logic are professionals on the make, who sense piles of government money just over the horizon. Speaking for *school counselors*, Jacquelin Greuling and Richard DeBlassie argue that they can assume the role of "true friend" towards troubled teens and so render "a unique, unmistakably gratifying and life-saving service to young people." One "promising" means toward this goal is for counselors to test "all youngsters" for "suicide ideation" and other forms of "psychological distress" and herd those children who do not measure up into school-run group counseling. *Social Workers*, meanwhile, view the "disordered personalities" of parents and "unbalanced" home environments as the cause of teenage problems. As a policy solution, they call for expanded "home visitation" where they can evaluate "intrafamilial communications along characterological lines." *Psychologists* note that "there is always the need for more and better counseling services and psychological staff, including mental health consultants" who "can provide more rapid and thorough attention to depression and alienation in students." As McGuire and Ely conclude, the "experts [are] unanimous about many young children needing help, and that enough is known so that more help . . . can be offered." Indeed, a whole industry has risen up in the last decade to fan the youth suicide crisis, including the American Association of Suicidology (and its dozens of affiliated crisis centers), the National Committee on Youth Suicide Prevention, and the Youth Suicide National Center.[6]

The schools are their principal target. As psychologist Irving Berkovitz coyly notes, public schools are the places "where the behavior and feelings of the majority of children first come to the close attention of professionally trained adults outside the nuclear family," i.e., the places where the experts get their turn at the expense of Mom and Dad. Parents are not trusted by students, Charlotte Ross argues; teenagers turn most often to their peers. She advocates school-based prevention programs for all children, training them "both as potential victims and potential rescuers." In addition, teachers—the true "gatekeepers of the young"—should be trained in the psychology of suicide prevention.[7]

Ross admits that most local communities, awash in "dangerous myths" about suicide, can be expected to oppose such enlightened approaches. Hence, the crisis advocates are focusing their attention on the state and federal governments. Cantor calls for "a presidential task force on youth suicide to get state legislators to recognize the need for education on a state level." Anne Spoonhour, mother of the dead Justin, says that her long-range goal is a federal solution to the problem: "Damn it, this is an epidemic, and it's the brightest, the best, and most sensitive who are at risk. We're losing them and we don't know why." Only the government can help.[8]

In this ocean of sentiment and words, honest, thoughtful, popular reports on the real situation are almost non-existent.[9] However, numerous research articles appearing over the last ten years in professional social work and psychology journals have gone far toward explaining the youth suicide phenomenon, particularly the rise in the adolescent suicide rate between 1957 and 1977. Surprisingly, given the historic secular orientation of these professions, the journal articles testify to the critical role played by religious belief and family structure in preventing youth suicide.

No discussion of suicide research can begin, though, without attention to the work of French sociologist Emile Durkheim. His classic 1897 study *Le Suicide* continues to cast a long, even determining shadow on the contemporary debate.

Durkheim's theory of suicide held that social integration depended on the subordination of the individual's desires and needs to those of the group. This submission of persons to collective life gave meaning to existence: "They cling to life more resolutely when belonging to a group they love, so as not to betray interests they put before their own . . . [T]he lofty goal they envision prevents them from feeling personal troubles so deeply." He concluded that group suicide rates would rise during periods of social disturbance, times when the norms governing society weakened and limits were unknown. The ongoing process of industrialization, he stressed, was loosening bonds throughout Western Europe as newer, individualistic values undermined older, collectivist ones. In consequence, "egoistic" and "anomic" suicides occurred more frequently. This was the result, he reasoned, of "society's insufficient presence in individuals."

In order to measure this social change, Durkheim focused on family and religion as the primary vehicles for collectivistic values. Concerning the former, he argued that a rise in the divorce rate would translate into a higher suicide rate. This would be particularly true among men, Durkheim reasoned, for while a man found his enjoyment "restricted" by marriage, "it is assured and this certainly forms his mental foundation." He also suggested that numerous children within a family would reduce the possibility of suicide. This would be particularly true for women, who tended to be more enmeshed in the daily flow of family life.

Turning to religion, Durkheim—himself a non-believer—argued that religion was not, in a sense, real. Rather, it was "the system of symbols by means of which society becomes conscious of itself; it is the characteristic way of thinking of collective existence." Dogma, in this view, was unimportant. Religion had meaning only as a mechanism for social cohesion.

In the modernizing world, Durkheim continued, even this role was decaying. As a means of imposing moral discipline on individuals, religion had already lost "most of its power" and would, in the future, decline further. The suicide rate would then rise. However, in a key turn of his argument, Durkheim stressed that the residual social function of religion could still be seen in the differential suicide rates of Catholics and Protestants. Catholics, he said, retained a relatively dense collective life, seen in a strict adherence to obligatory rituals and beliefs, which translated into higher integration and lower suicide rates. Protestants, in contrast, did not have to subordinate themselves to group ritual, and he theorized that their individualistic freedom would translate into a higher suicide rate. He compared suicide levels for Catholics and Protestants within five nations, and found that the rate of the latter was in all cases at least 50 percent higher.[10]

Durkheim's *Suicide*, and the Catholic-Protestant differential that lay at the heart of its theory, proved to be seminal to the emerging field of sociology. As late as 1972, it was still labeled "perhaps the only significant lawlike statement in sociology."[11]

Indeed, the experience of the twentieth century seemed to confirm Durkheim's thesis, with important consequences. Religious decline in the Western world, also labeled secularization, proceeded apace. Where the Catholic/Protestant differential in suicide still appeared, this could be readily explained by Catholicism's relatively higher degree of integration. Where it tended to disappear, this could be explained by the accelerated decay of social Catholicism: the "Protestantization" of the church. When sociologist Whitney Pope, in a comprehensive 1976 critique of Durkheim's *Suicide*, reported that the master had manufactured, distorted, or seriously misrepresented much of his data, most sociologists hardly batted an eye. The new evidence that there never had been a Catholic/Protestant suicide differential merely drove another nail into the coffin.[12] Religion, they concluded, was irrelevant to changes in the suicide rate.

Studies of European populations added fuel to the fire. French sociologist Andre Heim, assessing adolescent suicide, pointed to "the failure of the religious factor to influence suicide" in his country. An Israeli researcher, looking at continental European suicide rates, concluded that "neither [church] affiliation nor degree of religious involvement seems related in any significant way to suicide attempts." English psychologist C.D. Neal, using clinical data, reported the same result for England.[13]

Everywhere, it seemed, secularism had triumphed. Most sociologists affirmed that the religious influence on suicide rates, if it had ever existed, was now certainly dead. As American experts sought to explain the nation's rising incidence of youth suicide, it caused no surprise that the one factor never mentioned in their analyses was religion. Common denial that divorce and working mothers were linked to rising youth suicide further undermined serious attention to Durkheim's hypothesis. The new scholars proceeded to construct their response on a model rooted in psycho-social therapy. Backed by the police power and taxing resources of government, the therapeutic state would move to solve the problem.

Yet the truth could not be suppressed for long. Bryan Wilson, of All Souls College, Oxford, explained the systemic error in 1979. Sociology itself, he noted, could be seen as both a commentary on the secularization process and a manifestation of it. The founders of sociology—Karl Marx, Auguste Comte, Max Weber, Thorstein Veblen, and Durkheim—sometimes offered their "science of society" as an alternative to theology, and set its empirical orientation against the suprarational, metaphysical truths of Christian revelation. While describing the important functions of religion in traditional societies, Durkheim himself had emphasized that in advanced cultures religion was an anachronism, doomed to irrelevance. Similarly, he had declared that no scheme could save the family. Indeed, wrote Wilson, "Durkheim's whole enterprise might be summed up as the search for rational surrogates to fulfill the latent functions of the irrational." Society itself, he had concluded, must replace religion and family as the object of love. This secular orientation, Wilson concluded, critically weakened Durkheim's ability to understand social change and shape a true sociology.[14]

Sociologist Rodney Stark of the University of Washington argued that Durkheim, like many other social scientists, believed that since he had judged religious faith to be false, it could not have any real effect on suicide or any other measurable event. Nonsense, Stark replied: "it makes a difference if, on the one hand, one thinks one's problems are overwhelming and unsharable, or, on the other, if one thinks that Jesus knows and cares." He also noted that Durkheim, in regarding religion as a reflection of society, was forced to consider religiously *pluralistic* communities as inherently weak. It never occurred to the old sociologist that several intermingled faiths could generate independent, co-existing moral communities in which most individuals would find a high degree of social integration.[15]

Sociologist Steven Stack of Auburn University added that Durkheim's reliance on religious affiliation (Catholic or Protestant) was inappropriate. Vastly more important to measuring religious effect on suicide was the degree of personal adherence to a core of "life-saving" beliefs. Religion, Stack noted, assuages all manner of human disappointments. Suffering is more readily endured if eternal salvation and heavenly glory are offered as reward to those who persevere. Belief that God is watching and cares about human suffering has a similar impact. Religious communities generate real concern among their members for those in trouble. The Bible offers solid role models, such as Job, for those who remain steadfast in suffering. Belief in Satan galvanizes individuals into common action against a shared enemy. Belief in a responsive God and the power of prayer also has measurable results. Stack concluded that if all else was equal and so long as religions encouraged these life-saving values, faith "will help to reduce suicide."[16]

On the far side of Durkheim, contemporary sociologists have rediscovered religion as the central explanatory factor in changes in suicide rates. Stark and his associates, for example, have analyzed the relationship between church membership and suicide in the United States' 214 Standard Metropolitan Statistical Areas. They found "a very substantial and highly significant negative correlation" between the two, even after controlling for a series of variables (including rate of population growth, poverty level, and percent unemployed). In short, the higher the degree of church membership in a given urban area, the lower the suicide rate.[17] In a remarkable study, Stack calculated the relationship between church attendance (persons being asked: "Did you, yourself, happen to attend church or synagogue in the last seven days?") and suicide rate. As expected, he found a significant and negative relationship between the two. He also discovered the most dramatic relationship between these two variables to be among young persons, ages 15 to 29. This group, he related, produced an almost perfect correlation: young Americans experienced both the sharpest drop in church attendance and the most rapid increase in suicide rate over this period. Notably, the church attendance decline was more closely associated with an increase in young female, rather than young male, suicides. Stack also calculated an "elasticity coefficient" which showed that a one percent increase in church attendance by young adults would translate into a 1.4 percent decrease in suicide.[18]

Other researchers have come up with the same results. Writing in the *Journal of Clinical Psychology*, William Martin reported that the suicide rates during the 1970s for American Blacks, Whites, men, and women were negatively correlated with church attendance. He concluded: "religious involvement appears to be equally effective as a deterrent to suicide for all the subpopulations."[19] A team at the Universities of Chicago and Washington, using complex data from 42 different countries, found "a strong and highly significant" inverse relationship between "religious integration" and suicide rate. Indeed, the relation between the two variables proved to be exponential, meaning that "past some point or threshold the loss of only a small amount of religious integration is associated with a sharp increase in suicide rates."[20] Stack even explains the leveling off in the youth suicide rate after 1976 as an event related to religious change. In 1960, 46 percent of young persons, aged 18 to 29, attended church services in a given week. By 1976, that figure had fallen to 28 percent. Eight years later, though, it had climbed back up slightly to 31 percent, which predictably would have resulted in a stabilized incidence of suicide.[21]

Such data point to a common conclusion: religious belief saves lives, particularly among women and youth.

Similar findings reaffirm the continued importance of traditional family life as a protection against suicide. A little-noticed paper published in 1976 confirmed what common sense suggests: the highest suicide rates are found among families with unmarried, divorced, or widowed parents; the lowest rate is found among intact nuclear families.[22] Using nationwide data, psychologist David Lester found divorce rates to be the surest direct predictors of suicide rates.[23] Another study, using multi-national data, showed a direct relationship "of considerable strength and significance" between divorce and suicide rates.[24] Writing in *Social Forces*, two sociologists reported that Durkheim was correct in his explanation of the tie between suicide and family. Data from the World Health Organization for fourteen nations revealed that women with children were "substantially less likely to commit suicide" than their childless counterparts. In addition, the researchers found that marriage, while protecting both men and women from suicide, protected the former to a greater degree.[25] A psychiatric team reported on the positive relationship between "a high incidence of early father loss," through divorce or illegitimacy, and suicidal behavior among young women.[26] Stack showed that increased "female equality," as measured by the proportion of married women in the labor force, drove up suicide rates for both men and women, particularly the former.[27] A team headed by John Newman of the University of Chicago discovered the same results in studies of Chicago, Illinois, and Fulton County, Georgia: a direct and highly significant correlation between the suicide rate and the percentage of women in the labor force.[28] Another researcher discovered a clear relationship between "gender deviance" as children (behavior that violates gender norms, commonly labeled "sissy" or "tomboy" acts) and suicide attempts as adults.[29]

Here, too, research findings all point toward a common conclusion: the intact traditional family saves lives.

In his most recent paper, Stephen Stack draws together the variables of family and religion. He notes that they are linked by a common set of values: self-sacrifice, duty, honor, obligation, and caring for others. These values stand in conflict, he also says, with those of individualistic, material-oriented larger society. Using data for the United States between 1954 and 1978, Stack shows that indicators of spreading "domestic individualism" (divorce and mothers' participation in the labor force) and religious individualism (absence from church on a given Sunday) are both highly related to the total suicide rate. Indeed, when combined into a single measure (called the "domestic/religious individualism index"), the results for young persons aged 15–29 are particularly dramatic. Even after controlling for other variables (such as employment and news reports of suicides), the rise in the labor force participation rate of mothers, the increase in the divorce rate, and the decline in church attendance convincingly account for most of the rise in adolescent suicide in this period. Stack concludes that families and religions change together over time; that in a sociological sense the two institutions may represent the same set of collectivistic values; and that as these shared values decline, so will the relative importance of both institutions.[30]

Other studies explain how this process of change may have transpired. The evidence highly suggests, for example, that the decay first set in among the churches themselves. Using eight different indicators of "religious commitment" (including weekly church attendance, church membership as a percent of population, religious degrees awarded as a percent of all degrees, and monetary contributions), Robert Wuthnow convincingly demonstrates that there was a growth in religious commitment during the 1950–59 period and a downturn that began around 1960 and accelerated through 1972. Another researcher has shown a large increase between 1958 and 1971 in the percentage of Catholics who felt free to question church teachings. Such findings lend some credence to the argument of social historian Robert Bellah, who has criticized the religious revival of the 1950s for being "as artificial as the cold-war atmosphere that may have fostered it."[31]

Wuthnow's analysis further suggests that as young persons, armed with visibly impressive but internally weak faiths, began to taste the counterculture of the 1960s (measured by drug use, participation in demonstrations, approval of marijuana legalization, unmarried couples living together, and more freedom for homosexuals), they then renounced their religion. Put another way, the data indicates that "the dominant source of religious disaffection for many young people" was "prior identification with the counterculture."[32]

As Durkheim would have predicted, this massive challenge to American social norms created social anomie, or rootlessness. One manifestation of this was a dramatic drop in weekly church attendance by young persons. Another was growing rejection of traditional family values. Together, they produced the rise in adolescent suicides.

There are two options in confronting the problem. Americans can cast their lot with those who consider religion and the family to be dying or already dead. Representative of this view is William D'Antonio, past president of the Society for the Scientific Study of Religion. Albeit with a heavy heart, he argues that religion and the family "have come to the end of their long affair." The traditional Western family undergirded by religious morality, D'Antonio says, now "runs counter to the main thrust of American life," namely individualistic hedonism. The religion family complex can no longer serve its social control function in the face of a dominant ethic focused on careers and private pleasures. It is time for churches to abandon the futile defense of anachronistic dogma. Instead, they must "listen to the people" and "learn from them": cave into the present.[33]

With more sophisticated argument, Bryan Wilson says that the liberal individualism found in capitalist society must eventually overwhelm the cultural sphere of religion and family and instill pure hedonism. In this inevitable environment, "emotional gratification will no longer be moulded and channelled, and culture will lose its constraining and regulatory functions." Already in the American consumer society, he states, religion has become "just another consumer good, a leisure-time commodity, no longer affecting the centers of power or the operations of the system." Bellah takes a similar despairing position: there is a basic incompatibility between a liberal constitutional state predicated on individualism and a religious order resting on moral restraint. The United States, he says, is awash in luxury, dependence on the state, and ignorance: what eighteenth century philosophers understood to be the clear signs of decadence and corruption. Triumphant individualism in league with growing technocracy suggests that the U.S. is heading, "mildly and gradually, into something like Aldous Huxley's *Brave New World*.[34] Indeed, it is exactly this vision of the technocratic, therapeutic state that the advocates of a government solution to the youth suicide crisis would try to deliver.

The other option would drive Americans back to the brilliant, now disquieting insight of Alexis de Tocqueville, the nineteenth century French analyst of the American experiment. He saw that religion was the first of this nation's political institutions. It was the churches, he said, that inculcated the republican virtues in Americans and also gave them their first lessons on involvement in public life. More importantly, it was mores, not laws, that most contributed to the growth and success of American democracy. Such mores, Tocqueville insisted, could only be grounded in religious faith. He recognized that unrestrained individualism would quickly undermine a republican regime. The possibility for such naked pursuit of self-interest, Tocqueville continued, could be found in the commercial proclivities of the American people. However, religion and its handmaiden, the family, served in America as the powerful and needed restraints on individualism, turning the latter into "self interest rightly understood," in service of the public interest.[35]

From this perspective, religion and the family are not mere options for this nation; they are necessities if the American republic is to survive and prosper. Hence, the solution to the youth suicide problem—indeed the solution to the largest share of our public problems—is the recovery of those two institutions which restrain and channel the individual life toward life, virtue, and community.

Skeptics respond that such reconstruction cannot occur. D'Antonio argues that it is impossible to restore the traditional family, that hedonistic freedom has irreversibly triumphed over group solidarity. Wilson says that a sense of the sacred cannot be constructed at will: "If people actively and consciously begin to manufacture 'the sacred,' the very knowledge of their activity precludes our believing."[36]

Such paradoxes become meaningless in the context of two possibilities: first, that the traditional family unit is a natural creation rooted in the genetic code of humankind; and second, that God exists. In the former case, the corruption of the family unit no longer appears to be inevitable. Rather, such corruption is recast as a sort of cancerous transformation that might be cut away or altered by human effort. In the latter, it becomes evident that the "sacred" can break through, or return, whenever willed by God or rediscovered within Creation by humankind, using its new tools of social and physical science.

Relative to social problems such as the self-destruction of youth, this does not mean that Americans can call on governments to restore vigorous religions and strong families. Such acts, of course, cannot be performed by the state. The important tasks must be addressed outside Washington. For those religious groups that succumbed in recent decades to the allure of political activism and to theologies shaped by ideological fads, the need is to recover fidelity to God's word and will. As modern social research suggests, stronger families would follow, the youth suicide rate would decline, and the Republic would reclaim its soul.

Notes

1. These figures are from U.S. Department of Commerce, Bureau of the Census, *Statistical Abstract of the United States*, 1985 (Washington, DC: U.S. Gov't. Printing Office, 1985), pp. 79, 845.
2. Donald J. McGuire and Margot Ely, "Childhood Suicide," *Child Welfare* 63 (Jan.-Feb. 1984): 18–20 and Cynthia R. Pfeffer, "Suicidal Behavior of Children: A Review with Implications for Research and Practice," *American Journal of Psychiatry* 138 (Feb. 1981): 155.
3. Charlotte P. Ross, "Teaching Children the Facts of Life and Death: Suicide Prevention in the Schools," in *Youth Suicide*, ed. Michael L. Peck, Norman L. Farberow, and Robert E. Litman (New York: Springer Publishing Co., 1985), pp. 147-48, 156; and *Youth Suicide: What You Can Do About It* (Burlingame, CA: Suicide Prevention and Crisis Center of San Mateo County, 1985), p. 6.
4. Ross, p. 149; Joyce Jornovoy and David Jenness, "Teenage Suicide," *Good Housekeeping* (July 1984): 92; Mary Ann O'Roark, "The Alarming Rise in Teenage Suicide," *McCall's* (Jan. 1982): 16; and Charlotte Ross and Jerome A. Motto, "Group Counseling for Suicidal Adolescents," in *Suicide in the Young*, ed. Howard Sudak, Amasa B. Ford, and Norman B. Rushforth (Boston: John Wright Publishers, 1984), pp. 388, 390.
5. Anne Spoonhour, "The First Few Days are the Hardest," *People* (Feb. 18, 1985): 84–85; Richard Formica and Maryann Brinley, "What the Experts Don't Tell You About Teenage Suicide," *McCall's* (Oct. 1985): 84; Tania Pouschine, "By Their Own Young Hands," *Forbes* (Oct. 21, 1985): 163; Jurnovoy and Jenness, p. 84; Jeanne Thornton, "Behind a Surge in Suicides of Young People," *U.S. News and World Report* (June 20, 1983): 66; and interview with Pamela Cantor, "These Teenagers Feel That They Have No Option," *People* (Feb. 18, 1985): 84.
6. Jacquelin W. Greuling and Richard DeBlassie, "Adolescent Suicide," *Adolescence* 40 (Fall 1980): 595–96; Kathryn V. Den-Houter, "To Silence One's Self: A Brief Analysis of the Literature on Adolescent Suicide," *Child Welfare* 60 (Jan. 1981): 8; Irving H. Berkovitz, "The Role of Schools in Child, Adolescent, and Youth Suicide Prevention," in Peck, pp. 174–75; and Mcguire and Ely, p. 20.
7. Berkovitz, p. 170; Ross, pp. 151-52; and Charlotte P. Ross, "Mobilizing Schools for Suicide Prevention," *Suicide and Life Threatening Behavior* 10 (Winter 1980): 239–43.
8. "These Teenagers Feel That They Have No Options," p. 87; and Spoonhour, p. 83.
9. The rare exception is a 1983 report by *Newsweek*, which presents the real data and, among other insights, concludes that the rise in youth suicide between 1957 and 1975 was the consequence of the nation's "binge of social emancipation over the past decades." See "Teenage Suicide in the Sun Belt," *Newsweek* (Aug. 15, 1983): pp. 70f.
10. Emile Durkheim, *Suicide: A Study in Sociology*, trans. John A. Spaulding and George Simpson (Glencoe, IL: The Free Press of Glencoe, 1951), particularly pp. 209–10, 253–58, 270–1, 312.
11. Dominick LaCapra, *Emile Durkheim: Sociologist and Philosopher* (Ithaca, Cornell University Press, 1972), p. 147.
12. Whitney Pope, *Durkheim's Suicide: A Classic Analyzed* (Chicago: University of Chicago Press, 1976).
13. Andre Haim, *Adolescent Suicide*, trans. A.M. Sheridan-Smith (London: Tav-

istock Publications, 1974), p. 173; Benjamin Beit-Hallahmi, "Religion and Suicidal Behavior," *Psychological Reports* 37 (1975): 1303–06; and C.D. Neal, "Religion and Self Poisoning," *The International Journal of Social Psychiatry* 27 (Winter 1981): 257-60.

14. Bryan Wilson, "The Return of the Sacred," *Journal for the Scientific Study of Religion* 18 (Sept. 1979): 268–70.

15. Rodney Stark, Daniel P. Doyle, and Jesse Lynn Rushing, "Beyond Durkheim: Religion and Suicide," *Journal for the Scientific Study of Religion* 22 (Sept. 1983): 120–25.

16. Steven Stack, "The Effect of Religious Commitment on Suicide: A Cross-National Analysis," *Journal of Health and Social Behavior* 24 (Dec. 1983): 363–65.

17. Stark, pp. 125–27.

18. Steven Stack, "The Effect of the Decline in Institutionalized Religion on Suicide, 1954–1978," *Journal for the Scientific Study of Religion* 22 (Sept. 1983): 239–52.

19. William T. Martin, "Religiosity and United States Suicidal Rates, 1972–1978," *Journal of Clinical Psychology* 40 (Sept. 1984): 1166–69.

20. K.D. Breault and Karen Barkey, "A Comparative Analysis of Durkheim's Theory of Egoistic Suicide," *The Sociological Quarterly* 23 (Summer 1982): 326.

21. Reported in: Steven Stack, "A Leveling Off in Young Suicides," *Wall Street Journal* (May 28, 1986).

22. Friedrich V. Wenz, "Social Areas and Durkheim's Theory of Suicide," *Psychological Reports* 38 (1976): 1313–14.

23. David Lester, "Religion, Suicide, and Homicide," *Social Psychiatry* 22 (1987): 99–101.

24. Breault and Barkey, p. 326.

25. Nick Danigelis and Whitney Pope, "Durkheim's Theory of Suicide as Applied to the Family: An Empirical Test," *Social Forces* 57 (June 1979): 1081–1106.

26. Lynda W. Warren and C. Tomlinson-Keasey, "The Context of Suicide," *American Journal of Orthopsychiatry* 57 (Jan. 1987): 42.

27. Stack, p. 368.

28. John F. Newman, "Women in the Labor Force and Suicide," *Social Problems*, (1973): 220–30.

29. Joseph Harry, "Parasuicide, Gender, and Gender Deviance," *Journal of Health and Social Behavior* 24 (Dec. 1983): 350–61.

30. Steven Stack, "The Effect of Domestic/Religious Individualism on Suicide, 1954–1978," *Journal of Marriage and Family* 45 (May 1985): 431–47. See also: K.D. Breault, "Suicide in America: A Test of Durkheim's Theory of Religious and Family Integration, 1933–80," *American Journal of Sociology* 92 (Nov. 1986): 651–52.

31. Robert Wuthnow, "Recent Pattern of Secularization: A Problem of Generations?" *American Sociological Review* 41 (Oct. 1976): 852; Douglas Koller, "Belief in the Right to Question Church Teachings, 1958–1971," *Social Forces* 58 (Sept. 1979): 290–304; and Robert N. Bellah, "New Religious Consciousness and the Crisis in Modernity," in *The New Religious Consciousness*, ed. Charles Y. Glock and Robert N. Bellah (Berkeley: University of California Press, 1976), p. 339.

32. See Wuthnow, pp. 854–60.

33. See William V. D'Antonio, "The Family and Religion: Exploring a Changing

Relationship," *Journal for the Scientific Study of Religion* 19 (June 1980): 89–104; and William V. D'Antonio and Joan Aldous, *Families and Religions: Conflict and Change in Modern Society* (Beverly Hills: Sage Publications, 1983), pp. 10–14, 81–106.

34. Wilson, pp. 273, 277, 279; Robert Bellah, "Religion and Legitimation in the American Republic," *Society* (May/June 1978): 22; and Bellah, p. 350.

35. Alexis de Tocqueville, *Democracy in America* (Garden City, NY: Doubleday, 1969), pp. 287–301.

36. D'Antonio and Aldous, pp. 98–99; and Wilson, p. 278.

Conclusion:
Family Policy for a Free People

Lenin's famous question still looms before us: "What then is to be done?" Phrased differently, given the constraints of the family crisis, turmoil, and dissolution on the one side, and the awful power of the state to disrupt families, even through good intentions, on the other, how might we construct a positive family policy for the American future?

An answer can be found, I believe, in two lessons learned during the past four decades. The first of these is that the few successful examples of family-oriented federal social policy have been those based on an indirect, tax-relief-oriented approach. For example, the dramatic spread of home-ownership in the post-World War II era was the result of federal efforts to shore up mortgage markets, the continuation of the tax deductibility of mortgage interest, and the creation and expansion of the VA and FHA mortgage insurance programs, which indirectly subsidized home purchases without negating the principle of private responsibility. It is true that even this indirect intervention by the federal government came at some economic cost. Investment funds were diverted from other potential uses into home construction; natural market forces were tampered with. It is arguable, though, that the gains far exceeded the cost. Similarly, tax code changes in 1948 reinforced those families committed to the business of children. Creation of the joint return, and an increase in the value of the personal exemption to $600 served as indirect, albeit meaningful ways of affirming family creation, and were coincident with the blossoming of familism during the 1950s.

The second lesson is that the matriarchal welfare state, even when pursuing "pro family" goals, has produced family-disruptive results. The assorted crises that mark the history of our domestic policy debates—the poverty crisis, the ageism crisis, the teen pregnancy crisis, the overpopulation crisis, the juvenile delinquency crisis, the eugenics crisis, the child abuse crisis, the youth suicide crisis—have all become, intentionally or unintentionally, vehicles to expand the power of the state at the expense of the autonomy of its old adversary, the family. Paraphrasing that infamous comment by an American field commander in Vietnam, we have been

273

destroying the family in order to save it. The contemporary crisis, real as it is, derives in large part from these past assaults on family autonomy. We cannot allow this tragic irony to come full circle, and so bury the family in the robes of an activist family policy.

Based on these lessons, a family policy for a free people would take the following shape:

[1] *Reconstruct a viable suburban policy.* Rural America, once the well-spring of family-oriented America, has vanished as a culturally significant force in American life. Suburbia and exurbia, built on child-centered assumptions, emerged to replace the farm as a reservoir of familism, yet then fell victim in part to anti-family ideologues and the moral lassitude that characterized the 1960–80 period. Peasant America cannot be reconstructed; the numbers are no longer there. Yet the suburban vision can be restored, and the federal government can play a positive role.

That role must be based, as before, on an opportunity-oriented housing policy. During the 1970–80 period, inflation-driven housing costs, soaring mortgage rates, swollen fuel bills, and stagnant or declining real family incomes conspired to drive home ownership beyond the reach of the average new family. In 1970, 50 percent of American households could afford the median-priced new home; in 1980, only 13 percent could. By 1986, the situation had eased significantly; yet even then, home ownership increasingly necessitated two incomes, with anti-natalist effects. The traditional family unit, still the primary nursery of a majority of children in America, has found itself confined increasingly to the least desirable housing choices. Existing federal programs designed, in effect, to sustain the suburban mortgage market have simply proved inadequate for families with dependent children.

Accordingly, policymakers should look to new ways of delivering affordable mortgages to these young families. One possibility would be modified VA and FHA rules allowing lower (effectively subsidized) interest rates to purchasers with dependent children, with the difference to be made up by the borrower near the end of the loan. The tax code could also be amended to allow creation of IRA-like housing accounts, where young couples could save, tax-free, toward the purchase of their first home.

[2] *Construct a family wage through non-statist means.* The free market will not create a family wage. Only social convention, state action, or some combination of both can grant economic protection to the family in the business of raising children. Instead of the standard welfare-state solution to the family wage problem—state child allowances and the opportunity they create for state manipulation of families—we can return to that distinctively American form of social policy: tax credits and deductions keyed

to number and age of children, which would allow families with dependent children to keep more of their earned income.

Taken together, four steps would go far toward constructing a contemporary American family wage, and at the same time make some meaningful compensation for the inequities between generations that have been created by federal child care policy and the Social Security system since 1965: (a) increase the personal income tax exemption for each dependent child from $2,000 to $4,000; (b) transform the existing childcare tax credit into a universal credit at a set level, e.g. $500 per child to a maximum of $1500. This would be available to all American families with preschool children whether or not they use daycare (as a substitute for existing means-tested daycare programs, it could be made refundable); (c) transform the existing Earned Income Tax Credit, currently available to the working poor with one or more children as an offset to the payroll tax, into a universal Dependent Child Credit of $600 per child, up to the total value of the parents' payroll tax (in 1988, 15.02 percent of salary up to $6,759); and (d) provide an additional Dependent Child Credit of $600 to families in the year of a child's birth or adoption.

The impact of such a plan on a sample family with three small children, at varying income levels, is presented in Appendix A. When comparing this plan with provisions in place in 1988, under the terms of the Tax Reform Act of 1986, a family of five with reported earnings of $25,000 would retain $4,300 more in that year (net income would exceed reported income due to the availability of $1,788 in payroll tax paid by the employer), the maximum that any family with this structure would gain. A family earning $15,000 per year would retain $2,946 more than it does at present (it would also still be eligible for food stamps). This level of tax relief would decline in subsequent years as children grew older, and the family no longer was eligible for the Child Care Credit.

This plan would deliver significantly more disposable income to families with dependent children without disrupting free wage markets, without forcing an increase in overall tax burden, without increasing the size of government, without transforming families into a state-dependent class, and without using the policy vehicle as a lever for social engineering. The proposed program recognizes the perverse manner in which the tax burden has been shifted in recent decades. It grants meaningful recognition to contemporary childcare problems and gives maximum choice to parents, without discriminating against either the working mother or the mother-at-home. This scheme recognizes the perverse disincentive to children now found within the old-age pension component of the nation's Social Security system; it grants relief to parents who make the socially responsible decision to bear a child, without compromising in any way the revenues flowing into the Social Security trust fund. Finally, this plan even offers the advocates of tax credits and vouchers for religious and private schooling a constitutionally sound way of delivering the needed tax relief to their constituents.

The downside of the plan is that it would cost the federal treasury a considerable amount in lost income tax revenues: $30–45 billion annually. In the face of high deficits, such cost may seem prohibitive. The only relevant response is that the last twenty years have been witness to a kind of economic war, intended and unintended, against this nation's families. That must no longer continue. Either a reduction in expenditures or an increase in the base tax rate of 1.5 to 2 percent would pay for these measures, and so restore a profamily posture to American public life.

[3] *Defederalize 'family planning.'* In the ongoing conflict of sexual ethics, federal and state governments should be made to adopt a neutral stance. While the claims of success by the sexual modernists are clearly open to dispute, we do know that traditional controls over teenage sexuality do work, when given a chance to function. For example, careful studies have shown that black girls from father-headed families are *twice* as likely to be "non-permissive" sexually as compared to those from mother-headed units; that when mothers served their daughters as the primary source of sexual information, the latter were far less likely to have engaged in coitus; and that the teenage daughters (ages 15–16) of traditional white families report sexual activity less than half as often as daughters of non-traditionalists (9 percent compared to 20 percent).[1]

Accordingly, the need is to restore family planning to a normative model similar to that of the 1950s: birth control as a free choice within marriage; abstinence as the social expectation for unmarried adolescents; marriage as the solution of choice to an unplanned pregnancy; social stigma or shame attached to illegitimacy; and family planning as a private measure, conducted wholly independent of state encouragement, provision, or control.

[4] *Reprivatize the family.* The legal battle over the autonomy of the family is far from over. Aggressive defenders of family rights are needed to continue the fight, attorneys such as William Ball of Harrisburg, Pennsylvania, and activist, grassroots organizations such as *Vocal* (Victims of Child Abuse Laws), headquartered in Minneapolis. Fortunately, while the courts have generally supported the *parens patriae* doctrine and the projection of state authority into the family, there has been a notable line of dissent. In its 1944 decision in *Prince v. Massachusetts*, the U.S. Supreme Court did say that "the state's authority over children's activities is broader than over like actions of adults." Yet the majority opinion also affirmed that "it is cardinal with us that the custody, care and nurture of the child reside first

in the parents, whose primary function and freedom include preparation for obligations the state can neither supply nor hinder. And it is in recognition of this that [our] decisions have respected the private realm of family life which the state cannot enter." Chief Justice Warren Burger, in his 1979 decision to *Parham* v. *J.R.*, argued even more forcefully that "the statist notion that governmental power should supersede parental authority in all cases because some parents abuse and neglect children is repugnant."

At the state level, too, several recent court decisions have reinvigorated the natural law defense of family rights as a viable element of the American legal tradition. For example, in a stunning 1982 decision, the Utah Supreme Court struck down a provision of that state's Children's Rights Act which allowed for the complete termination of parental rights upon a decision by judicial authority that "such termination will be in the child's best interest." Writing for the majority, Justice Dallin Oaks stated: "This parental right [to rear one's children] transcends all property and economic rights. It is rooted not in state or federal statutory or constitutional law, to which it is logically and chronologically prior, but in nature and human instinct." He noted that much of the rich variety in American culture had been transmitted to children by parents "who were acting against the best interest of their children, as defined by official dogma." There was no surer way to destroy authentic pluralism, Oaks added, than by terminating the rights of parents who violated the "trendy" definitions and "officially approved values imposed by reformers empowered to determine what is in the 'best interest' of someone else's child."[2]

Judicial rebukes notwithstanding, the institutions of the therapeutic state follow their own bureaucratic logic, and continue to expand. The helping professions have accumulated sufficient power to ensure that necessary retreat in one activity (e.g. among the juvenile courts in wake of *In Re Gault*) is more than compensated for by expansion in another sphere (e.g. child neglect and abuse).

Freedom and autonomy for the family can be won, in part, by cutting back the aggregate size, funding, and power of bureaucratic agencies in the "child and family protection" business. Such tasks cannot be undertaken lightly, for two centuries of entrenched growth lie behind the vested interests that guide the state's governance of families. Moreover, budget reductions in the areas of "child protection" and "family services" will predictably bring howls of protest and charges that legislators are abandoning children to the inhuman monsters who are or might be their parents. These plaintive cries might best be countered by media- or legislative-led inquiries into specific cases of state abuse of children in foster care, "shelters," or medical exam rooms.

Another strategy for reprivatizing the family is to substitute vouchers, whenever possible, for monopoly state welfare services. Such devices, which give benefit recipients the equivalent of cash to spend among a range of service providers, both public and private, would work best in areas such as the care of the severely disabled and means-tested daycare. Vouchers are important because they reverse existing power relationships between state welfare officials and client families. This tends to reduce the subtle arrogance that state therapists naturally bring to their tasks, while encouraging personal responsibility among recipients and efficiency and true service among providers.

A third strategy toward liberating the family would involve reform of the neglect and abuse laws existing in most states. Changes should recognize the perverse incentives that now reward state authorities who increase the number of innocent families charged with neglect and abuse. Specific reforms could include: precise legal definitions of abuse and neglect, which would sharply limit the discretion of welfare investigators; guaranteed legal representation, rules of evidence, and due-process in child removal proceedings; the protection of children from abuse by state therapists; holding state therapists liable to civil action by parents; holding everyone except medical doctors legally liable for their reports of abuse; and insuring respect for diverse values in child rearing.

[5] *Restore the spiritual element to the public square.* Family life will not thrive in a vacuum. Sociologically and historically, familial bonds normally depend on the support of religion for the preservation of the family's moral authority. Driven by a series of adverse court decisions bonded philosophically to the secular assumptions of its governing and media elites, the American commonwealth has waged quiet war in recent decades against the symbols and partisans of the sacred.[3] American life has been denuded of what Peter Berger calls our "sacred canopy." Reinvigoration of the family in America ultimately depends on a restoration of religion to its historic, albeit unwritten, role as authenticator and guide to this unique experiment in republican government.

Governments cannot, of themselves, "restore" religion. They can, though, become more hospitable to the religious impulse. Local communities should be left free to celebrate in public ways the spiritual bonds that hold them together. Religious schools and home schools should be freed from the regime of state regulation. Public schools, and the textbooks used therein, should cease subtle campaigns that are generally antireligious, and specifically hostile to the Judeo-Christian faiths.

Even concerning measures of family health such as fertility, the results should be positive. One consistent finding in studies of differential fertility is that strong religious faith translates into larger families. This appears to have relatively little to do with strictures against birth control and a great deal to do with reverence towards creation and life and obedience to God's perceived will. Indeed, America's existing pockets of high marital fertility are found exclusively among religious groups: Mormons in Utah; the Amish and Hutterite farm communities; fundamentalists concentrated in the South; Hassidic Jews; and traditional Catholics.[4]

The central lesson of the last one hundred years is that the state can disrupt, but it cannot save families. That task can only be achieved through a revitalized, family-affirming culture. We need a literature that celebrates, rather than denigrates, the familial virtues. We need a popular culture that defends what is wholesome and decent in American life. We need normative social arrangements that reinforce Americans who make a commitment to children and home. We need an educational system that, without apology, presents and upholds marriage, fidelity, and children as the essential framework for the good life. Except at the margins, these are clearly not tasks of government. A familial culture will either emerge out of the popular sentiments of the people, or it will not appear at all. It cannot be imposed by the crude hand of bureaucracy.

Accordingly, a family policy for a free people will largely be one involving the creative disengagement of the state and the reconstruction, to the degree possible, of the natural family economy. From nature, the family can claim prior existence to the state and the exercise of prerogatives that no government can rightfully impair. For families in America, the central task of the next decade is to win back the authority and autonomy which are their due. The alternative can be starkly drawn: the continued socialization of families and childrearing, to their ultimate disappearance, and the ongoing destabilizing of a free and responsible people.

Notes

1. Julian Roebuck and Marsha G. McGee, "Attitudes Toward Premarital Sex and Sexual Behavior Among Black High School Girls," *The Journal of Sex Research* 13 (May 1977): 109–12; Graham B. Spanier, "Sources of Sex Information and Premarital Sexual Behavior," *The Journal of Sex Research* 13 (May 1977): 73–88; and Kristin A. Moore, et al, "Parental Attitudes and the Occurrence of Early Sexual Activity," *Journal of Marriage and the Family* 48 (November 1986): 777–82.
2. *In re J.P.*, 648 P. 2nd Utah 1364 (1982).
3. For the definitive analysis of these developments, see: Richard John Neuhaus, *The Naked Public Square: Religion and Democracy in America* (Grand Rapids: Wm. B. Eerdmans, 1984).
4. See: Nan E. Johnson, "Religious Differences in Reproduction: The Effects of Sectarian Education," *Demography* 19 (Nov. 1982): 495–99; Julia Ericksen and Gary Klein, "Women's Roles and Family Production Among the Old Order Amish," *Rural Sociology* 46 (Spring 1981): 282–96; Tim B. Heaton and Sandra

Calkins, "Family Size and Contraceptive Use Among Mormons, 1965-75," *Review of Religious Research* 25 (Dec. 1983): 102–13; Gordon F. DeJong, "Religious Fundamentalism, Socio-Economic Status, and Fertility Attitudes in the Southern Appalachians," *Demography* 2, No. 4 (1965): 540–48; and Michael Lee Yoder, "Religion as a Determinant of Fertility Among White Americans, 1965," Ph.D. Dissertation, University of Wisconsin–Madison [1980].

Appendix

I. Components of Family Tax Relief Plan

[1] Increase the personal exemption, for dependent children only, to $4,000 per child.

[2] Grant a $500 Child Care Tax Credit to all parents for each preschool child (through age six), to a maximum of $1500.

[3] Grant a refundable and indexed Dependent Child Credit of $600 to families for each child, up to the total value of the families' and employers' combined payroll tax for the year (15.02 percent of salaries and wages, 13.02 for the self-employed).

[4] Grant an extra Dependent Child Care Credit of $600 to families in the year of a child's birth or adoption, with the same ceiling.

II. Effects on a Sample Family with Varying Income

A. Assumes father employed with a taxable income of $25,000 a year; mother, not in paid labor force, caring for three small children at home (ages 7, 4, and 6 months as of Dec. 31).

	Under Current Law	Under Family Relief Plan
Family income	$25,000	$25,000
Standard Deduction	5,000	5,000
Personal Exemption	10,000 (2,000 × 5)	16,000 (4,000 × 3) (2,000 × 2)
Taxable Income	10,000	4,000
Income Tax	1,500	600
Payroll Tax	1,878 (3,756 with employer's portion)	1,878 (3,755 with employer's portion)
Child Care Tax Credit	none	1,000
Dependent Child Credit	none	1,800
Extra Credit During Year of Child's Birth	none	600

NET ANNUAL INCOME, AFTER FEDERAL TAXES	Income:	25,000		25,000
	Less income tax:	− 1,500		− 600
	Less payroll tax:	− 1,878		− 1,878
		$21,622	Child Care credit:	+ 1,000
			Depend. Child Care Credit:	+ 2,400
				$25,922

NET GAIN: $4,300

B. Assumes father employed, with a taxable income of $15,000 a year; mother, not in labor force, caring for three children at home (ages 7, 4, and 6 months, as of Dec. 31).

	Under Current Law	Under Family Relief Plan
Family income	$15,000	$15,000
Standard Deduction	5,000	5,000
Personal Exemption	10,000 (2,000 × 5)	16,000 (4,000 × 3) (2,000 × 2)
Taxable Income	-0-	-0-
Income Tax	-0-	-0-
Payroll Tax	1,127 (2,253 with employer's portion)	1,127 (2,253 with employer's portion)
Child Care Tax Credit	none	1,000*
Dependent Child Credit	200 (Earned Income Credit est.)	1,800
Extra Credit During Year of Child's Birth	none	600

*refundable

	Under Current Law	Under Family Relief Plan
NET ANNUAL INCOME, AFTER FEDERAL TAXES	Income: $15,000 Less income tax: Less payroll tax: − 1,127 E.I.C. + 200	$15,000 − 1,127
	$14,073	Child Care credit: + 1,000 Depend. Child Care Credit: + 2,253
		$17,126

NET GAIN: $3,053

C. Assumes father employed, with a taxable income of $40,000 a year; mother, not in labor force, caring for three children at home (ages 7, 4, and 6 months, as of Dec. 31).

	Under Current Law	**Under Family Relief Plan**
Family income	$40,000	$40,000
Standard Deduction	5,000	5,000
Personal Exemption	10,000 (2,000 × 5)	16,000 (4,000 × 3) (2,000 × 2)
Taxable Income	25,000	19,000
Income Tax	3,750	2,850
Payroll Tax	3,004 (6,008 with employer's portion)	3,004 (6,008 with employer's portion)
Child Care Tax Credit	none	1,000
Dependent Child Credit	none	1,800
Extra Credit During Year of Child's Birth	none	600

NET ANNUAL INCOME, AFTER FEDERAL TAXES

	Under Current Law	Under Family Relief Plan
Income:	$40,000	$40,000
Less income tax:	− 3,750	− 2,850
Less payroll tax:	− 3,004	− 3,004
	$33,246	
Child Care credit:		+ 1,000
Depend. Child Care Credit:		+ 2,400
		$37,546

NET GAIN: $4,300

D. Assumes father employed, with taxable income of $20,000 per year; mother, employed part-time, earning $10,000 per year; two preschool children in day care, one in school (ages 7, 4, and 6 months, as of Dec. 31).

	Under Current Law	Under Family Relief Plan
Family income	$30,000	$30,000
Standard Deduction	5,000	5,000
Personal Exemption	10,000	16,000
		(4,000 × 3)
		(2,000 × 2)
Taxable Income	15,000	9,000
Income Tax	2,250	1,350
Payroll Tax	2,253	2,253
	(4,506 with employer's portion)	(4,506 with employer's portion)
Child Care Tax Credit	960	1,000
Dependent Child Credit	none	1,800
Extra Credit During Year of Child's Birth	none	600

NET ANNUAL INCOME, AFTER FEDERAL TAXES			
	Income:	$30,000	$30,000
	Less income tax:	− 2,250	− 1,350
	Less payroll tax:	− 2,253	− 2,253
	Child Care Credit:	960	
		$26,457	
		Child Care credit:	+ 1,000
		Depend. Child Care Credit:	+ 2,400
			$29,797

NET GAIN: $3,340

Index